TABLE OF CONTENTS

on Children and Teens

ENDORSEMENTS

"Medic!" When a wounded soldier shouts that word, they hope the person scrambling to their side is properly equipped. When the wounded kids in our neighborhood seek help from us, they also deserve properly prepared responders. This book provides great resources for effective, God-honoring ministry. Every youth worker should have this book in their "first responders" backpack. Where was this book when I was in youth ministry?!?! May God use it in great ways to help the wounded kids all around us.

-- David Wheeler, Professor of Congregational Ministry, Johnson University

This is a terrific book for anyone working with kids in pain. Gary Zustiak (Zus) has gathered all his notes from many decades of teaching and put them into one readable volume. This is an interactive book with many helpful exercises. The book is practical and can be used immediately as a basic resource. By reading this book you will be more effective and have more confidence in working with troubled youth. Many issues faced by teens simply require a caring person coming alongside them. However, Zus also stresses the need in many situations to refer to a trained professional. Extremely helpful, this a book you will be pulling of the shelf many times.

-- Les Christie, Professor Emeritus, William Jessup University

Intensive Care is simple, yet profound, in that rarely is there a resource that has depth mixed with personal application for the counselor, mixed with ready-to-use practical steps to help the teen toward health. This book is a well-researched and an incisive resource for those ministering to hurting teens. Dr. Zustiak is constantly researching the latest harmful trends among youth and searching for appropriate responses--always starting with God's Word! Using *Intensive Care* with youth in crisis will be like having Dr. Zustiak in the counseling chair next to you. Believe me, you will be forever grateful to God as your teens make steps toward health and wholeness in Christ. *Intensive Care* presents careful and thorough research on a variety of crisis issues with teens and then walks the youth worker through the practical steps to help the teen in crisis.

-- Bob Witte, Director of the Ministry Center, Ozark Christian College

ACKNOWLEDGEMENTS

At the risk of leaving a few people out, let me acknowledge and thank a few friends, colleagues, youth group members and family for their immeasurable support and encouragement through the writing of this book. This is not just the fruit of my labors, but the sum contributions of everyone.

I will start by thanking the ministers I have had the privilege of working with and being mentored by them: Thomas Shepherd, Marvin Scherpf, and Chuck Wigton. You were all patient with me when I was a rookie and you went to battle for me with the elders and leadership when I messed up. Thank-you for your grace!

I cannot thank enough some of the key members of the different youth groups that I was privileged to lead. Your allowing me into your lives to share the love and grace of Jesus was my greatest pleasure. Thank you, Randy, Carlene, Velma, Verna, Evelyn, Debbie, Carleen, Kevin, Kelly, Mike, Jim, Dan, Kay, Connie, Jolene, Doug, Sherrie, Lance, and David—and so many more.

The influence, input and opportunities to serve with Christ in Youth was a huge blessing to my life. Word cannot express how much the National Youth Leaders Convention and the International School of Youth Ministry shaped my life and ministry. Thank you: Paul Smith, Andy Hansen, Steve Sigler, John Mouton, Robin Sigars, Kevin Greer, Tony Allmoslecher, Brenda Hawkins, Les Christie, David Roadcup, Bill Baumgardner, Jude Champagne, Mike Temm, Jayson French, Jason Miller, Pat Fancher and Terry Ohmart.

This book could not have been written without the gracious support of Ozark Christian College who allowed me to take a year sabbatical to put the book together. The leadership and my colleagues at OCC have been supportive and encouraging throughout the entire process. Thank you: Matt Proctor, Damien Spikereit, Doug Aldridge, Chad Ragsdale, Peter Buckland, Terry Bowland, Mark Scott, Bob Witte, Karl Wendt, John Hunter, Gerald Griffin, Jessica Scheuermann and Woody Wilkinson.

I am grateful to my late father, George Zustiak, and my mother, Janice Zustiak who raised me up in the church and who taught me the values of integrity, honesty, hard work, kindness, perseverance, and a belief in myself and my abilities. Your support through the years is greatly appreciated. (I know I wasn't the easiest to raise, so thanks for not giving up on me during the rebellious teenage years!) Thanks to my brother, Randy, for not ratting me out!

To my three sons, Joshua, Aaron and Caleb: I am as proud of you and your families as I can be. You have taught me more about life and ministry than you will never know. I am so grateful that God gave you to me and I pray that you will continue to love and serve Jesus all the days of your life. I take great joy in seeing how you parent your children and love your spouses.

The greatest support and encouragement has always come from my wife and best friend of forty-seven years (so far) of shared ministry together. Mary has contributed in significant ways to every ministry that I have ever held and has made sacrifices behind the scenes so that I could do what I felt God has called me to do. Thank-you for allowing me to pursue my dreams. I love you and appreciate you so much.

FOREWORD

Intensive Care is a MUST HAVE resource for ALL YOUTH WORKERS!

I would make sure that every one of my volunteers as well as professional staff had a copy of this book for easy referral and to utilize as a springboard of response, a foundation of wise counsel in addressing a multitude of issues that confronts today's youth culture.

This book is so insightful, yet easy to read. The first quarter of the book is an invaluable training and guide which has the potential to transform the "average" youth worker into a helpful listener and spiritual counselor, a true friend to a teen in need. The remaining pages of this book are chock full of references and quotes, thorough statistics and clear explanation of the reality of eleven different topics that undoubtedly will be experienced within the realm of youth ministry.

Students we love and care for are dealing with the ramifications of such challenges and need to be ministered to by caring and concerned adult mentors. It is our high responsibility to be prepared to respond effectively with compassion and commitment to the struggles faced by the students God has placed in our fold!

Teaching God's truth in a manner that can be absorbed and applied to everyday lifestyle is the high calling of church youth ministry. Upon that responsibility, building trust and relationships that allow us to speak to the soul and the needs of the students we work with is the reality of where Gospel teaching really makes a difference. This work is invaluable as a guide to help you become an effective youth worker to today's generation of students!

Dr. Gary Zustiak has written this wonderful tool from a rich background of years of intensive youth ministry experience, college age instruction and endless hours of counseling with thousands of students. This book is thorough (a Zustiak trait), practical, insightful and a gem of a resource from where any youth minister can gain invaluable nuggets of guidance and applicable understanding as well as helpful steps of action in response to a student's struggle. A young person's trajectory could be altered for the better and for eternity by a concerned and caring youth worker who applies what they gain from reading this work.

I wholeheartedly recommend that you add this to your "must read" resources . . . and for every volunteer youth worker in your church!

--Andy Hansen, President, Christ In Youth

INTRODUCTION

Many caring adults believe the object of comforting or advising a young person is to make that young man or woman happy. The object of ministering to youth, however, is not happiness but wholeness. --Josh McDowell and Bob Hostetler in *Handbook On Counseling Youth*[1]

Teenagers have long been considered to be hostile, moody, withdrawn, whiny, narcissistic, aggressive, rebellious, and unpredictable. Even Anna Freud, who specialized in treating young people, considered adolescent behavior to be so close to neurotic and psychotic disorders that differentiating between normal adolescents and those who had pathological problems was a very "difficult task"! --Les Parrott III, *The Comprehensive Guide to Youth Ministry Counseling*[2]

Tim[3] was eleven years old when his mother sat him, his little brother and father down in the living room to tell them that she was leaving. She was in love with another man and was only going to be home long enough to pack her bags and then she would be out of their lives forever. No amount

> **The object of ministering to youth is not happiness but wholeness.**

of tears, pleading or promises to change would dissuade her. She walked out of their lives leaving a path of emotional devastation behind. It would be years before Tim recovered from this blow.

Bonnie was going into her senior year of high school when she finally worked up the nerve to talk to her youth minister. She came from a blended family of five brothers and sisters—it was a case of "his, hers and ours." Taking a deep breath, and looking down at the floor she said, "My step-father has been making me sleep with him from the time I was eleven years old."

Ken always felt different from other boys for as long as he could remember. His father was away from home a lot on business and he spent most of his time with his mother and sisters. He didn't like the rough-housing that all the neighborhood boys engaged in and when he cried because he got hurt they would all tease him, calling him "sissy." When an older counselor at camp molested him in his cabin while the other boys were gone it confirmed in his mind that he must be a homosexual.

Kathy always struggled with her weight. In grade school the other students called her names like "chubby" and "fatso." She is now a freshman in college and is extremely concerned about her body image. She limits her meals to diet sodas, plain yogurt, carrot sticks, salads and sugarless gum. She exercises almost two hours daily. She has stopped having her monthly periods and has to wear several long-sleeved shirts at a time to keep warm and to hide her emaciated figure from others.

Fifty percent of today's youth may experience a major crisis before reaching the age of eighteen. They will be hospitalized, appear in court, have major parental conflicts, be crippled in an accident, attempt suicide, abuse alcohol or drugs, drop out of school, get pregnant, contract a sexually transmitted disease, be arrested, be raped, pay for or have an abortion, witness an act of violence, or experience something else of this magnitude. Many will endure multiple crises![4]

> Studies show that at least one in five children and adolescents have a mental health disorder.

"Today's youths live in a world where complex problems are everyday occurrences. Surviving the teen years without suffering permanent scars is a real challenge for many young people."[5] Divorce, incest, homosexuality and eating disorders are only a few of the serious struggles that plague many teenagers trying to grow up in today's society. According to the National Alliance for Mental Illness, 20% of youth ages 13-18 live with a mental health condition.[6] It is disturbing to compare what was once considered the main problems of youth growing up in the 50s and 60s with those in the 90s and the new millennium. In Clyde Narramore's book, *Counseling Youth*, published in 1966, his table of contents listed the problems of children and youth as: aggression and hostility, attention getting, bedwetting, dating, dress and grooming, educational and vocational planning, homesickness, lying, parental conflict, sex problems, spiritual problems and withdrawal and shyness.[7] In Josh McDowell's, *Handbook On Counseling Youth*, published in 1996, his table of contents contained: suicidal thoughts, tendencies, and threats, parental divorce, masturbation, pornography, abortion, homosexuality, AIDS, rape, ritual abuse, drug and alcohol abuse, and eating disorders.[8] The following chart allows you to see the difference in a side by side comparison.

Narramore - 1966	McDowell - 1996
1. Aggression and Hostility	1. Suicidal Thoughts and Threats
2. Attention Getting	2. Parental Divorce
3. Bedwetting	3. Masturbation
4. Dating	4. Pornography
5. Dress and Grooming	5. Abortion
6. Educational and Vocational	6. Homosexuality

Planning	
7. Homesickness	7. AIDS
8. Lying	8. Rape
9. Parental Conflict	9. Ritual Abuse
10. Sex Problems	10. Drug and Alcohol Abuse
11. Spiritual Problems	11. Eating Disorders
12. Withdrawal and Shyness	12. Premarital Sex

It could be argued that the problems of youth have not really increased, but only society's awareness of them and willingness to acknowledge them. Regardless of whether the problems have truly increased in number and intensity or whether it is just our awareness of them, no one can deny there is a tremendous need for willing and trained adults to come along side of hurting teens and help them navigate successfully through the various crises and problems they encounter as a part of growing up.

The purpose of this book is to provide some essential insights and practical techniques for those who engage in the ministry of counseling youth. It is not intended to be a substitute for professional training or treatment, but a basic resource for those involved in lay counseling or pastoral care of teenagers. It is my prayer that this resource will equip you to serve more effectively and confidently as you minister to the various needs of the young people God has placed in your care. Consider this possibility: if **you** don't provide young people with the help they need now, *they may never get it from any other source!* Without your prayerful intervention, their difficulties may become worse. "Problems don't just solve themselves. They usually become more exaggerated and more serious. Later they will require a longer period of time to solve."[9]

Trust and allow God to work through you to bring real hope and healing to hurting adolescents. "A man finds joy in giving an apt reply— and how good is a timely word!" "A word aptly spoken is like apples of gold in settings of silver."[10]

CHAPTER ONE

CHARACTERISTICS OF AN EFFECTIVE COUNSELOR

(DO YOU HAVE WHAT IT TAKES?)

"Empathy is feeling your pain in my heart." Kids respond to people whom they sense have a feel for what they're going through. –Rich Van Pelt, *Intensive Care: Helping Teenagers in Crisis*[11]

Leaders must not wait until they feel "good enough" to make a difference. Accepting this myth may prevent leaders from fulfilling the very role that students need most: loving them and being there with them. The most important instrument of healing a leader can have is herself. Why? Because *who* a person is in relationship to hurting teenagers is more important than *what* a person can do in terms of professional competence. --Les Parrott III in *Reaching a Generation for Christ*[12]

Empathy is feeling your pain in my heart.

I never wanted to be a "professional counselor." I just wanted to be involved in youth ministry and be the most effective youth minister that I could possibly be. It was my privilege to be hired as a part-time youth minister in a medium sized church my freshman year of Bible College. I entered into this ministry opportunity with all eight cylinders running strong. I played guitar and led the youth group in contemporary worship before it was even called contemporary worship! The wild and crazy games I came up with from my library of *Idea Books* wowed the teens and they looked forward to the next student event to see what bizarre thing I would come up with next. The Wednesday night Bible studies came right out of my gospels class that I was taking at college. Whatever I learned in college that week was what I passed along to the students. It seemed the deeper I took them and the more I challenged them with biblical insights, the more they liked it. The church people were always very complimentary when I preached for the monthly youth service. As far as my skills in biblical exegesis, apologetics, homiletics and practical ministry were concerned, I was very confident that I could meet the needs of the students entrusted to my care.

I just wasn't prepared for the depth and the intensity of the counseling needs that I encountered in my youth ministry. Serious problems such as rape, incest, homosexuality, drug and alcohol abuse and suicidal thoughts needed much more than just a prayer from me and some hastily quoted verses of scripture. The depth of inadequacy that I felt was overwhelming. I loved these teens and really wanted to help them, but it was obvious that what they needed was beyond what I could give them at the time. It was this first ministry experience that convinced me to go to graduate school and pursue a Master's Degree in Pastoral Care and Counseling.

The training and education that I received in graduate school proved invaluable to me in terms of my confidence and skill level in treating the various counseling issues that I encountered as a regular part of my ministry. However, I learned a very important lesson concerning one's effectiveness in counseling when I was serving as a Youth and Counseling Minister after graduate school.

> **The single most important factor in effective counseling is the personhood of the counselor.**

My policy was that I would see people on a short-term basis, but if the problem required some long-term, intensive treatment I would refer them to a professional counselor. One of the counselors that I would use was a very godly man. He was a licensed professional counselor (LPC) and also served as an elder in our church. Our children played together in the neighborhood and our families would often share a meal together. While Fred[13] was qualified professionally and spiritually to be a counselor and I had confidence in him, I encountered a troubling phenomenon when I would refer clients to him. After about four or six weeks (sometimes less than that) the people I referred would call me at the office and try to convince me to take them back as clients. When I questioned their experience with Fred they would be very apologetic and say something like, "Well, I am sure he is a very nice man and he may be a licensed counselor but I just didn't get the feeling that he really cared for me. I mean, he just seemed so cold and distant." It was then that I realized one's personality contributed as much to a successful counseling experience as one's training and education.

> **The effectiveness of your counseling is determined primarily by the quality of your personality.**

The single most important factor in effective counseling is the personhood of the counselor. Regardless of one's education, training, theoretical orientation, or counseling techniques, it is now widely accepted that if certain qualities are not brought to the helping relationship, little chance of successful intervention exists.[14]

You see, while Fred was a Christian and qualified as a counselor professionally, his very reserved and quiet personality did not communicate to his clients that he understood and cared for them. As a result, his clients interpreted his reflective and introverted personality as a lack of concern. Dr. Keith Olson sums it up well:

> You are the main ingredient in counseling. The effectiveness of your counseling is determined primarily by the quality of your personality. The techniques that you use and the skills you possess, although important, are secondary to the quality of your being.[15]

Don't misunderstand! Learning counseling techniques is very important. Years of specialized training, classes, supervision and continuing education all help the counselor to develop and refine their skills. But in the end, a counselor's style will be very much a reflection of their unique and caring personality. "Research findings have shown that in general, therapeutic change in clients results from client and therapist factors more than from techniques."[16]

Qualities of an Effective Counselor

To gain a better insight into the importance of personal characteristics and effective counseling, fill out the following chart and reflect on what you discover about counseling effectiveness and personal characteristics. Think about the different people who have made a significant impact on your life. Try to remember especially those people whom you deemed helpful during your teenage years as you were struggling with developmental and relational problems. List the person's name in the first column, try to identify a specific characteristic or helping quality they exhibited and write it in the second column and finish by describing your personal response to their help.[17] Some people may have more than one characteristic. I have given some personal examples to help you get started.

Exercise 1.1 – Helping Qualities

HELPING PERSON	HELPING QUALITY	MY RESPONSE
Glen	Always made himself available - he was never too	Trust and a sense of security knowing I could

	busy to listen	call on him whenever I needed
Kenny	Showed unconditional love	Did not feel "judged" or inferior just because I had a problem
Chuck	Encourager—always found something positive to say	Improved my self-esteem and motivated me to keep trying and not give up
Paul	Speaking the truth in love—confronted me and held me accountable	Learned to take responsibility for my life and choices and to be honest about my failings

Look over the helping qualities in the list. I believe that what you will find is that the qualities that were deemed "helpful" are qualities that can be found in just about any caring person. You don't have to have a Ph.D. or a Harvard education in order to make a significant difference in a young person's life.

> I have no methods. All I do is accept people.
> –Paul Tournier

However, research has shown that there are certain characteristics that are found in the most successful counselors. You will want to try and incorporate those into your life if you wish to be the most effective counselor to youth that you can be.

The Discovery of the "Big Three"

The search to discover what makes some counselors successful and some unsuccessful (and some even harmful) has led researchers to an overwhelming conclusion. There are certain personality characteristics that provide the core of effective counseling when adequately integrated within the counselor's person.[18]

It has been said that there are no superior therapies but only superior therapists. In other words, it doesn't matter as much what particular therapy you have been trained in, if you have the essential personality characteristics that communicate genuine concern and caring, then you will be a successful counselor of youth.

What are the essential personality characteristics of effective counselors? Research has proven that clients of therapists improve if the therapist expresses high levels of 1) accurate empathy; 2) unconditional positive regard or warmth; and 3) genuineness or congruence.[19] These findings have been supported by subsequent research and is found in practically every textbook on counseling and psychology. It would be helpful to define in more detail each particular characteristic.

> **All successful counselors possess high levels of:**
> 1. **Empathy**
> 2. **Warmth**
> 3. **Genuineness**

Accurate Empathy – Empathy is the ability to communicate to another that you feel their pain. As far as it is humanly possible, you are sharing in their experience along with them whether it be grief, anger, depression or hopelessness etc. Empathy "implies both the capacity to enter into the feeling states and understandings of another person but also the capacity to communicate this to the person."[20] Empathy is different from sympathy, it is deeper and stronger. With sympathy, you feel sorry *for* someone—but you are personally removed from the situation. With empathy, you feel sorry *with* someone—you enter into their situation and try to understand and experience it from the viewpoint of the client. "Sympathy is standing on the shore and throwing out a lifeline while empathy is jumping into the water and risking one's safety to help another."[21]

Unconditional Positive Regard or Warmth – This is simply another way of saying "unconditional love" (Romans 5:8,10). Jesus loves us enough to die for us *just as we are*. He came and provided salvation for us even though we didn't deserve it nor could we earn it. It is nonjudgmental acceptance of people. "Paul Tournier, the renowned Swiss counselor, said, "I have no methods. All I do is accept people."[22] Caution: this does *not* mean that the counselor approves of all the current behaviors and choices of the teenager, but simply that he accepts the teenager as a worthwhile human being, made in the image of God and deserving of respect and care. "It is friendliness and consideration shown by facial expression, tone of voice, gestures, posture, eye-contact, and such non-verbal behavior as looking after the helpee's comfort."[23]

> Warmth is non-judgmental. It is neither approving nor disapproving. Rather it accepts the individual, not requiring change or growth in order to invest time and energy in him or her. This issue here is acceptance, not evaluation. . . It is a freeing kind of love. It frees the teenager from the tyranny of pleasing the counselor in order not to feel guilty. It frees the teenager to be his or her own person, rather than the person someone else wishes.[24]

"If we are to respect the other person we are required to see him or her again, *from God's perspective,* to relate to him or her as though he or she is a person of worth, regardless of what life has done or what the person has done in his or her life."[25]

Genuineness or Congruence – This trait refers to the necessity of the counselor's behavioral and affective display to match what he is communicating to the teenager. It must also be in harmony with the content currently being communicated by the teenager. In other words, if the counselor is verbally communicating words of care and concern, but his tone of voice and body language is sending a message of boredom and indifference, then he is not being congruent or genuine. Another example of failing to exhibit congruence would be if the teen is sharing about a very painful experience and the counselor has a smile on his face and a very self-satisfied demeanor. The counselor must communicate by their body language, facial expression, tone and rate of voice and expressed emotions that they are genuinely *with* the teenager and understanding the teen's current experience whether it be joy, depression, hopelessness or confusion. "Genuineness means that the helper's words are consistent with his actions. He or she tries to be honest with the helpee, avoiding any statement or behavior which could be considered phony or insincere."[26] "Genuineness cannot be faked. Either you sincerely want to help or you are simply playing the sterile role of a "helper"—hiding behind masks, defenses, or facades. In other words, authenticity is something you *are*, not something you *do.*[27]

While these three traits have been found to be critical for effective counseling, they do not guarantee success nor are they the *only* traits needed. They are necessary but not all-sufficient.

Additional Traits That Contribute to Successful Youth Counseling

The following traits/characteristics are also very helpful for the person counseling with teenagers. Remember that you do not have to possess all of them, but the more of them you can incorporate in your life the higher the probability will be that you will be a successful counselor to teens. This list is not meant to be exhaustive and you are encouraged to discover other traits that teens find helpful in those who counsel them.

> **God gave you two eyes and two ears so that you would do twice as much observing and listening as you do talking!**

A good listener – Someone has said that This is especially true for the effective counselor. Active listening is an essential skill for the one who wants to successfully work with youth. The road to the heart is through the ears. A good listener should be able to restate back to the teen the content and feelings behind his statements without judging them, adding to them, correcting them or leaving anything out. This does *not* mean that the counselor merely acts like a parrot and just repeats verbatim what the teen said, but is able to capture the content, feeling and meaning of the teen's statements and restate them in his own words in such a way that it communicates a total grasp of what the teen is thinking and experiencing.

> Adolescents do not readily lay out their thoughts and feelings even for a compassionate counselor. Counselors who build a therapeutic relationship with adolescents do it the old-fashioned way: They earn it. An adolescent's real concerns are often closed off and opened only by continued and careful listening.[28]

> **Usually the teen wants to "test the waters" before actually getting to the real problem.**

Teens share their stories not only by the words they use, but also by *how* they say it, by what they choose *not* to say and by what they find *painful* to say. If you will really listen you will be alert to these unspoken messages as well.

Patience – It is a rare teen who will make an appointment to talk to a counselor and who will actually open up and begin talking about the core issue that is bothering them. Usually the teen wants to "test the waters", so to speak, before actually getting to the real problem. In this way, they are able to gauge whether or not the counselor is trustworthy and will actually be helpful to them or merely be another adult who thinks he has all the answers before really listening.

> Trying to solve a young person's problem before the problem is fully understood is a common therapeutic mistake. It takes patience and time to unwrap the salient features of a teenager's problem. Like a complex jigsaw puzzle with hundreds of interlocking pieces, a young person's struggle cannot be solved in a matter of minutes.[29]

Availability – While our lives and work schedules all seem to be busier than ever, the effective youth counselor knows that they must make time for young people when a crisis arises. We must communicate our availability to them.

> **Availability must be coupled with approachability.**

Caution: It is possible to be physically present with a teen, but not really "with them." "Physical presence must be coupled with an emotional focus for the availability to be meaningful and helpful."[30] Availability must also be coupled with approachability. There are a good number of youth workers who pride themselves on spending lots of time with their students by visiting them on campus, taking them out for cokes after school and attending many school social functions. While they may be physically present, they are not truly approachable, because certain aspects of their personality keep the students at arm's length.

A sense of humor – It has been said that "laughter is the best medicine." There is something very therapeutic about a good, hearty laugh. Recent medical studies

> **There is something very therapeutic about a good, hearty laugh.**

have pointed out the physiological benefits of laughter. "A study done at the University of Maryland Medical Center suggests that a good sense of humor and the ability to laugh at stressful situations helps mitigate the damaging physical effects of distressing emotions."[31] The incorporation of humor in a counseling setting is a developed skill that requires good judgment, timing and sensitivity. The correct and timely use of humor with a teenager can open up dialog and create huge insights into the teen's world.

But, a word of caution: humorous intentions can be misinterpreted. A teen might misconstrue the use of humor as a personal put-down or as the counselor not taking the teen's problem seriously. Proceed with caution, but don't be afraid to use humor when you have deemed it appropriate both to the situation and to the individual teen involved.

Competency – Anyone who wants to counsel teens should follow the physician's rule of thumb concerning treatment. I would summarize it in this way: Do no harm. If what you are doing helps, keep it up. If what you are doing doesn't help, stop it. If you don't know what you are doing, don't do anything.

When I find myself scheduled to meet with a neurosurgeon who is going to be operating on my back to remove a ruptured disk, I don't really care if the receptionist tells me the doctor has the greatest sense of humor. It is of no great interest to me that he can hit a 3-point shot four out of five times on the city league basketball team. The fact that he has a wonderful tenor voice in the church choir is of no importance to me. There is only thing I want to know if this guy is going to be cutting open my back—Is he a competent surgeon? Because if he isn't, nothing else matters!

Parents and teens have a right to expect competency from us too. This doesn't mean that you need a Ph.D. in clinical psychology before you listen to a depressed teen's story, but it does mean that you must know your limitations. It is of paramount importance that you are able to recognize when the issues are so severe that a referral is needed and you can do so with confidence.

> Do no harm. If what you are doing helps, keep it up. If what you are doing doesn't help, stop it. If you don't know what you are doing, don't do anything.

There are a number of good resources to help train the willing worker on the essentials of counseling youth. You are encouraged to take appropriate college courses and to attend as many weekend seminars as you can in order to sharpen your counseling skills. If you aren't in a position to be able to attend a college class, there are a number of counseling training courses available through the internet and on DVD.

Spiritual sensitivity and vibrancy – The Christian counselor who wants to influence teenage lives in a positive way must be firmly grounded in the faith and have a vibrant and growing relationship with Jesus Christ. A knowledge of God's word serves as the foundation for all counsel. "The fear of the Lord is the beginning of wisdom, and the knowledge of the Holy One is understanding" (Proverbs 9:10). The skilled counselor will utilize a variety of psychological methods and techniques, but all of them must be tested, not only scientifically and pragmatically, but primarily against the written Word of God.

Being a Christian does not give a counselor some mystical power for healing people's psychological brokenness. It does, however, bring him or her into conscious spiritual living. Being a Christian opens us to the possibility of living our lives at a higher level of personal integration. Spiritual and psychological energies can be focused together for more effective counseling. . . Being a Christian does not guarantee being a good counselor. But being alive to spiritual reality within yourself can help you assist young counselees in their spiritual and psychological growth.[32]

> "A gossip betrays a confidence, but a trustworthy man keeps a secret" (Proverbs 11:13).

Confidentiality – Nothing will kill your effectiveness as a counselor more than a violation of confidentiality. When something that was revealed in the sacred confines of the counseling session is then used as an illustration in a sermon/lesson or a "prayer concern" the young person feels betrayed. It doesn't matter if the counselor believes the information has gone public, the counselor should always protect the privacy of the young person by not sharing with others what was told to them in confidence. "A gossip betrays a confidence, but a trustworthy man keeps a secret" (Proverbs 11:13).

Having said that, you need to know that the confidentiality rule is not absolute. In fact, there are times when the professional counselor is required to break confidentiality by law. Even if you are not bound to the same rules and requirements as a professional counselor, it would still be helpful to follow the same guidelines. Confidentiality is to be broken is cases of: 1) physical or sexual abuse; 2) suicide, and 3) homicide (the intention to physically harm another person). A professional consultation is not considered a violation of the confidentiality rule. This is where the counselor is not sure on how to proceed with the troubled teen and consults with another professional about the facts of the case, while keeping the identity of the client confidential.

The youth counselor is bound to encounter situations that do not require them to break confidentiality, but believes that it would be in the best interests of the teen to do so. Situations like teen pregnancy, drug addiction, date rape, etc., cry out for parental involvement. In cases like this, I try to gently guide the teen to an understanding that this information must be shared. I offer to provide a safe environment for the information to be shared or even to share the information myself if the teen is too scared. In doing so, the teen does not feel like confidentiality has been broken because they have had a voice in the process and it did not take place apart from their knowledge.

Humility – "The best counseling will come from our taking the position of humble dependence upon God for His enlightenment and wisdom, in the work of counseling."[33] I am reminded of the words of Jesus in John 15:4-5: "Remain in me, and I will remain in you. No branch can bear fruit by itself; it must remain in the vine. Neither can you bear fruit unless you remain in me. I am the vine; you are the branches. If a man remains in me and I in him, he will bear much fruit; apart from me you can do nothing." Keeping this truth in mind will prevent us from thinking that we, as counselors, have all the answers. We must still seek to draw upon all of our training and experience in the counseling area and consult with others when necessary, but ultimately, we need to acknowledge our limitations as imperfect vessels and continually seek God's wisdom.

> The best counseling will come from our taking the position of humble dependence upon God for His enlightenment and wisdom, in the work of counseling.

Unique Characteristics of a Christian Counselor

> The first requirement for anyone wanting to contribute as a Christian counselor in healing and restorative work with distressed and troubled people, is a vital relationship with Jesus.

"The first requirement for anyone wanting to contribute as a Christian counselor in healing and restorative work with distressed and troubled people, is a vital relationship with Jesus. This will always be the 'foundation distinctive' for Christian counselors."[34] Having an understanding of biblical principles and being able to apply them to the counseling encounter is important, but it is not as important as the counselor's relationship to Jesus Christ. Whatever other qualities the counselor possesses naturally or seeks to develop through training, these will always be secondary to the importance of a relationship to Jesus that is vibrant and growing.

Unique Assumptions – The Christian counselor is going to possess some basic beliefs about the inspiration and authority of the Bible, the attributes of God (i.e., God is a compassionate, forgiving, sovereign God), the nature of humankind (i.e. made in the image of God, but fallen), and that the forgiveness of sins and the hope of eternal life is available through Jesus Christ. Wholeness, restoration and healing is the desire of

God for all people. These beliefs are going to guide the counselor as they seek to come along side of the young person and provide godly guidance and counsel.

God is not as concerned about a person's happiness as He is their holiness.

Unique Goals – The main goal of Christian counseling is the facilitation of spiritual maturity and growth. Like other counselors, Christian counselors do seek to help the client deal with the problems that are presented. But solving problems is *not* their primary objective. Rather, their goal is to help people understand their problems, and their lives, in light of their relationship with God and then to make responsible choices in light of this knowledge. The Christian counselor works with the client to alleviate their problems because he wants the client to experience the abundant life in Christ (John 10:10). But problems should never be the primary focus. The focus should be on helping the client become a whole person as he or she lives out life as a child of God. God is not as concerned about a person's happiness as He is their holiness.

> Genuine soul care is never exclusively focused on any one aspect of a person's being to the exclusion of all others. If care is to be worthy of being called soul care, it must not address parts or focus on problems but engage two or more people with one another to the end of the nurture and growth of the whole person.[35]

> Historically Christian soul care has involved four primary elements: healing, sustaining, reconciling, and guiding. *Healing* involves efforts to help someone overcome an impairment and move toward wholeness. These curative efforts can involve physical healing as well as spiritual healing, but the focus is always the total person, whole and holy. *Sustaining* refers to acts of caring designed to help a hurting person endure and transcend a circumstance in which restoration or recuperation is either impossible or improbable. *Reconciling* refers to efforts to reestablish broken relationships. The presence of this component of care demonstrates the communal, not simply individual, nature of Christian soul care. Finally, *guiding* refers to helping a person make wise choices and thereby grow in spiritual maturity.[36]

Unique Methods – Besides using the standard counseling skills and techniques of professional therapy, the Christian counselor is also going to incorporate prayer, Bible reading, confession, meditation, worship and devotional literature when appropriate.

> When religious resources are used in counseling, it is crucial that they be employed with care and sensitivity. In particular, it is important that a pastor understand how they are experienced by the person who is seeking help. Prayer, scripture reading, and other religious resources carry heavy, negative emotional freight for some people. They can also easily be used in ways that arouse inappropriate guilt or unnecessary discomfort or block creative dialogue.[37]

When using a particular religious resource in counseling it is important that the Christian counselor think through why he is choosing that resource at that particular time. It could be that the resource of choice is the most appropriate and helpful for the situation at hand. But, it could also be a way of avoiding talking about an uncomfortable subject, or it might be a way of providing premature reassurance, possibly even a way of relieving one's own anxiety or distress. "Religious resources should always be used in ways that empower the person, never in ways that might diminish his or her sense of initiative, strength, or responsibility. They must facilitate rather than block the owning and catharsis of negative feelings."[38]

> **When religious resources are used in counseling, it is crucial that they be employed with care and sensitivity.**

Conclusion

You may be saying to yourself, "There is no way I can measure up to all of these expectations. I might as well give up on being a counselor." Take heart! There is no counselor or therapist who possesses all of these characteristics. But you should be aware of them and their importance in the counseling process and be willing to try and develop them to some degree in your life.

Possessing the aforementioned characteristics or traits will greatly enhance your chances of being an effective youth counselor, but I would caution you that there are no guarantees. Even the best professional counselors are not immune to oversights or blunders. But do not let fear of failure keep you from involving yourself in the life of a troubled teenager. "If you are a counselor in training, give yourself permission to make mistakes and learn from them. No one expects you to be a 'perfect' counselor right out of the gate. So, don't give up if you initially fumble your way through the practice of counseling struggling adolescents."[39]

Exercise 1.2 - Positive Counseling Characteristics

Rate yourself on possession of the following positive counseling characteristics. Use the scale provided: 1 = poor; 2 = below average; 3 = Average; 4 = Above average; 5 = Excellent. Simply check the box that best describes you. If you are brave, ask a trusted friend to take the exercise on your behalf. Look for discrepancies in your scores.

Characteristic or Trait	1	2	3	4	5
Accurate Empathy					
Unconditional Positive Regard or Warmth					
Genuineness or Congruence					
A Good Listener					
Patience					
Availability					
A Sense of Humor					
Competency					
Spiritual Sensitivity and Vibrancy					
Confidentiality					
Humility					

1. What are your counseling strengths? How can you capitalize on them?
2. Where are your weaknesses?
3. What can you do to improve the areas where you are the weakest?
4. How would you rate a person whom you respect as a good counselor in each area?

CHAPTER TWO

WHAT A TEEN IN CRISIS NEEDS FROM A COUNSELOR

(COUNSELING INSIGHTS FROM THE BOOK OF JOB)

Though not all crises or problems are spiritual (in their cause or in their correction), they are interrelated with a person's spiritual beliefs and spiritual state. –Josh McDowell, *Handbook on Counseling Youth*[40]

It's not our responsibility to define what crisis should or should not be for teenagers. But it *is* our responsibility and privilege to respond. –Rich Van Pelt, *Intensive Care*[41]

One of the best ways we can learn what people in crisis need is by examining case studies of people who have successfully survived a crisis. The biblical book of Job serves as a great case study and is a rich source of information and insights on what to do and what *not* to do for people in crisis. While Job was definitely not a teenager when he experienced his crisis, I believe the principles and insights gained from examining his crisis and the response of his "counselors" serves as a universal guide on how to effectively minister to people of all ages who find themselves in the midst of a crisis. "A crisis is any event or series of circumstances which threatens a person's well-being and interferes with his routine of daily living."[42]

Exercise 2.1 – Insights from the Book of Job

Read through the following passages from the book of Job. From a counseling perspective write down what you believe Job really wanted and needed as a hurting person as compared to what Job actually received from his peer counselors. You may need an additional piece of notebook paper to write out all of your answers.

What Job Wanted	What Job Got
1:1; 10:7; 27:5	4:7-8; 11:6; 22:5
1:18-20	8:4
2:11	2:12-13
3:3,11	4:5-6; 5:2

6:14	6:15-16
6:26	6:26
7:11; 10:1	8:2
12:3; 13:2	13:4
13:5-6,13,17; 21:2	13:12
13:15	42:5, 10-12
16:5	16:2-4
16:20-21	18:2
17: 11	17:12
19:21	19:13-15,19
30:24	30:9-10

What Job Wanted and What Job Received From His Counselors

Let's see how many insights into the counseling process you were able to discern from the previous exercise. In Job 1:1; 10:7; 27:5 he needed for his counselors to treat him with dignity, as a man of integrity, even though he found himself in the midst of a serious crisis and great personal pain. But his counselors' theology would not allow them to give him the respect that he desperately needed in this crisis. From their standpoint, if a man was suffering as much as Job was, it had to be the punishment of God (4:7-8; 11; 6; 22:5). Their counsel was to try and get Job to acknowledge his sin, but when Job continually proclaimed his innocence they became angry with him.

This is a difficult issue because it is true that *sometimes* a person's pain is the direct result of sin. The plagues on Egypt were sent by God to punish Pharaoh and the Egyptian people because of the hardness of Pharaoh's heart. God decreed to the Israelites if they would be obedient to him that he would not bring on them any of the diseases that he brought on Egypt (Exodus 15:26). When King Jeroboam stretched out his hand to give the command to seize the man of God who had prophesied against him, God caused his hand to shrivel up so that he couldn't pull it back (1 Kings 13:4). Galatians 6:7 says, "Do not be deceived: God cannot be mocked. A man reaps what he sows." A person who abuses alcohol and ends up dying with cirrhosis of the liver has brought this upon himself through his sin. The woman who loses her home, family and respect of her friends because of her involvement in an extramarital affair is reaping what she sowed. In all of these cases it would be correct to try and bring the counselee to a place of repentance and to take responsibility for their actions. However, the danger is in *always* assuming that a person's pain is the direct result of personal sin.

In John 9:1-3 the disciples came upon a man who was blind from birth. They asked Jesus, "Rabbi, who sinned, this man or his parents, that he was born blind?" Jesus replied, "Neither this man nor his parents sinned, but this happened so that the work of God might be displayed in his life." In Luke 13:1-5 the people were telling Jesus about the Galileans who had been killed by Pilate in the middle of offering their sacrifices. The people assumed that since these men were killed in the very act of worship that somehow, they were greater sinners than anyone else. But Jesus refuted their assumption. Jesus also brought up the incident of the tower of Siloam falling over and killing eighteen people. He said that these people were not anymore guilty than all the others living in Jerusalem at the time.

So, what insights does the youth counselor learn from all of this? The most important is that we must treat every teenager who comes to us with a problem with great dignity and respect. It is not our job to judge and to try and determine whether or not the teen deserves what they are experiencing or if they have brought it upon themselves. The counselor must come alongside of the teenager and accept the young person as they are and extend unconditional love. By honoring the teen in this way, it will establish a foundation of trust that will allow the teen to be transparent and welcoming to the involvement of the counselor in their life.

Placing blame does not bring about healing.

"Loss is one of the most difficult, painful and psychologically disruptive experiences that everyone will encounter."[43] In Job 1:18-20 Job needed people who understood the depth of his pain at losing his entire family. Job tore his robe and shaved his head which was his culture's way of expressing profound grief and sorrow. Instead of comforting Job in his grief, Job's counselor suggested that the tragedy that happened to his children was brought on by their own sin (8:4). Placing blame does not bring about healing. It is especially damaging when the counselor is wrong in their assessment!

There may be a time and place in counseling for confrontation and accountability, but not when the sting of sorrow is fresh and the grief at losing everything is still overwhelming. The sensitive youth counselor knows when genuine empathy is called for and will offer it graciously to the hurting teen.

In 2:11 Job's three friends hear about his troubles and set out to meet with him in order to sympathize and comfort him. What Job needed was the support and presence of his friends. There is a saying that says: "Shared sorrow is half sorrow. Shared joy is double joy." When a teenager is going through a rough time, such as the divorce of his parents or the death of a grandparent, he needs to be surrounded by caring friends and adults. Even though nothing can be done to change the situation, just the presence of concerned people makes the grief easier to bear.

When Job's friends saw the depth of his despair, they wept aloud, tore their robes and sprinkled dust on their heads. They sat in silence with him for seven days and nights. Some people might think that his friends failed him because they didn't do or say anything. The truth is just the opposite. Job's friends communicated accurate empathy in the culturally acceptable manner. Just their presence was a comfort to Job. They didn't have to say anything or do anything. In fact, there was nothing they could say or do which would actually change the situation. The most loving thing they could do was to try and share the experience with him. Understand as a counselor, you do not have to talk all the time or "have the answers." Sometimes your presence is all the teen needs to gain strength and courage to face the difficult days to come.

Job is so devastated by his loss that he wishes he had never been born (3:3, 11). This is another way of expressing deep grief and sorrow. He needed empathy and understanding but what he received from his counselor was a stern rebuke (4:5-6). He was told to "buck up and take it like a man!"

In 6:14 Job pleads for unconditional love to be given to him. He argues that a true friend will remain devoted to another even if one is in such despair that he gives up on God. But what Job received from his counselors was conditional acceptance. He called them "fair-weather friends" (6:15-17).

If you are involved in youth ministry for any time at all it won't be long before you see some students who "crash and burn." It may be drugs, alcohol, crime, premarital sex or homosexuality that causes them to drop out. What I have noticed in my years of ministry is that it is rarely

32

a sudden and unforeseen event. Youth workers and peers can usually see it coming. The sad thing is that as they see it coming they begin to remove themselves from the life of the teen who is struggling. It is a judgmental attitude that says, "Unless you are good enough and keep it together I won't hang around with you." The youth counselor who is wise knows that offering unconditional love does not mean approval of all the choices that a struggling teen makes, but simply that they are going to model the same kind of attitude that God displays towards lost and struggling people (Romans 5:6-8).

In 6:26 Job was simply asking that his counselor's treat his sharing of his crisis with respect. Have the courtesy to accept my experience at face value without questioning it. But his counselors dismissed the validity of his experience and made him feel like his words meant nothing—they totally invalidated him by not allowing his story to speak for itself.

> **A person in crisis needs an opportunity to talk, confident that those thoughts and feelings are not falling on deaf ears.**

A universal need of people in crisis is to find a safe place to "vent." Venting is a form of catharsis[44] where the counselee just "lets it all out." It is a kind of emotional lancing of a wound—it relieves the pressure and the pain. This is what Job was referring to in 7:11 when he spoke of "not keeping silent," "speaking out in the anguish of his spirit," and "complaining in the bitterness of his soul." Job's counselors did the very opposite of what he needed and told him to "shut up" (8:2)

Teens especially need a place to vent because their parents often misinterpret it as anger and resentment directed at them and try to repress it, when in reality the teen is just trying to work through the strong emotions pent up inside of them. A good counselor will allow a teen to vent, not taking it personally or feeling threatened by the strong release of emotions and the verbal barrage that pours forth. There are times when this is all that is needed to help the teen regain their emotional equilibrium. The counselor doesn't have to change anything, solve any problems or even give new insight—all that is required is that they be a good listener.

A person in crisis needs an opportunity to talk, confident that those thoughts and feelings are not falling on deaf ears. None of us appreciates being asked a question when there's no obvious interest in our reply. Few kids ever have the privilege of really being listened to by an adult who will take the time that's required and who will work hard at understanding what's being said.[45]

One reason why people are reluctant to share their struggles with other people is that they do not want to be looked down upon just because they are currently struggling with a problem. This was Job's concern in 12:3. He felt that his counselors were acting in a condescending and judgmental way towards him. They had determined that Job's crisis was "deserved"—that he was an evil man who was being punished by God. Job wanted to be treated with respect, dignity and as an equal with his counselors. In other words, his current crisis did not make him inferior to his friends just because their lives were not in crisis at the time. Not only did Job not get treated with respect, but his counselors actually portrayed him to be worse than he actually was! They lied about him (13:4)!

Hurting teenagers already have enough self-esteem issues they struggle with just as a natural part of growing up. They do not need their counselors to add to their pain by making them feel like "second-class" citizens because they struggle with difficult issues. "Kids and families sometimes fear that if we *really* knew the truth about them, we'd want nothing to do with them. They, like the disfigured serviceman, have the validity of that fear confirmed all too often."[46] A good counselor communicates total acceptance of the individual as a child of God made in His image and redeemed by the precious blood of Christ.

Job cried out for his counselors to simply be good listeners (13:5-6, 13, 17; 21:2). He said, "If you will just listen carefully to my words that will be consolation, relief and comfort to me."

> **In giving hope to people facing desperate situations, we must be careful not to offer simplistic answers or false hope.**

There is a difference between hearing and listening. Hearing is the gaining of information for oneself. Listening is caring for and being empathetic toward others. In listening we are trying to understand the feelings of the other person, and we are listening for his sake. Hearing is determined by what goes on inside of me, what effect the conversation has on me. Listening is determined by what is going on inside the other person, why my attentiveness is doing for him.[47]

In the previous chapter I talked about the value and importance of being a good listener, but instead of patient listening Job's counselors gave him maxims and proverbs (13:12). In other words, instead of allowing him to vent they responded to his despairing situation with trite sayings and religious adages. It was the kind of fluff that Hallmark cards are made of: "Just let go and let God." "When God closes a door, He opens a window." "When life gives you lemons, make lemonade." These kinds of remarks, even though they are well-intentioned, tend to be insulting and come across as superficial and lacking in genuine concern and understanding of the situation. "In giving hope to people facing desperate situations, we must be careful not to offer simplistic answers or false hope."[48] Your mom was right: "If you don't know what to say, don't say anything at all!"

When teens experience a devastating crisis such as the death of a family member, severe illness or a natural disaster like Katrina they will often interpret the event as the abandonment of God. What teenagers need, and what Job needed, is to be assured that God has not forsaken them in the midst of the crisis (13:15).

Joseph experienced one crisis after another. First, his brothers beat him up and threw him into a well. Next, they sold him into slavery. Then his master's wife tried to seduce him and when he rejected her efforts she falsely accused him of attempted rape. Joseph was then placed in the king's prison. He had every reason to believe that God had forsaken him and yet in the midst of all of this the Bible declares three times in the chapter that "the Lord was with Joseph."[49] Job is similarly vindicated by God at the end of the account (42:5, 10-12). A helpful youth counselor will know how to assure the struggling teen that God is still with him, even when it doesn't *feel* like it.

> **A helpful youth counselor will know how to assure the struggling teen that God is still with him, even when it doesn't *feel* like it.**

Job continues to instruct his counselors on what he desires from them. He needs encouragement, comfort and relief (16:5). But what he gets is a lecture—a long-winded one at that (16:3). Advice giving is probably one of the most misused elements of the counseling experience. Rarely is advice giving very helpful to the counselee and it takes the focus off of the client who needs to be heard and understood and places it on the counselor. Teens feel like they get talked to plenty. What they need is someone who will really listen.

When Job feels distant from God and unsure of his standing with Him, he needs a counselor who will go to God on his behalf (16:20-21).

Prayer can be a powerful tool in counseling youth as long as it is used appropriately. It is inappropriate and unhelpful when prayer is used just to avoid dealing with a difficult issue or as a "magic wand" that will automatically make it better without the hard work of going to the source of the problem and taking responsibility for working through it.

In 17:11 Job shares once more about the depth of his pain. From his perspective, his life is over. His plans are shattered and the desires of his heart are crushed. He needs for his counselors to acknowledge the intensity of his heartache and to understand how profoundly broken he is. Instead, his counselors minimize his pain with false optimism and empty platitudes (17:12).

Job cries out to his counselors to have pity on him and his situation for he feels that God has struck him down (19:21). But instead of support, his family, friends and closest associates have removed themselves from Job's life. Job's abandonment in his time of need is complete. Not only has his main source of support failed him when he needed them the most, but some actually turned against him (19:13-19).

The last kindness that Job seeks from his counselors is simply consideration for his situation. You don't kick a man when he is down. You deal gently with him and show sensitivity concerning the crisis that he is in (30:24-25). Yet Job found himself being mocked, rejected and some even had the audacity to spit in his face (30:9-10). In their opinion he deserved what he was experiencing. They added insult to injury.

Exercise 2.2 – Personal Evaluation of Crisis Needs Skills

Please place an "**X**" on the lines to indicate where you perceive yourself to be presently with respect to the specific crisis needs skills from the book of Job. This will provide you with a fair assessment of your strengths and areas where you need to improve.

Treat with dignity	------------------------------------	Condemnation
Compassion	------------------------------------	Place blame
Available	------------------------------------	Unavailable
Empathy	------------------------------------	Harshness
Unconditional love	------------------------------------	Conditional love
Respect	------------------------------------	Rejection
Allow venting	------------------------------------	Prohibit venting
Treat as equal	------------------------------------	Treat as inferior
Careful listener	------------------------------------	Offer trite sayings
Vindicated by God	------------------------------------	Rejected by God
Encouragement	------------------------------------	Insensitive lectures

Intercessor to God	----------------------------------	Failure to pray
Acknowledge pain	----------------------------------	Minimize pain
Support	----------------------------------	Abandonment
Gentleness	----------------------------------	Callousness

It's inevitable as you work with teenagers that you are going to encounter them in the midst of a crisis. In fact, you may feel that you simply move from one crisis to another! Exhibiting the right characteristics and possessing a knowledge of what is helpful and what is not helpful will greatly enhance your ability to minister to the teens who have been entrusted to your oversight. Caring for those in need is a reflection of God's character, it imitates Christ's work and is an essential function of the body of Christ.

Helpful Resources

Miller, Ashley. "Top Eight Attributes of an Effective Counselor."
      Chron.com. Accessed: March 21, 2017.
      http://work.chron.com/top-eight-attributes-effective-counselor-
      22250.html
"What Are the Characteristics of an Effective Counselor? Careerigniter.
      Accessed: March 21, 2017.
      http://www.careerigniter.com/questions/what-are-the-
      characteristics-of-an-effective-counselor/

CHAPTER THREE

A MODEL FOR COUNSELING

(THIS IS HOW IT'S DONE, PEOPLE)

Counseling is serving as a *facilitator and catalyst of change*. We do not change anyone, but we help people change. Counseling is a process of assisting people to solve their own problems. –Dave Carlson in *The Youth Leader's Sourcebook*[50]

Without accurate listening the counselor is rendered totally ineffective. Listening is not so much a technique that the counselor uses or does as it is a required ingredient for all counseling. –G. Keith Olson in *Counseling Teenagers*[51]

Counseling is a function that ministers have always performed, at least in an informal way in many situations. Research has shown over and over again that people's first choice of a person to help them when they have a problem is a member of the clergy.[52] This is true whether the person with the problem is particularly religious or not. People prefer a counselor who approaches therapy from a religious background. The same is true for the young people that you work with. Whether they are talking to their youth minister or one of their adult sponsors whom they have come to trust, they want to know that the guidance they are going to receive comes from a Christian perspective.

Religious counselors have a status and resources that secular counselors do not have. Pastors bring to counseling the dimension of faith and the resources of worship and prayer. They endeavor to reveal a way of life that has cosmic worth and significance. They help people to recognize themselves as beings of worth in the sight of God.[53]

The Significance of Relationship in Counseling

How does one go about successfully caring for a struggling adolescent? Where do you begin? How do you begin? It has been proven time and time again that the most important ingredient in helping teens through difficult issues is the relationship you build with them. Helen Perlman, in her book, *Relationships: The Heart of Helping People*, states:

"What is the common element, the red thread, that seems to run through every successful effort by one person to influence another in benign and enabling ways? The answer seems to be 'relationship.'"[54]

> Relationship is the essence of counseling being done by clergy. To be sure, such counseling may incorporate a wide variety of methods and techniques, but the essential component that brings about the resolution of difficulties is the therapeutic relationship between the minister and the counselee.[55]

> **It has been proven time and time again that the most important ingredient in helping teens through difficult issues is the relationship you build with them.**

Moreover, Clarkson has written: "A wealth of studies demonstrates that it is the relationship between the client and the psychotherapist, more than any other factor, which determines the effectiveness of psychotherapy."[56] Yalom affirms, "It is the relationship that heals. This is the single most important lesson the therapist must learn."[57] Coleman makes the same emphasis. "Actually, the doctor-patient relationship is not a tool or instrument of psychotherapy; it is the primary process itself. It is the stage and the play, and not merely the way in which the lines are read."[58]

You can easily see that more than any other single issue it is the relationship in counseling that is the curative agent. If any healing takes place through counseling with youth, it occurs through relationship. Even though there are many different schools of psychotherapy, it is the importance of the counselor-client relationship that is the common healing element among them.

Therefore, since the relationship between the client and the counselor is the main vehicle through which healing takes place, it should be a priority for the counselor of youth to learn all that you can about what makes for a healthy relationship.

The counseling relationship does not develop instantaneously. If building a meaningful and helpful relationship with a teenager as a part of youth ministry takes time, it is even more so with personal counseling. You must be aware that the counseling relationship, important as it is, cannot and must not, be forced. It must be allowed to grow slowly and naturally until it is strong enough to allow the sensitive sharing and communication that must develop in order for healing to take place.

The Essence of Counseling Is Helping People Solve Their Own Problems

One of the most common misconceptions about counseling is that counseling is either giving people advice or solving people's problems for them. Nothing could be further from the truth. The essence of counseling is coming along side of a young person and through active listening, reflection and asking the right questions, you provide the young person with new insights that allow them to make a more informed decision concerning a problem that is troubling them.

> **The emphasis in counseling is on preparing a person and helping him process information and feelings rather than on giving him an answer and final end product.**

Since most of us have more training in witnessing and preaching than in counseling, our tendency is to teach, preach, and give answers more than to listen, ask questions, and paraphrase what we hear others telling us. In many ways, it is easier to proclaim what we know than listen to what people are asking for and need. The emphasis in counseling is on preparing a person and helping him process information and feelings rather than on giving him an answer and final end product. . . It is merely one way, a uniquely different way, of helping people get to the answers they need and utilizing the answers in their daily life.[59]

It is tempting to try and solve a young person's problem for them. Because of your maturity, education and life experience you may truly know what decision or action would be the best choice in a given situation. However, if you just impose your will on the young person and make them follow your direction, you do damage to them in two ways. First of all, by denying the young person the opportunity to wrestle through the issue to their own conclusion, you create an "emotional cripple." There is an important aspect of character building that only comes through choosing your own course of action and having to live with the consequences, whether for good or for ill. If you are the one who always takes responsibility to solve the young person's problem, then they will never develop confidence in their own problem solving skills. They will never know the satisfaction of working through a difficult issue to a satisfying conclusion.

> **Rather than *doing* *for* the hurting person, the counselor *does* *with* the person as an affirmation of his worth and dignity.**

The second problem with attempting to solve a young person's problem for them is that it takes the responsibility for their life and places it on you. In the student's mind, if they follow your direction and it doesn't work, it is not their fault, it's *yours!* This is very damaging because people will only grow and get better when they take responsibility for their own life.

Counseling is helping a person get his own information in his own language and using it in his own way. Many people confuse *giving* counsel with *offering* counseling. Generally, it is easier to tell someone the answer than to help him discover ways to get to the answer. A key difference between counseling and giving counsel is the skill of *thinking with*, more than *thinking for*, another person. Counseling then utilizes the active participation of the personal seeking help. . . Rather than *doing for* the hurting person, the counselor *does with* the person as an affirmation of his worth and dignity.[60]

Three Important Questions

Before you enter into a counseling relationship of any kind with a young person, you must ask yourself three very important questions. How you answer these questions will determine whether you should enter into this relationship or refer them on to someone else immediately.

The first question is: "Do I have the time that the problem demands?" Most emotional and psychological problems are years in the making. They will not go away overnight. Some problems require two to three sessions a week or they will require meeting regularly for an extended period of time from nine to twelve months or more. Before committing to the relationship, make sure you have the time available that the problem requires.

> **Greater harm could be done to a young person through unskilled or inadequate counseling even if it is done with well-meaning intentions.**

The second question is: "Do I have the skill or training that this problem requires?" There are some counseling situations that require little in the way of specialized training, but only good listening skills and a quality relationship. Others, such as eating disorders, multiple personality disorder and homosexuality are not treatable without some specialized training. Greater harm could be done to a young person through unskilled or inadequate counseling even if it is done with well-meaning intentions.

The third question is: "Do I possess emotional stability with this issue?" A youth leader may have the time and the training required for a particular problem, but if the leader has unresolved issues related to this same type of problem in his own life, these may interfere with the counseling process. It would be best to refer the young person to someone who has resolved those conflicts or who is comfortable dealing with the particular issue.

The Basic Elements

In order to be effective in counseling youth, one must have a model or pattern to work from. Upon examining a variety of models, it was found that there is no agreement on the exact number of steps or the names for the steps, but there does seem to be some similarity in the various definitions and steps in the counseling process of some major models of counseling. Study the following examples and look for common principles or goals.[61]

Van Pelt	Carlson	Olson	Doyle	McDowell
Accepting	Engaging	Relationship building	Relationship building	Listen
Reassuring	Empathizing	Defining problems	Exploration and understanding	Empathize
Listening	Exploring	Establishing goals	Decision Making	Affirm
Processing	Experimenting	Working toward goals	Working	Direct
Focusing	Evaluating	Terminating	Termination and Follow-up	Enlist
Planning	Exiting	Follow-Up		Refer

Exercise 3.1 – Finding Common Elements

Spend some time studying the counseling steps suggested by the various therapists listed above, then write down in your own words what you feel are the common elements or common steps in counseling from the overview of these models.

_____

_____

_____

Connect with the Teen

> **Don't be afraid to take the initiative, as many teens are too afraid or simply don't know how to approach you with a serious issue.**

In most situations, teens will seek you out when a problem is overwhelming them. They will hang around after a youth meeting and ask if you can "talk for a while" or they will call you at the office and say that they "needs to talk." If a teen you know is hurting and they have not contacted you, there are times when it is acceptable for you as a youth worker to take pastoral initiative and approach a young person and give them the opportunity to "unload." Don't be afraid to take the initiative, as many teens are too afraid or simply don't know how to approach you with a serious issue. They will be grateful for the chance to talk. But, you must be sensitive about this and not come across as "pushy" or intruding where you are not wanted. Use wisdom on when to approach a young person and when to refrain from bringing up the issue. How the teen interprets your invitation greatly depends upon the strength of your relationship previous to the problem. If you have already developed a solid, caring relationship I am confident they will welcome and not resent your invitation to talk.

Once contact has been made and a counseling appointment is set up be sure to affirm the teen that seeking out help was the right thing to do. Reassure them that even though it feels really bad right now, it will get better. "People facing crisis often lose their perspective. They are sure the despair and panic they feel at the moment will never leave them."[62] Prepare them by giving a brief explanation of the purpose of counseling, what to expect, etc. Be careful not to promise what you cannot deliver. Do not offer false hope or simplistic answers.

You will need to set a specific time to counsel with the young person. When setting up the appointment it is very important that you make it clear to the teen that your meeting time has limits. In other words, there will be a specific starting time and an ending time. The reason for this is that if you make your counseling appointment sound "open ended" then the teen will take forever to get to the real problem. By setting time limits it helps to facilitate getting to the core issue sooner. Experienced counselors know that the first problems teens share are often not the major or central ones. Teens will start by disclosing safer, less threatening problems first. Then, after they gain confidence in your ability and willingness to accept them in spite of their imperfections, they will be more willing to share their most private and serious problems with you. Plus, it has been my experience that most teens can't handle more than an hour's worth of deep introspection and reflection. If your session goes more than an hour it produces too much material to be handled effectively. Time limitations are healthy for everyone.

You will need a safe place to meet. For most youth pastors the obvious place to meet is the church office. If you don't have an office, then an appropriate room in the church will work. The room you choose to do counseling in must provide a comfortable setting to talk and protect the confidentiality of the teen. The room must also protect you from any false accusations. By this I mean that you should only do counseling during office hours

> **Experienced counselors know that the first problems teens share are often not major or central ones. Teens will start by disclosing safer, less threatening problems first.**

when other staff are in the building for accountability and protection. If you must do counseling after office hours, then you need to arrange for another staff member or appropriate person to be in the building at the same time. Never, never, never do counseling in a parked car or in an isolated or remote area! I do not recommend counseling in public areas like restaurants, malls or parks because it does not provide a secure area. Others can easily listen to the conversation and if the young person has some very serious issues to discuss they will not want others privy to that information.

Besides having a safe place to counsel, you must prepare the environment before the session. You prepare the setting by getting rid of distractions (turning off your cell phone, having the administrative assistant hold all calls and "drop-ins"), making sure the room environment is as comfortable as possible (temperature, furniture arrangement, background music, lighting, etc.), and you must clear your desk of all work. You don't want to make it appear that the teen is taking you away from something important. You must communicate in nonverbal ways that your unpressured priority is to listen to them and help solve the present crisis.

Exercise 3.2 – Distractions

List 5 things that could be distracting during a counseling interaction. Think of what you could do to eliminate them.

1. _____   2. _____

3. _____   4. _____

5. _____

Once the date, time, place and environment is set you must also prepare yourself for the counseling encounter. Be sure to arrive early enough that you do not feel rushed or pressured. Review what you know about the general goals and techniques of counseling. Assess what you know about the teen and the present crisis. If you have an idea of what the teen is struggling with (i.e. eating disorder, depression, addiction, etc.) you can prepare by reviewing what you know about this problem and how to best help someone dealing with this issue. It is very important that you pray and ask God to help you be sensitive to the guidance and direction of the Holy Spirit as you counsel.

Exercise 3.3 – Evaluating Your Counseling Setting

Think about the setting where you will be doing most of your counseling. Evaluate the counseling setting for its strengths and weaknesses.

General Description:

_____

_____

Contextual Strengths:

_____

_____

Contextual Deficits:

_____

_____

Understand the Teen

Once you have connected with the teen and you are ready for the counseling encounter, you must have a purpose—a plan of what you are trying to accomplish. Teens need to know that you understand their current situation and what they are feeling. The way you accomplish this is to communicate accurate empathy. There are a number of simple but very important techniques that will help the counselor communicate empathy to the teen.

> Leona Tyler outlines three goals for the initial counseling session: to establish an adequate foundation for the counselor-counselee relationship; to begin facilitating the counselee's opening-up process that will help him or her delve deeply into anxiety-producing, psychologically significant material; and to provide counselees with the basic structure of counseling that will help them gain the greatest benefit from their future counseling sessions.[63]

You must pay attention to your position and your posture. If you are seated behind a desk it can communicate distance, detachment and a lack of interest to the teen. You need to come out from behind your desk and sit in a chair that is close enough to communicate involvement but not so close that it invades their personal space. As you face the teen you should sit squared with the teen, leaning forward slightly and making good eye contact.

"Elton Mayo said, 'One friend, one person who is truly understanding, who takes the trouble to listen to us as we consider our problems, can change our whole outlook on the world.'"[64] You must be able to communicate accurate empathy through mastering the technique of "active listening." This means that not only must you be able to listen well, but you must also be able to articulate back to the teen what you have heard. This requires listening not only to the explicit message, but learning to listen for the implicit message as well.

> Active listening involves listening with all senses. As well as giving full attention to the speaker, it is important that the 'active listener' is also 'seen' to be listening - otherwise the speaker may conclude that what they are talking about is uninteresting to the listener.

> Interest can be conveyed to the speaker by using both verbal and non-verbal messages such as maintaining eye contact, nodding your head and smiling, agreeing by saying 'Yes' or simply 'Mmm hmm' to encourage them to continue. By providing this 'feedback' the person speaking will usually feel more at ease and therefore communicate more easily, openly and honestly.[65]

> **What teens say and how they say it tells you much about how they see themselves and the world around them.**

What a teen says and *how* they say it tells you a lot about how they see themselves and the current situation. You need to pay special attention to posture, facial expressions and overall appearance. As the teen shares their story listen carefully to the rate, volume and tone of their voice. Be on the lookout for any discrepancies or incongruencies in the teen's behavior or appearance. What teens say and how they say it tells you much about how they see themselves and the world around them. "A client could say 'She left without saying goodbye' in a tone of voice that communicated anger, indifference, hurt, pleasure, revenge, or any combination of these and other feelings. The words will be the same; the message will be entirely different in each case."[66] You will have to rely on tone of voice, body language and other hints to determine what was actually communicated.

The following are needed in order to develop good listening skills:

- Being able to set aside your own conflicts, biases, and preoccupations so you can concentrate on what the counselee is communicating.
- Avoiding subtle verbal or nonverbal expressions of disapproval or judgment about what is being said, even when the content is offensive.
- Using both your eyes and your ears to detect messages that come from the tone of voice, posture, gestures, facial expressions, and other nonverbal clues.

> **It is the responsibility of the counselor to create the conditions which will facilitate open, honest and complete communication.**

- Hearing not only what the counselee says, but noticing what gets left out.
- Waiting patiently through periods of silence or tears as the counselee summons enough courage to share something painful or pauses to collect his or her thoughts and regain composure.
- Realizing that you can accept the counselee even though you may not condone his or her actions, values, or beliefs.[67]

Gerard Egan, in his book, *The Skilled Helper*, emphasizes the importance of body language by the counselor to communicate attending or active listening. He uses the acronym SOLER to summarize the skills that the counselor should learn and employ to communicate that they are actively following the client's narrative.[68] These skills or behaviors are:

> **S** – Facing the person *squarely* rather than at an angle which would communicate less involvement.
> **O** – With arms and legs uncrossed, the counselor conveys an *open* attitude to the counselee. A closed posture signals defensiveness.
> **L** – When two people are in close conversation, they tend to *lean* toward each other. Such leaning signals availability or involvement.
> **E** – Although direct *eye* contact may cause some people to feel uncomfortable, looking directly at the other's eyes is an indication that you want to be deeply involved. Shifting your gaze periodically allows your conversational partner to look away during times of deep thought.
> **R** – Communicating a *relaxed* manner says you are at home with this person. Staying calm and comfortable yourself will let the other person know that you are composed in the conversation.[69]

Teens need to feel a sense of trust, genuineness and compassion from the one who is counseling them. It is the responsibility of the counselor to create the conditions which will facilitate open, honest and complete communication. By incorporating active listening techniques into your counseling repertoire, you will create an environment where the teen will feel safe and encouraged to share their current concerns.

Caution! While active listening is important, you must be careful that it is not misused. There are five obstacles that must be avoided in active listening:

- Don't minimize or trivialize the teen's problem. Be careful of saying statements that may be interpreted as minimizing by the teen, i.e. "I'm sure things will get better soon." Or to say, "You must have been disappointed," when they were beyond disappointed, i.e. devastated, or furious, etc.
- Don't deny the teen's problem. By denying a statement, i.e. "I'm no good," you may miss the feeling expressed behind the statement. Arguing or denying the problem may cut off communication.

- Don't be a parrot. Avoid verbatim responses. Seek to paraphrase the entire message of fact and feelings and implication back to the teen.
- Don't over-interpret. Avoid projecting your own feelings on to the teen. Listen accurately and avoid reading in your own ideas and feelings.
- Don't overuse active listening. There is a time for confrontation or redirection or clarification.[70]

Exercise 3.4 – The Revolving Discussion Sequence

You will need to find a willing partner in order to perform this exercise. It is called the Revolving Discussion Sequence. In the Revolving Discussion Sequence, the first partner will talk for two minutes. The listening partner cannot ask any questions, disagree, interrupt or do anything but listen for those two minutes. At the end of the two minutes, the listening partner must say back everything that the speaking partner said without adding to it, leaving anything out, changing or disagreeing with what was said. Then switch roles.

You cannot impose your own experience on the teen. You must try to see the situation from the teen's perspective.

The Revolving Discussion Sequence exercise forces you to increase your listening skills because you cannot be thinking about what you are going to say when the person stops talking because you will miss the content of what they are sharing. Practice being able to paraphrase accurately and completely what people share with you.

However, in an actual counseling situation you will be able to ask for clarification or for the teen to repeat something that you missed. When you are engaging in active listening in the counseling session, it is important that you are able to restate back to the teen the basic *content* of what they are sharing which may be summarized as the 5WH: who, what, why, when, where, and how. The response to content clarifies the details and the specifics of the teen's experience. A good response will rephrase what the teen has said in a fresh way. A good format for responding to content is: "You're saying _____," or "In other words _____," or "What I hear you saying is _____."[71]

Being able to restate the content of a teen's story is only the beginning. A good counselor will not only be able to communicate an

49

understanding of the content, but also the *feelings* behind the content. In order to discern the feelings behind the content, the counselor must ask themselves "the empathy question." The empathy question is: "How would I feel if I was *this person* in this situation saying these things and doing these things?" It is *not*: "How would *I* feel in this situation?" Each person has their own strengths, weaknesses, preferences and a history that makes them unique. You cannot impose your own experience on the teen. You must try to see the situation from the teen's perspective. For example, if my wife told me that our cat had been run over by a car, I would dance a jig that would rival Riverdance! (I think "cat" is ancient Ugaritic for useless, annoying, hairy creature.) But if my son was told that his cat had been run over, he would be very sad because his cat is his children's pet and brings much joy to his family. His feelings are going to be much different than my feelings. That is why the counselor must answer the empathy question as best as possible from the perspective of the teen and not themselves.

The answer to the empathy question is always a feeling word, i.e. you feel sad, angry, frustrated, hopeful, lonely, etc. According to Carkhuff, there are just seven basic feeling words (happy, angry, sad, confused, scared, strong, or weak) with three different levels of intensity (high, medium or low).[72] When choosing the correct feeling word, the counselor must choose the correct category of feeling words and the correct intensity of the word (See Feelings Chart). Once the selection has been done, use the simple format, "You feel _____."

Feelings Chart[73]

Happy	Sad	Angry	Scared	Confused	Strong	Weak
Excited	Hopeless	Furious	Fearful	Bewildered	Potent	Overwhelmed
Elated	Depressed	Seething	Afraid	Trapped	Super	Impotent
Overjoyed	Devastated	Enraged	Threatened	Troubled	Powerful	Vulnerable
Cheerful	Upset	Agitated	Edgy	Disorganized	Energetic	Incapable
Up	Distressed	Frustrated	Insecure	Mixed-up	Confident	Helpless
Good	Sorry	Irritated	Uneasy	Awkward	Capable	Insecure
Glad	Down	Uptight	Timid	Bothered	Sure	Shaky
Content	Low	Dismayed	Unsure	Uncomfortable	Secure	Unsure
Satisfied	Bad	Annoyed	Nervous	Undecided	Solid	Bored

After capturing the content and feeling of the teen's story, the counselor must then combine them together to communicate an understanding of the *meaning* behind it all. The simple, but effective formula that captures both content and feeling and expresses meaning is, "You feel _____ because _____." Sometimes a teen will express multiple feelings and content. It is important for you to communicate an understanding of all the major feelings and content. The teen needs to be reassured that you understand *all* of their story.

Exercise 3.5 – Content – Feeling - Meaning

Fill in the appropriate response to the following statements using the formulas given in the previous paragraphs for communicating an understanding of content, feeling and meaning.

1. "I think Michelle is super and it has been great to go out with her most of my senior year, but she is starting to talk about our future together. She seems so sure of her love for me. I really like her a lot, but I am not sure if I am ready to make a commitment to marriage."

Content

_____

_____

Feeling

_____

_____

Meaning

_____

_____

2. "I just found out that Fred has been writing horrible things about me on his blog site. Man, I thought we were friends. I don't care if I ever see him again. I feel like flaming him!"

Content

_____

_____

Feeling

_____

_____

Meaning

_____

_____

3.　　"My dad just got a promotion and we have to move to another city. I know I have no choice in the matter, but I hate leaving my senior year. I'll never have the kind of friends that I have here."

Content

_____

_____

Feeling

_____

_____

Meaning

_____

_____

Explore with the Teen

In order to do effective counseling with youth, one must have a model or pattern to work from. Almost all of the models emphasize the importance of developing a meaningful relationship with the teen and using active listening techniques to develop a rapport with the teen. A part of this relationship building process will naturally involve listening to the young person present their "problem." It is very important that the young person feels "heard and understood" and not rushed through the counseling process. However, it is not beneficial to dwell on the problem too long. Kollar, a proponent of solution-focused pastoral counseling, writes: "Unfortunately, in regard to counseling, the search for the root cause often intensifies and maintains the problem. The counselor's desire to ascertain the cause directs the interview into deficiency conversation."[74] In other words, focusing on the problem only makes it worse! Solution focused pastoral counseling tries to reframe the teen's perception of themselves and their problem to focus their energies on what a future solution would look like instead of dwelling on the painful and disappointing past.

In light of this insight, after you have connected with the teen and have communicated an understanding of their current situation then you must explore the various options for change or a solution to their problem. The most crucial aspect of this stage in counseling is personalizing. Personalizing is guiding the teen to take responsibility for their life and for their recovery. No one ever recovers from a crisis or emotional distress until they come to the place where they are willing to accept responsibility for their own recovery. If the teen wants to blame their parents, teachers, peers or society for all of their problems then they are not in a position to get well.

> No one ever recovers from a crisis or emotional distress until they come to the place where they are willing to accept responsibility for their own recovery.

When a teen comes to see you for counseling, they are going to approach the counseling session from one of three positions. The first, and the one you hope for, is the "willing position."[75] This is where the teen wants to change and is motivated to do the hard work of counseling. The teen may not know exactly what is wrong with their life but will be open to exploration and the wisdom and guidance of the counselor.

The second position is the "blaming position."[76] This is where the teen will show up for a counseling session and share with you details about their situation, but puts the blame and responsibility squarely on someone else. The teen might interpret all the problems in their life as the fault of their parents, ex-boyfriend or ex-girlfriend, the coach, a teacher, etc. The problem is always someone else's fault. Other people have to change, but not them.

The third position is that of an "attending position."[77] This is the teen who finds themselves in counseling unwillingly. Perhaps the parents have forced the teen to see the youth pastor and are threatening to withhold privileges (like a cell phone, access to the family car, attending homecoming dance, etc.) if they don't comply with their demand. This teen doesn't really want to be in counseling, but is there because someone else has forced them to be there.

The counselor's task is to discover ways to move the teen to become a willing participant in the counseling process. Without the teen taking a willing position and being responsible for their life change, counseling will not accomplish the desired result.

Gestalt Therapy teaches the value of taking personal responsibility for one's own health and gives the illustration that you are not responsible for the rain outside, but if you are caught in the rain either get an umbrella or choose to come in out of the rain. Don't continue to stand in the rain and complain about getting wet![78]

To make a serious application, you might have a young girl reveal to you that her uncle sexually molested her when she was a child. She is *not* responsible for her uncle molesting her. She was a child who could not defend herself against an adult. But what she *is* responsible for is her response to the abuse *now*. She can choose to do a number of things. She can confront the uncle, report the incident to the appropriate authorities, she can write a letter to him and pour out her pain or she can join a support group. There are a number of options for her in which she can take responsibility for her present and future mental health.

The counselor must help the teen take responsibility by facilitating their understanding of where they are in relation to where they want or need to be. A very simple and practical way to do this is to build upon the formula that was given previously to communicate meaning. All you do is add the word "you" to your response to the teen.

> **Taking responsibility is the most critical transitional step to taking action that will resolve the problem.**

"You feel _____ because you _____." The key ingredient is the personal implication. No one ever solves a problem or gets well until they come to the place where they take responsibility for their own life and quit trying to blame others for all of their problems. Taking responsibility is the most critical transitional step to taking action that will resolve the problem. Once the problem is identified and personal responsibility accepted, then you set out with the teen to create a goal that captures the essence of where they would like to be in terms of emotional, mental and spiritual health.

A good place to start in helping the teen work towards this goal is to look at their life and identify those things that are causing or contributing to the problem. In other words: "What is missing that contributed to the problem?" "What is present in the teen's life that contributes to the problem?" It may be that you, as the counselor, will have to confront some discrepancies at this point. The teen may say one thing, but actually be working or acting in the opposite way. A good formula for the type of confrontation that is needed is, "On the one hand, you say/feel/do _____, while on the other hand you say/feel/do _____."[79]

After identifying the deficits in the teen's life that are contributing to the problem, the counselor should lead the teen in identifying the assets in their life that may help in solving the problem. These consist not only in what the teen already possesses in their life that will help resolve the issue, but also what they may have the ability to add or do that will contribute to helping resolve the problem. The simple formula for conceptualizing deficits and assets would be: "You feel _____ because you cannot _____ and you really want to _____." "You feel _____ because you are going to _____."[80]

A good place to start is to help the teen identify the times when the problem is *not* present. In other words, "no matter what the problem is that the individuals are seeking counseling for, that problem does not happen all the time."[81] The counselor will then try to help the teen identify the key issues/strengths/behaviors that have contributed to a more positive situation and encourage the teen to simply do more of that. These "exceptions" to the problem need to be clarified and should then be used to develop goals for the counseling that follows.

Sometimes a student will have a difficult time in coming up with a measureable goal. The student is not sure what needs to change, but only knows that the present situation is painful and undesirable. If you cannot help the teen identify exactly what it is they want to achieve through the counseling process, you might employ a technique developed by Alfred Adler that he simply called "the question."

It went as follows: "If I had a magic wand or a magic pill that would eliminate your symptom immediately, what would be different in your life?" Corollary questions were "How would your life be different if you did not have this problem?" and "What would you do if you were well?"[82]

Initiate a Plan with the Teen

Once you have worked with the teen to develop a clear goal of where they want to be in relation to where they are now, then you must assist the teen in working out a specific plan that will facilitate reaching the goal. Caution: You don't want to make the plan so large a task that the teen feels overwhelmed and gives up even before trying. The secret is to set up a series of smaller steps that are easily within reach and within the capabilities of the teen considering their particular deficits and assets. (Hint: Think about the concept of "baby steps" as presented in the movie, "What About Bob?") The goal that you help the teen set up must be one that is measurable and includes the 5WH and some kind of standard that will let the teen know when they have reached this goal. It is also important to describe the reason for and methods to accomplish the goal. It cannot be vague and unmeasurable. The formula to use in communicating the goal to the teen would be: "You want to _____ (5WH of behavior) as indicated by _____ (standards)."[83] An example of a good goal would be: "You want to gain the trust of your parents as indicated by their allowing you to set your own curfew."

Besides setting a measurable standard for a goal, you need to determine all of the ingredients of the goal. It is important to include all of the people or things involved. You also want to describe the reason for and methods to accomplish the goals. This involves describing when and where the activity will occur.

As stated before, the counselor will need to help the teen set up a series of easily attainable sub-steps that will eventually reach the ultimate goal that has been identified. Most of these sub-steps are by nature sequenced by contingency, i.e. each step is dependent upon the successful completion of the previous step.

Besides developing specific steps and sub-steps to reach the goals, the counselor should help the teen by setting up a specific timetable in which each step and sub-step is reached. The major emphasis in scheduling is starting times and completion times.

Very important to the successful completion of a program are built-in reinforcements as each step is accomplished. Reinforcements are simply something that is important and meaningful to the teen that will serve to motivate them to accomplish their steps. To be effective, they must come from the teen's frame of reference.

Positive reinforcements or rewards are the most potent reinforcements. Teens will work hard for things that are meaningful to them. You want to avoid employing negative reinforcements. By that, I mean, punishments. The use of punishments for not reaching a step or goal can cause avoidance reactions and sabotage the initiating process. The only kind of negative reinforcement should be the absence of rewards for not reaching a goal or step.

Finish with the Teen

At some point in the counseling experience you must determine when and how the counseling relationship is going to end. The best conclusion is when both of you agree that the problem has been solved and there is no longer any need for more counseling sessions. When you sense that this is the case it is often helpful to begin spacing out the counseling sessions from once a week to once every other week to once a month and then to cease meeting altogether. Even with this preferred scenario it is still good to schedule a "check-up" sometime in the future to verify that healing and resolution has truly taken place.

Sometimes the teen will end the counseling relationship by simply not showing up or keeping appointments. When this happens, it may mean that the teen was not really serious about wanting to solve the problem or was looking for a "quick fix" and didn't want to commit to the difficult road of real change. It could also be that what you were offering as a counselor wasn't helping and the teen didn't want to hurt your feelings by telling you to your face, so they just quit coming. There are

> **There are times when you as a counselor are doing everything correctly as far as technique and skills go, but there is just an inappropriate fit between the two of you.**

times when you as a counselor are doing everything correctly as far as technique and skills go, but there is just an inappropriate fit between the two of you. Sometimes your personalities just don't "click" and it interferes with the counseling process. Other issues such as racial differences, cultural differences, age differences, and gender differences can also be the cause of an ineffective counseling experience.

You may also engage in a counseling relationship and very quickly realize that you are in "over your head" and the problems presented by the teen demand professional attention. It could also be that you are qualified to deal with the specific issues but that they demand more time than you can give. When this is the situation, you must make a referral. There will be more on the proper way to make a referral in the next chapter.

Practice, Practice, Practice!

Congratulations! You have now worked through the basic skills of short-term counseling and have a concrete plan to follow which will serve as the foundation for your counseling encounters with the teens entrusted to your care. You should commit to memory the basic steps of the counseling process: 1) connecting with the teen, 2) understanding the teen, 3) exploring with the teen, 3) initiating a plan with the teen, and 4) finishing with the teen. You will need to work in a most intense and disciplined manner to hone all of the various skills needed to be a competent counselor. Practice, practice, practice until you can process these responses in your own mind naturally and comfortably as you counsel with confidence and effectiveness.

Helpful Resources

Edgette, Janet Sasson. "How to Talk to Teenagers Who Don't Want to Talk to You." Alternet.Org. Accessed: March 21, 2017. http://www.alternet.org/personal-health/how-talk-teenagers-who-dont-want-talk-you

Horne, Rick. "God's Counsel About Counseling Youth." Biblical Counseling Coalition.org. Accessed: March 21, 2017. https://biblicalcounselingcoalition.org/2015/07/21/gods-counsel-about-counseling-youth/

Marvin, Betsy. "Can We Talk? 10 Starbucks Counseling Basics."
    Seedbed.com. Accessed: March 21, 2017.
    http://www.seedbed.com/can-talk-10-starbucks-counseling-
    basics/

Selected Bibliography

Carkhuff, Robert R. *The Art of Helping*. 9th ed. Amherst, MA: Human
    Resource Development Press, 2009.
Egan, Gerard. *The Skilled Helper*. 10th ed. Pacific Grove, CA: Brooks/Cole
    Publishers, 2013.
McDowell, Josh & Hostetler, Bob. *Josh McDowell's Handbook On
    Counseling Youth*. Nashville, TN: W Publishing Group, 1996.
Parrott III, Les. *The Comprehensive Guide to Youth Ministry Counseling*.
    Loveland, CO: Group, 2002.
Parrott III, Les. *Helping the Struggling Adolescent*. Grand Rapids, MI:
    Zondervan, 2014.

Exercise 3.6 – Skills and Abilities for Effective Counseling

Rate yourself on the following skills and abilities with respect to effective
counseling. Be honest! 5 = Always, 4 = Most of the time, 3 = Sometimes, 2
= Hardly ever,1 = Never

Skills and Abilities for Effective Counseling	1	2	3	4	5
I integrate theology and the biblical insights into my counseling.					
I build relationships with teens easily.					
I understand the importance of the counselor-client relationship in the counseling process.					
I allow sufficient time to pass in order to build strong relationships with the teens in my care.					
I try to solve teen's problems for them.					
I am comfortable with allowing teens to make their own decisions about their life.					
I like to give answers or offer advice in counseling.					
I have the time to offer teens that counseling demands.					
I have the basic skills or training needed to handle most problems.					
I am comfortable talking about difficult issues such as incest, abuse, homosexuality, abortion, drugs,					

alcohol, etc.					
I am able to take "pastoral initiative" and approach a teen if I believe they are hurting and need help.					
I have an office space that is conducive to effective counseling.					
I do everything in my power to eliminate distractions during a counseling session such as turning off the cell phone, etc.					
I am able to set boundaries and time limits for the counseling session.					
I have a specific plan or goal in mind as I begin counseling.					

The following charts may be helpful by providing you with a visual of the steps that are taken in a typical counseling encounter. Remember that while the techniques you use are important, they are only secondary to the quality of your personality and the strength of the relationship that you have developed with the teen.[84]

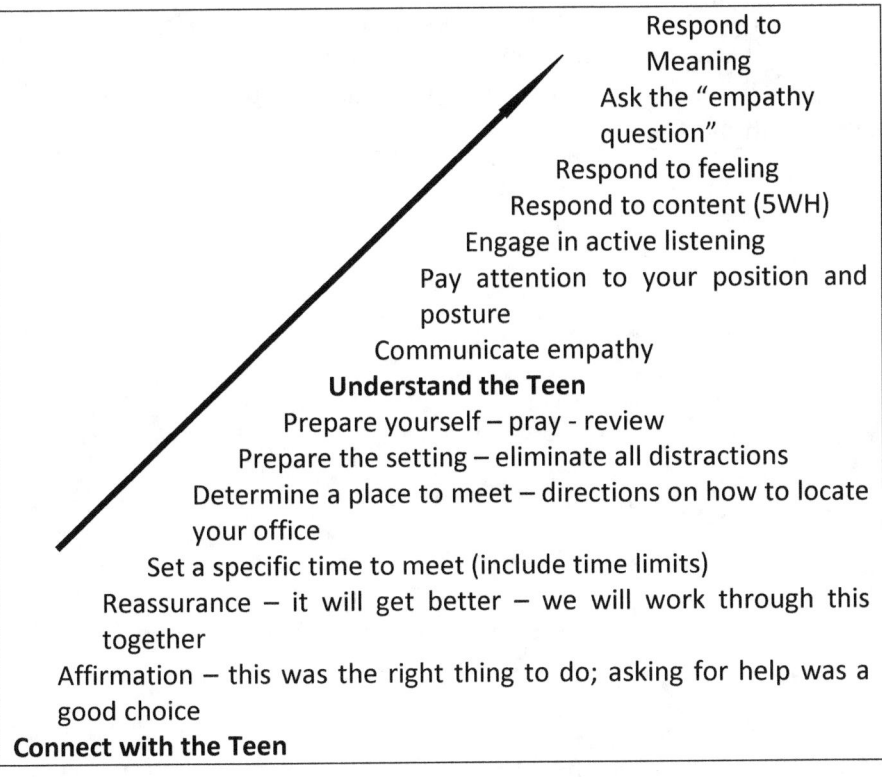

Respond to Meaning

Ask the "empathy question"

Respond to feeling

Respond to content (5WH)

Engage in active listening

Pay attention to your position and posture

Communicate empathy

Understand the Teen

Prepare yourself – pray - review

Prepare the setting – eliminate all distractions

Determine a place to meet – directions on how to locate your office

Set a specific time to meet (include time limits)

Reassurance – it will get better – we will work through this together

Affirmation – this was the right thing to do; asking for help was a good choice

Connect with the Teen

Follow-up
Refer
Accomplish goal
Finish with the Teen
Develop reinforcements of goal
Set up a time-table to reach the goal
Have a reason and method for the goal
The goal must be broken down into sub-steps
The goal must be measurable - (5WH) of behavior
Develop a clear goal
Initiate a Plan with the Teen
Identify assets – look for "exceptions"
Confront discrepancies
What is present that contributes to the problem?
What is missing that contributed to the problem?
Personalizing – take responsibility for recovery and release blame
Explore with the Teen

CHAPTER FOUR

MAKING A COUNSELING REFERRAL

(WHEN YOU KNOW THAT YOU ARE IN OVER YOUR HEAD)

Choosing to refer a young person, parent, or family to the kind of help that can make a long-term difference is not an admission of weakness; it's a sign of strength. –Rich Van Pelt in *Intensive Care*[85]

Sometimes the best counseling process is to facilitate a referral of the counselee to a source of help that is especially well-suited to meet the specific needs of the case. Just because someone comes to a counselor for help does not imply that counselor is the best source of care for the particular counselee. –G. Keith Olson in *Counseling Teenagers*[86]

"Preacher, I have never told this to anyone before and I don't know how to tell you, but I think I'm gay. I have always felt different and I don't know what to do."

"Yeah, you're right. I have changed. I have been smoking meth for the past six months. I was hooked on the first smoke. I have been stealing and prostituting myself for money to support my habit.

"I need your help! The FBI and CIA have me targeted. They have all my phones tapped and they have been following me. The grand, sand, stand, planned is overly etched, sketched and fetched."

What would you do if any one of the previous statements came up in a counseling session with a young person? You would probably panic. But, there is no need to. There is a proper and safe way to deal with these kinds of situations. As was stated in the last chapter, the good counselor must know their limitations. You must know when a problem is of such a serious nature that it can only be solved by trained professionals. Knowing when and how to make a referral is one of the most important skills that a minister or youth worker needs to learn. The following exercise is designed to help you understand this need.

Exercise 4.1 – (Possible Answers Found at the End of the Chapter)

Beginning with each letter of the alphabet, write a problem that teens struggle with which you might encounter in a counseling situation. Spelling does not count and you can use words that sound like the letter as well as those that actually begin with it. Examples might include: Alcoholism, Boredom, Career choices, Divorce of parents, etc. Come up with as many as possible for each letter. Allow yourself five minutes to complete this exercise.

A_____   N_____

B_____   O_____

C_____   P_____

D_____   Q_____

E_____   R_____

F_____   S_____

G_____   T_____

H_____   U_____

I_____   V_____

J_____   W_____

K_____   X_____

L_____   Y_____

M_____   Z_____

The Need to Refer

Go back over your list, and circle the problems that you feel are of such a serious nature that they require professional help. These are the kinds of problems that untrained youth workers are not adequately trained to deal with. Good intentions will not help the problem and may even make the problem worse. Only a trained professional will know what kind of action to take to best help the teen.

Look over the list again, and place a check by the problems that are really best suited for an untrained youth worker. These are the kinds of issues that simply require a caring person who will be a good listener, offer support and insight. Are there any problems that might require both a friend and a professional?

It is important to note that there are some problems such as rape, incest, alcoholism, homosexuality, suicide and others that the untrained youth worker needs to refer to a professional. These problems are beyond the skill and training level of the average youth worker. The mental health or physical life of the teen may be in jeopardy if one unskilled or untrained tries to deal with the problem.

On the other hand, notice that there are a good number of problems, such as loneliness, discouragement, unrealistic expectations, boyfriend & girlfriend problems, etc., that the youth worker may be the best person to help solve them. There are times when an understanding, loving, listening ear is all that is needed and it would be a shame if the person had to pay a professional to fulfill that need. Gary Collins lists a number of actions that the nonprofessional counselor can do which would be very helpful in a counseling situation:

- Give support in times of need.
- Encourage expression of emotion.
- Help counselees to get intellectual insight into their problem behavior.
- Confront counselees with sin, irresponsibility, self-defeating behavior, or inconsistencies in their lives.
- Teach social skills.
- Encourage and guide counselees as they try new ways of coping with problems, making decisions, or struggling to avoid falling into sin.
- Help people to find and use information.
- Work to eliminate undesirable behavior.
- Help Those who are searching for meaning or purpose in life.
- Guide those who have theological problems and are seeking answers.
- Challenge counselees with the need to commit their lives to Christ and to grow as disciples.
- Refer counselees when professional or other help is necessary.[87]

There are times when an alliance of both a supportive youth worker and a professional can work together to make up the best healing team for a hurting person. The professional deals with the complicated relational and background issues and the youth worker acts as an encourager, supporter and accountability partner.

There is a place for everyone in the healing community. But it is important that the youth worker knows their limits and knows where to go when a professional referral is called for. Anytime you encounter a young person who is suicidal, hearing voices, is severely depressed, threatening to harm another person or is talking and acting is a bizarre manner, then a referral to a mental health professional is called for. One should remember that a referral does not represent pastoral failure. No one is skilled enough to handle every problem that an adolescent might bring. Making a referral doesn't mean that you are incompetent or don't care about the teenager. Referral is often a way to communicate to your teen that you want the very best for them. It can be a significant step to helping struggling teenagers with their problems.

> It is important that the youth worker knows their limits and knows where to go when a professional referral is called for.

> One of the reasons that pastors do not have time to do their pastoral ministry is that they insist on doing it all themselves. They have failed to build a detailed knowledge of their community as to the agencies, professional and private practitioners, etc., who could help them in their task.[88]

Different Types of Referral

Not every referral needs to mean a termination of the counseling relationship. The counselor may make a referral in order to have some specific tests given or an evaluation done which will give some direction for the counselor. A referral of this kind may involve sending the client to a physician for some specific medical tests to see if there is a relationship between the problem (i.e. depression) and some organic deficiency or problem. If this turns out positive, can the problem be treated medically? If so, by whom? Is continued therapy needed or recommended after receiving the medication?

The youth worker might want the troubled teen to take some specific personality tests, such as the MMPI, 16PF, Myers-Briggs or the Taylor Johnson. These can only be administered and evaluated by someone who has been trained to use these instruments. A referral to a local psychologist or psychotherapist would be in order. A written letter of release should be requested of the teen so that the youth worker could see the results and confer with the professional administrating and evaluating the test.

When making a referral, the youth worker should state only the facts of the case. Professional judgments should be left out. State only what has been observed and not the meaning that you give it. State what the teen tells you and not your interpretation of it. Do not try and impress the person to whom you are making the referral with your knowledge, insights and grasp of psychological theory, technique, etc. Just present the facts as related by the teen. Include what you have already tried in the way of therapy and help and the results that those efforts have achieved. Give a short statement on the general family and social adjustment of the person being referred.

> **To be effective, referral must be responsible, timely, appropriate, and it must consider financial resources.**

Some Cautions to Heed When Making a Referral

"Referral is a necessary component in any crisis intervention program. To be effective, referral must be responsible, timely, appropriate, and it must consider financial resources."[89] A referral is not something that will always be received enthusiastically by the young person, especially if they came to you first for help and a good rapport has already been developed. If you want the referral to be received in the most positive way, there are a number of guidelines that you should follow.

If you make a referral, it is important that you do not over-exaggerate the counselor's ability to the teen. Do not make promises that the counselor cannot keep. This is not fair to the counselor and it may set up unrealistic expectations for the teen that may ultimately cause them more harm than good.

Prepare the teen for the fact that therapy is often a tedious, time consuming and expensive process. Remind them that there are no miraculous short-cuts and that patience and perseverance are called for.

Before suggesting referral, it would be helpful to check with the referral source first in order to be sure that a referred person can be accepted for help. Many counselors have a limited number of clients that they can see.

Be careful to make the referral in such a way that the referral is not seen as a rejection by the teen, but the most effective help that you can provide and is evidence of genuine concern. Try to involve the teen as much as possible in the decision to refer. If the teen "claims ownership" for the decision, they will probably be more likely to actually follow up on the suggested referral.

Avoid making a referral too soon or too late. Some refer too soon because they fear failure in the counseling situation and don't want to risk seeing a hard situation out to the end even if they have the time and the skills that are necessary. Others fear a lawsuit and refer simply as a way of

> **Be careful to make the referral in such a way that the referral is not seen as a rejection by the teen.**

avoiding a potential legal situation. Churches have been sued and the minister or youth worker is no longer exempt. But this should not keep people from reaching out and caring when they are able.

Reasons Why Ministers and Youth Workers Often Resist Making Referrals

> **Another false idea often found among ministers is the idea that a minister should be able to deal with every problem that is presented to him.**

Some ministers and youth workers operate under the false assumption that the gospel should be adequate to meet the needs of all sorts of conditions and problems. For them, a referral is seen as an admission that the gospel is inadequate. It is seen as a betrayal of the gospel. But this is an unfortunate misunderstanding of what the sufficiency of the gospel really addresses.

Another false idea often found among ministers is the idea that a minister should be able to deal with every problem that is presented to him. To refer is seen as an admission of his own inability or weakness. Closely related to this is the fear that someone else may be more capable of meeting the problems of life than the minister. He sees the referral as a threat.

Some ministers have a fear or distrust of the "world-view" of the professional counselor. They are concerned that a teen referred to a secular counselor might have his religious views "psychoanalyzed" out of him. Indeed, there is some truth to this concern. This is the reason why the minister or youth worker must do good research before making a referral.

> Just because a person has a degree . . . does not mean that he or she can help our kids and families with their problems. We must become familiar with the counselors'

treatment methods and faith perspective so that the help kids and their families receive will harmonize with rather than conflict with the beliefs of our church and youth programs.[90]

Let us not forget, however, that God is sovereign and powerful. He does not require people—include you and me—to have perfect theology before we are used. If we search the Scriptures, we find that God sometimes even uses nonbelievers to accomplish His divine purposes. A nonChristian counselor, like a nonbelieving physician or lawyer, may at times use his or her professional skill to guide a counselee through a crisis or help restructure a personality, both of which may get the person to a point where he or she is more ready to accept Christ and move toward becoming a disciple.[91]

There is an interesting correlation between the number of referrals a minister makes and his education level, social status and theological position. Ministers with little education have low referral rates, whereas clergy with the highest education have the highest referral rates. Ministers with low social status in the community have low referral rates. On the other hand, ministers with high status have high referral rates.[92]

Many ministers with a seminary education have received, as a part of the core of their education, training in pastoral care skills. Some have advanced training or degrees in pastoral care and counseling. These have a lower referral rate because they elect not to refer because they see themselves as having the time and skills needed for the presenting problem.

Some are slow to refer because they have no ready access to the resources for referral or are unaware of the possibilities for healing available to them in the community. Others are slow to refer because they simply do not know the process.

When Should You Make a Referral?

If you have a limitation of time you should refer. With sermon preparation, calling, Bible study and administrative work, many youth workers simply do not have the time to spend with the teen that the problem warrants. There are problems brought to the youth worker that are within their scope of skill and resources, but for which they simply do not have sufficient time and therefore, must refer.

Youth workers with a limitation of skill or experience should refer. Some problems are going to be obviously out of the youth worker's range of skill or experience. Sometimes it is hard to tell if a problem is beyond the youth worker's skill or experience. They may feel comfortable dealing with the problem, but if after a fifth or sixth session the youth worker becomes aware of certain factors that were not brought out in the first session, they may want to refer. The duration of the counseling problem may serve as an indication in and of itself of a need to refer.

There are times that a youth worker may have the skill and the time available but is not emotionally comfortable with the issue. If the presenting problem brings us unresolved conflicts in the youth worker's life, they should make a referral. If the youth worker is going through a stressful period in their own life because of finances, marriage, career or leadership, they may not have the emotional reserves left that are required to adequately deal the problem at hand.

Whom Should the Youth Worker Refer?[93]

- Teens who can be helped more effectively by someone else.
- Teens who do not respond to their help after five or so sessions.
- Teens whose needs obviously surpass their time and/or training.
- Teens with problems for which effective specialized agencies are available in their community, i.e. chemical dependency problems, unwanted pregnancy, legal aid, and the mental illness.
- Teens who show bizarre or extremely aggressive behavior.
- Teens who appear to be severely disturbed emotionally.
- Teens with severe financial needs.
- Teens who need medical care or institutionalization.
- Teens who need intensive psychotherapy.
- Teens who are severely depressed or suicidal.
- Teens who need legal advice.
- Teens who stir strong feelings of dislike or sexual arousal in the counselor.

Some Principles to Follow in Making a Good Referral

The youth worker should learn who and what is available in their community before they need them. Conscientious youth workers who are committed to making responsible referrals will need to keep an up-to-date file of people and agencies whose care they respect and to whom they are comfortable making referrals. One of the first tasks a youth worker should do when moving to a community is to complete a community and ministerial survey that informs them of all the available people and agencies. After the survey is completed, the youth worker should solicit recommendations and warnings from trusted veteran youth workers in the community about the results of the survey. Once a referral agency or person is selected the youth worker should compile the following information and have it readily available:

- Name of the agency, program or individual
- Spiritual qualifications (is this a Christian counselor or agency?)
- Educational and professional qualifications
- Address
- Office phone number, crisis line number, cell phone (if available)
- Type of services rendered (individual counseling, group, drug intervention, etc.)
- Admission requirements (if any)
- Referral procedure
- Costs (hour, sliding scale, third party payment, etc.)
- Hours of operation

> There may even be a situation where you will need to attend the first session with the teen to help alleviate their fears.

It is usually best to be straightforward and frank with the teen when preparing to make a referral. You should give the teen your observations that concern you and the reason why you are suggesting a referral. An example might be, "I am really concerned about you because you have contacted me twice within a week and both times you were in tears and feeling pretty hopeless. Because I care about you and want the best for you, I am going to recommend that you make an appointment to talk to one of my recommended Christian counselors in the area." When the teen is ready and prepared to go to a professional, the youth worker should help make the appointment as soon as possible. However, be ready for some resistance to the idea of a referral by the teen. This hesitation may stem from the basic fear that "if I need professional help, I must be crazy." Reassure the teen that you don't think they is crazy and educate them about the various reasons why people seek out professional help. Another area of resistance may come from the teen who sees the need for professional counseling as a "sign of weakness." Assist the teen in understanding that reaching out for professional help in the area of counseling is no different than needing a physician when there is a physical problem. It is a sign of maturity and wisdom to seek out help from those more qualified than yourself.

There may even be a situation where you will need to attend the first session with the teen to help alleviate their fears. An example might be a girl who has revealed to you that she has become sexually active and is worried that she is pregnant. She may be paralyzed with fear about going to the crisis pregnancy center by herself. If the pregnancy test is positive, she may also need you to accompany her home to help break the news to her parents and then counsel them on future options. Another example might be a young boy who has shared with you through tears that he was sexually molested. He may not have the courage to tell his parents or the police without your support and presence. Note: when working with teens, it is almost always necessary to involve the parents in the decision to seek professional counseling.

Warning! Not all parents will be enthusiastic about the idea of their son or daughter needing professional help. Some parents resist the idea of taking their son or daughter to a psychiatrist or psychologist because they falsely believe it will reflect poorly on the family. They will be more concerned about maintaining outward appearances than the actual emotional and mental health of their son or daughter. If

> **Note: when working with teens, it is almost always necessary to involve the parents in the decision to seek professional counseling.**

there is concern on the part of the youth worker about the genuine physical and emotional welfare of a teen whose parents refuse to provide help, the youth worker may need to solicit the involvement of a social-welfare worker who can intervene without parental consent.

Sometimes a referral is a simple matter of providing the correct information of a group or agency to meet the teen's need. Other times the referral is a difficult process because the teen resists seeking help or even acknowledging the seriousness of the problem. Mentioning the possibility of referral as a possibility early in any counseling relationship makes it easier to accept when it is presented.

The youth worker should be careful to make the referral in such a way that the referral is not seen as a rejection by the teen. Pains should be taken to assure the teen that the referral is not a rejection, but the most effective help and concern that the youth worker can provide and is evidence of the youth worker's genuine care.

The minister should explain the general nature of the help that the teen may expect to receive by the person or agency referred to. Once the teen has accepted the idea of referral it is best to let the teen make their own appointment with the new counselor.

Some Considerations When Selecting a Counselor for a Referral

- Who sponsors the counselor? Mental health? County, State or Federal Government? Local hospital? Counseling Clinic? Private practice? Church?
- How long has the person been in the community?
- Has the person been adequately trained?
- Is the counselor a person of basic spiritual integrity?
- Has the counselor been reasonably successful in dealing with the problems of others?
- Does he come recommended by other clergy and professionals in your community?

Characteristics of a Poor Referral

When the youth worker continues a counseling relationship beyond their limit of ability, training and experience it is potentially dangerous to the teen. It should be made as soon as the situation indicates that a referral is in the best interests of the teen.

Poor orientation of the teen for a referral is a problem. Teens are very sensitive and referrals demand tact. When the youth worker refers the teen to someone who is not properly trained or qualified there can be serious repercussions.

Conclusion

The main thing to keep in mind is that the youth worker must always have the teen's best interests at heart. Sometimes the very best thing we can do for the teens we care about is to refer them to someone else whose training and expertise will better serve them. Remember, referral does not mean that you as a youth worker are incompetent or trying to get rid of the teen. No one person is skilled enough to counsel everyone, and referral is simply the best way to show your desire provide the best help possible.

Exercise 4.2 – Counseling Referral

Rate yourself on the following issues pertaining to counseling referral. Be honest!

5 = Always, 4 = Most of the time, 3 = Sometimes, 2 = Hardly ever,1 = Never

Counseling Referral	1	2	3	4	5
I can identify the problems that are beyond my ability to help.					
I can identify the problems that I am qualified to help a teen with.					
I have the time that counseling teens requires.					
I am comfortable talking about difficult issues with a teen.					
I am familiar with the different types of referrals that may be needed.					
When making a referral, I am careful not to exaggerate the counselor's ability or make promises they can't keep.					
I prepare the teen for the fact that counseling is often a tedious, time consuming and expensive process.					
I check with the referral source before making a referral					
I make referrals in a prompt manner when required.					
I have a well-developed and researched referral list.					
I involve the parents of the teen in making a referral.					
I am careful in not making the referral seem like a "rejection."					
I can easily identify the teens who require a referral.					
I make myself available for follow up after a referral.					

Exercise 4.1 Possible Answers

Abuse, AIDS, Anger, Anxiety, Alcohol, Anorexia

Bulimia, Bitterness, Bashful, Boredom

Crisis,   Choosing a mate/college/vocation, Cancer

Depression, Dating, Drugs, Divorce, Dropping Out

Eating Disorders, Envy, Ecstasy, Effeminate

Family, Friends, Facing Death, Fag, Fat, Fetish
Gambling, Grades, Guilt, Grief, God's Will

Homosexuality, Homeless, Helpless, Hopeless

Incest, Inferiority, Interpersonal Problems, Identity

Jail, Job, Judicial Issues, Juvenile Delinquency

Kleptomania, Special "K", Keggers, Killing

Lust, Loneliness, Love, Trouble with the Law

Masturbation, Mental Disorders, Marital Issues

Narcotics, Non-Christian Parents

Oral Sex, Over-Protective Parents

Pornography, Premarital Sex, Parents

Queer, Quiet, Quarreling, Questions

Rape, Rebellion, Racial Issues, Runaway

Sexual Abuse, Sibling Rivalry, Singleness

Tattoos, Teasing, Terrorism, Transgender

Underachievement, Unhappy, Unstable

Violence, Vocation, Vane, Venereal Disease

War, Witchcraft, Weary, Wedlock, Weed

X-Rated Movies, X-boyfriends/girlfriends

Yielding to Temptation

Zero Tolerance, Zoned Out, Zits

CHAPTER FIVE

SUICIDE PREVENTION AND INTERVENTION

As a friend of mine who works with suicidal young people recently said, "Some kids think suicide is a fad. They have a big problem and they say, 'I think I'll try suicide this week. If it doesn't work, I'll try something else next week.'" Next week!!? –Paul G Quinnett[94]

David Elkind points out that it is often difficult to identify teens who are contemplating suicide partly because "teenagers in particular are often reluctant to reveal the problems they are experiencing or their inner thoughts. Unfortunately, many teens also conceal their inner pains and fears so that even their parents and closest friends have no idea that they are suffering and considering suicide. –Josh McDowell & Bob Hostetler[95]

A Case Study[96]

Sherri saw herself as a fairly normal teenager. She believed she had a large number of friends, but by her own admission she could never talk to them about serious issues or share her feelings with them. As a result, most of her relationships were shallow and she felt lonely because she had to deal with everything by herself.

There was a lack of communication in her home and she grew up learning to hide her emotions. She became depressed and cried often, both in public and in private. Her friends saw her personality change from a bubbly, outgoing person to a withdrawn, reclusive one. She started spending lots of time in her bedroom listening to songs that had death as their main theme and even began to write original poems about wanting to die. She began to drop veiled hints to her friends about her thoughts of suicide saying things like, "I'm not going to have to deal with this life much longer" and "you won't have me around forever." She gave away some of her most prized possessions, her Taylor guitar, her iPad and Harry Potter collection.

On a Friday night, when the family was gone she went into her bedroom and swallowed 50 pills that she had taken from her parent's medicine cabinet. She put on some music, laid down on her bed and went to sleep never to wake up.

Now her family and friends have to try and make sense of this tragedy. Her parents are wracked with guilt and her friends are confused.

How could they have missed the signs? What could they have done to prevent this senseless tragedy?

Statistics on Adolescent Suicide

- There is one death by suicide in the U.S. every 12.3 minutes.[97]
- Rates of suicide in the U.S. have risen almost steadily between 1999-2014, with the greatest percentage increases occurring among girls aged 10-14 and men aged 45-64 years of age.[98]
- The suicide rate is more than three times higher for men than for women (20.7 compared with 5.8 per 100,000 in 2014).[99]
- The suicide rate for females aged 10-14 had the largest percent increase—200%.[100]
- Suicide ranks second as a cause of death among young people ages 15-24.[101]
- Each day in our nation there are an average of over 5,400 attempts by young people grades 7-12.[102]
- There is a relationship between depression and suicide; the risk of suicide is increased by more than 50 percent in depressed individuals. Aggregated research findings suggest that about 60 percent of suicides were depressed.[103]
- Among those sexually abused as children, odds of suicide attempts were 2-4 times higher among women and 4-11 times higher in men compared to those not abused.[104]
- Suicide is the second leading cause of death for college-age youth and ages 12-18.[105]
- More teenagers and young adults die from suicide than from cancer, heart disease, AIDS, birth defects, stroke, pneumonia, influenza, and chronic lung disease, *combined*![106]
- Four out of Five teens who attempt suicide have given clear warning signs.[107]
- Among students in grades 9-12 in the U.S. during 2013:
  - 17% of students seriously considered attempting suicide in the previous 12 months.
  - 13.6% of students made a plan about how they would attempt suicide in the previous 12 months.
  - 8.0% of students attempted suicide one or more times in the previous 12 months.
  - 2.7% of students made a suicide attempt that resulted in an injury, poisoning, or an overdose that required medical attention.[108]

- A survey of 1,986 teens in *Who's Who Among American High School Students* found that 30 percent of these young people had considered suicide, 4 percent had attempted it, and 60 percent said they knew a peer who had attempted suicide or had killed himself.[109]

The statistics concerning adolescent suicide will vary some depending upon the specific survey or authority consulted. Some claim that teenage suicide is the second leading cause of death among adolescents, while others list it as the third cause of death. One thing they are all in agreement on is that adolescent suicide is probably highly under-reported. There are a number of automobile accidents that are highly "suspicious" in nature which don't get listed as a suicide because the coroner doesn't want to bring any additional pressure to an already grieving family. The fact that many insurance policies won't pay if the victim is a suicide often puts pressure on the coroner to overlook some obvious signs of a suicide in an attempt to help the grieving family. No matter how many suicides actually take place, even one is too many. It is a tragedy that young people with so much promise end up contemplating suicide because they feel overwhelmed by temporary pressures and problems.

> **Youth workers need to be trained to recognize the signs of a possible suicide and have a proven plan of action that will increase the chances that an intervention will be successful and a life saved.**

Suicide is a preventable tragedy. Youth workers need to be trained to recognize the signs of a possible suicide and have a proven plan of action that will increase the chances that an intervention will be successful and a life saved. If youth workers acquire a knowledge of some of the most common contributing factors that lead to an adolescent suicide attempt it will help them to spot a potential victim before they can harm themselves.

Exposing Some Common Myths About Suicide

It is important to dispel some common myths about suicide. These myths have accumulated through the years and actually hinder people from becoming involved in the life of a young person who is at risk.

<u>People who talk about suicide don't commit suicide</u>. Research in the St. Louis area found that 69% of those who completed a suicide communicated their intent to kill themselves an average of three times, the maximum number of communications by one individual was twelve. 60% communicated their intentions to their spouses, 50% communicated to relatives, including in-laws, 33% communicated to friends, and less than 20% communicated to physicians, job associates, ministers, police and landlords.[110] Sometimes the warnings are indirect. Suicidal people will drop hints like: "I'm going away" or "You won't have to worry about me anymore."

<u>Suicides usually happen without warning</u>. Nothing could be further from the truth. It is just a matter of knowing what to look for. There are usually behavioral, emotional, and verbal clues that a young person is at risk. The youth minister must learn what to look for in order to recognize the signs. A list of common signs follows later in this chapter.

<u>Suicidal people can't be talked out of it if they are really intent on dying</u>. Most people who are suicidal are ambivalent about it. They don't really want to die, but they want the pain to stop and so they think death is the only way to bring relief. Most teens would rather live if you could help them find a solution to the emotional, psychological or physical pain that is causing the suicidal ideation.

<u>An individual's drastic improvement following a serious crisis means the suicidal risk is over</u>. Just the opposite is true! Drastic improvement after a long period of depression or crisis usually means that the person has developed a suicidal plan and is simply counting down the days until it is enacted. The reason this brings about such drastic relief is because the person believes they only have to "put up with life" for a few more days and then there will be relief.

<u>Suicide is a problem of a specific class of people.</u> Suicide is found in every demographic area: young, old, rich, poor, black, white, male, female, married, single, educated and uneducated. There is no demographic group that is immune to the dangers of suicide.

> "Suicide feels like a total dismissal, the cruelest possible way a person could tell us that they are leaving us behind."
> –Albert Y. Hsu

<u>Talking about suicide causes suicide by planting the idea in a person's head</u>. One of the most important things a pastor can do for someone who is suicidal is to ask them directly if they are thinking about suicide. Talking openly is quite possibly the most caring thing you can do. Talking about it may generate helpful

alternatives for the person who is suicidal and relieve some of the emotional and psychological pressure that has built up.

If a person is a Christian, he will not commit suicide. Christians can become depressed just like anyone else. Some very famous and influential ministers struggled with depression. C.H. Spurgeon and Martin Luther both wrote about their battles with the darkness. Francis Schaeffer struggled with suicidal thoughts.

People who kill themselves are just being selfish. Suicide might look like a selfish rejection but one must take into consideration the hopelessness and depression that the deceased experienced. Albert Hsu writes: "Suicide feels like a total dismissal, the cruelest possible way a person could tell us that they are leaving us behind."[111] But he also notes that what is helpful is to realize that the suicidal person doesn't kill himself to abandon anyone. He does it to end his pain, not to cause pain for others. The best gift you can give someone suicidal is to start that conversation for them.

Some Common Stresses That Contribute to Adolescent Suicide

> Teens' lives are fashioned around an achievement orientation and if they don't make the football team, the cheerleading squad or get straight A's then they tend to think that they are failures and life is over.

The adolescent experience, in and of itself, is fraught with landmines that could blow up in the teen's face. Teens struggle with self-esteem issues and generally have poor communication skills. Their lives are fashioned around an achievement orientation and if they don't make the football team, the cheerleading squad or get straight A's then they tend to think that they are failures and life is over. They generally have poor problem solving skills, make narrow commitments, operate under high stress and have an inadequate network of social support.

Teens also live with daily family problems. They have poor communication with their parents and may spend an inordinate amount of time in conflict. They experience significant losses in the form of divorce, death of a parent or grandparent, the loss of employment for the father or mother and an unplanned move to a new school where they have to make new friends. Their family system may include dual-career parents, single parents, blended families, abusive parents, parents experiencing a mid-life crisis or parents who are dealing with severe personal problems such as a drug or alcohol addiction or a mental illness.

Teens also struggle with a number of personal problems. Some experiment with drugs or alcohol. By their own admission many are lonely and depressed. They feel the pressure to succeed and to get accepted into a good college. Relationship issues are often confusing and hurtful as they breakup with their current love interest.

Reasons Why Adolescents Attempt Suicide

There are a number of reasons why a teen might make a suicide attempt. The following are a summary of some of the most common.[112]

To escape from an intolerable situation. It is important to note that "intolerable" might be anything in the mind of a developing adolescent. Any time a teen feels hopeless and does not possess good problem solving skills, the situation might be seen as "intolerable."

To punish the survivors. Suicide is a hostile act and sometimes the hostility is directed towards the survivors. It may be a teen's parents or a boyfriend or girlfriend who jilted them.

To gain attention. Are there young people who really don't want to die, but who just want some attention? Undoubtedly, yes. But, that doesn't mean that you shouldn't take every suicide threat seriously. If you ignore or dismiss an attempt as merely an attention-getting device, then the teen may be challenged to prove you wrong with the next attempt.

To manipulate others. A teen may threaten suicide to keep a boyfriend or girlfriend from breaking up with them. The teen may also threaten suicide as means of manipulating his parents into allowing him to have a certain privilege.

To join a deceased loved one. Many times, teens are especially close to an older relative such as a grandparent, aunt or uncle who has died. They attempt suicide in order to restore the relationship that was severed.

To avoid punishment. Because teens don't always have the best problem-solving skills, they may choose suicide rather than face a punishment they see as intolerable. If a teen has committed a crime and is facing some serious prison time, he may choose suicide rather than face the potential homosexual rape and abuse that is common in prison.

To avoid becoming a "burden". This motive is more common among the elderly who have contracted some kind of fatal disease such as cancer or multiple sclerosis. They don't want to be a burden to their families, so they take their own lives. While it is most common among the elderly, I know of a young boy in a large Hispanic family who took his own life because the family was very poor and his mother was concerned with how she would be able to feed everyone. The boy took his life and left a suicide note stating that he hoped that one less mouth to feed would make it easier for his younger brothers and sisters.

<u>To pursue an irrational and impulsive whim</u>. As stated before, teens are always the most logical in their thought processes. They may see a movie like Romeo and Juliet or Thelma and Louise and decide it would be very "romantic" to end one's life is such a way. They decide to end their lives on a Friday night and can't wait to see what an impact it has on the school culture on Monday. What they don't realize is that they won't be around to enjoy being the center of attention because they will be dead!

<u>The changing moral climate</u>. Teens are growing up in a postmodern culture where there are no absolutes. The prohibition and stigma that was once associated with suicide is very quickly fading. The State of Oregon has passed a physician-assisted suicide law. Many do not hold a Christian belief in a final judgment and heaven or hell. They have no reason to fear death, so it is seen as a viable alternative to their problems.

Learn the Signs of a Possible Suicidal Risk

Most of the crisis intervention experts will maintain that in approximately 80% of all suicide attempts, the person who took their life gave definite, identifiable clues as to their intention. With this insight, youth workers can take a significant step towards suicide prevention by learning the warning signs.

The concerned youth worker needs to be cautioned, however, that the presence of a single sign may mean very little. But, if there are a number of indicators in a teen's life, this cluster of clues should be given the proper attention and appropriate measures taken.

- Any suicidogenic situation - any situation which may be considered "traumatic"
- Sudden changes in behavior - either listless or reckless
- Giving away prized possessions
- Withdrawal from family or friends
- Drugs or alcohol abuse
- Unusual neglect of appearance
- Radical personality change

- Preoccupation with themes on death
- Unexplained or unusually severe, violent or rebellious behavior
- Running away
- Tends to dwell on problems
- Does not want to converse
- Hidden or veiled statements hinting at suicide - verbal clues
- Conversation centers continuously on withdrawing, quitting and hopelessness or has a tone of despair
- Previous attempt
- Noticeable change in eating or sleeping habits
- Persistent boredom
- Exaggerated and/or extended apathy
- Attempts to secure means
- A history of depression
- A history of being abused as a child
- Inability to tolerate frustration
- Making a will
- Feelings of being unwanted
- Inability to communicate
- Writing a suicide note
- Mental illness
- Identifies with the LGBT community
- High expectations—a perfectionist
- Anyone suffering acute & chronic stress

The youth pastor must be aware of the signs of a young person who is at risk for suicide and be willing to intervene. You must get involved, show interest and support in the young person, and be available to help. You must be willing to listen and allow for the expression of intense emotions. Be nonjudgmental of what the teenager shares with you and don't act shocked because this only creates distance. Don't allow yourself to be sworn to secrecy or make promises that you cannot keep. Most of all, you must take action. The practical steps that you must take to prevent a suicide are presented in the next section. Learn them. Memorize them. Use them.

Guidelines for Suicide Intervention

Talking to a young person about their suicidal thoughts and feelings can be extremely difficult for anyone. But if you're unsure whether someone is suicidal, the best way to find out is to ask. You can't make a person suicidal by showing that you care. In fact, giving a suicidal person the opportunity to express his or her feelings can provide relief from loneliness and pent-up negative feelings, and may prevent a suicide attempt.

Here are some ways to start a conversation about suicide:

- I have been feeling concerned about you lately.
- Recently, I have noticed some differences in you and wondered how you are doing.
- I wanted to check in with you because you haven't seemed yourself lately.

Questions you can ask:

- When did you begin feeling like this?
- Did something happen that made you start feeling this way?
- How can I best support you right now?
- Have you thought about getting help?

What you can say that helps:

- You are not alone in this. I'm here for you.
- You may not believe it now, but the way you're feeling will change.
- I may not be able to understand exactly how you feel, but I care about you and want to help.
- When you want to give up, tell yourself you will hold off for just one more day, our, minute—whatever you can manage.

When talking to a suicidal person, do:

- Be yourself. Let the young person know you care, that they are not alone. The right words are often unimportant. If you are concerned, your voice and manner will show it.
- Listen. Let the suicidal person unload despair, ventilate anger. No matter how negative the conversation seems, the fact that it exists is a positive sign.
- Be sympathetic, non-judgmental, patient, calm, accepting. Your teen is doing the right thing by talking about their feelings.

- Offer hope. Reassure the teen that help is available and that the suicidal feelings are temporary. Let the teen know that his or her life is important to you.
- If the teen says things like, "I'm so depressed, I can't go on," ask the question: "Are you having thoughts of suicide?" You are not putting ideas in their head, you are showing that you are concerned, that you take them seriously, and that it's OK for them to share their pain with you.

When talking to a suicidal person, don't:

- Argue with the suicidal person. Avoid saying things like: "You have so much to live for," "Your suicide will hurt your family," or "Look on the bright side."
- Act shocked, lecture on the value of life, or say that suicide is wrong.
- Promise confidentiality. Refuse to be sworn to secrecy. A life is at stake and you may need to speak to a mental health professional in order to keep the suicidal person safe. If you promise to keep your discussions secret, you may have to break your word.
- Offer ways to fix their problems, or give advice, or make them feel like they have to justify their suicidal feelings. It is not about how bad the problem is, but how badly it's hurting your friend or loved one.
- Blame yourself. You can't "fix" someone's depression. Your teen's happiness, or lack thereof, is not your responsibility

Once you confirm that a young person is at risk, you must act immediately. Dr. Paul Quinnett has designed a very simple, but very effective procedure to follow if you believe someone may be suicidal. The procedure is referred to as "QPR: Ask a Question—Save a Life."[113] The initials QPR stand for: Question, Persuade and Refer. You do not have to be a professional counselor in order to understand and implement this procedure with someone who is suicidal. Anyone who has had a minimum of training can follow this procedure and prevent an unnecessary tragedy. Much like CPR or the Heimlich Maneuver, the fundamentals of QPR are easily learned.

"Q" stands for "question." If you believe a young person may be suicidal because they have exhibited some of the classic signs of suicidal risk or if they have given some verbal signs (whether director or veiled), then do not hesitate to question them directly by asking, "Are you contemplating suicide?" or "Are you thinking of harming yourself?"

You may not be comfortable with coming out directly and asking them if they are thinking of committing suicide. In that case, you could begin by taking a less direct approach and acknowledging the teen's distress by asking, "Have you been unhappy lately?" "Have you been very unhappy lately?" "Have you been so very unhappy that you wished you were dead?"

The important thing is for you to find a way of asking the question that is comfortable for you. The exact wording is not as critical as is the need for you to make the specific inquiry. Don't worry that you will offend a teen by asking the question. Many are actually very relieved to be able to talk about it and to know that someone is actually paying enough attention to them to notice the depth of their pain.

> Don't worry that you will offend a teen by asking if he is thinking of harming himself.

But if you ask the question and you receive a "Yes" response from them, you must now do something with this information. It is now time to apply step two, which is to **"Persuade"** them to get help. The first response you need to make as a concerned youth worker after hearing the confirmation of a suicidal intent is to simply be a good listener. Listening can be life-saving. "Listening takes time, patience, courage, but it is always right. Advice tends to be easy, quick, cheap and wrong."[114] To become a better listener, just follow these simple guidelines:

- Give the person your full attention.
- Do not interrupt them when they are speaking and only speak when the other person has finished.
- Do not rush to judgment or condemnation.
- Get a grip on your own fear concerning the situation so that you can focus all of your attention on the other person.

The goal of persuasion is simple. All you need to accomplish is to convince the person who is thinking of harming themselves to get some help. You could say something like: "Will you go with me to see a counselor?" (Or a minister or a doctor or any kind of professional person they are willing to see). "Will you let me help you make an appointment with . . . ?"

> **Listening can be life saving. Listening takes time, patience, courage, but it is always right. Advice tends to be easy, quick, cheap and wrong.**

Some teens who are suicidal may agree to get some help, but not follow through with their promise. The more hopeless they feel the more difficult it will be for them to follow through. That's why it is preferable for you to take them to the professional helper immediately. If you can't get the teen to go with you immediately, then try to get them to make a commitment to go on living and not harm themselves until they are ready to see someone. The best way to get this commitment is to have them sign a "No Harm" agreement. (An example of a No Harm agreement can be found at the end of this chapter.)

The last step in the QPR model of intervention is to make the **Referral**. The best way to do this is to personally accompany the teen to the referral professional or agency. The next best referral is when the teen agrees to see a professional and you are convinced that they will actually keep their word. The third best referral is getting the person to agree not to harm themselves and to seek professional help in the near future. Above all, you must know where professional help is available and help direct the teen to them. Some referral possibilities would be: 1) Crisis or Suicide Prevention Center; 2) Physician; 3) Mental Health Center; 4) Mental Health Professionals; 5) Ministers; 6) and State and Local Mental Health Associations.

When a student reveals to you that they are considering suicide, besides working towards persuading them to get help, you should do a risk assessment. This will give you a good idea of how serious the teen is about committing suicide. This will help you to know how "hard" you should push them towards accepting your recommendation to seek professional help. The following acronym should be memorized and followed when trying to determine the seriousness of the risk: S-L-A-P.

> **Always take a suicide threat seriously! Don't ignore the warning signs.**

S - How Specific are the details of the "plan of attack." The greater the details, the higher the degree of risk.

L - What is the Lethality Level of the proposed method? Is the teen threatening to take a dozen aspirin or put a shotgun to the head?

A - What is the Availability of the proposed method? A gun is a very specific and a very lethal method, but if the teen does not have one readily available to use, then you know you have some time to persuade him to get help.

P - What is the <u>Proximity</u> of helping resources? The greater the distance from those who could rescue him in an emergency, the greater the degree of risk.

Always take a suicide threat seriously! Don't ignore the warning signs. Be sincere, this will build trust and establish a positive basis for the encounter/relationship. Communicate your concern for the well-being of the teen. Be honest, caring and compassionate. Avoid overwhelming the teen by asking too many questions. It is better to allow the teen to speak and to listen actively for clues. Do not offer promises you cannot keep. Avoid unrealistic assurances. Remember that you are not responsible for a teen's life. The choice is theirs. But you may give hope and remind the teen that suicide is a permanent solution to a temporary problem.

Behaviors to Avoid When Working with Depressed or Suicidal Teens

<u>Do not allow yourself to be sworn to secrecy by the suicidal teen</u>. Often the teen actually wants you to tell because he doesn't know how to ask for help himself. It is easier to apologize to him the next day when he is still alive for breaking a confidence than it is to apologize to his parents at the funeral for not telling.

<u>Do not leave the student alone if you believe the risk for suicide is immediate</u>. Don't let him leave the room without you. Stay right with the student until you have persuaded him to seek professional help and you have accompanied him to the referral agency or professional.

<u>Don't act shocked at what the student tells you</u>. Remain calm and empathetic to the student's pain and possible scenario. A student may have committed some sin or act that he finds unforgiveable and thinks that suicide is the only way to make the situation "right." You must be able to listen to his confession without reinforcing his fears through your reaction and possibly pushing him towards harming himself.

<u>Do not stress the shock and embarrassment that the suicide would be to the teen's family before you are certain that is not exactly what they hope to accomplish</u>. There are times when a teen considers suicide as an act of revenge and his goal is to inflict as much pain as possible. If you try to argue him out of the act by stressing the pain that his parents/girlfriend/coach would experience, you may be unwittingly reinforcing the decision to harm himself.

Do not debate whether suicide is right or wrong. To be sure, there is a time for teaching against suicide as a solution for the personal pain that a teen is experiencing, but when the teen is in the middle of the act it is *not* the time. The pain interferes with the ability to think rationally. The hurting adolescent doesn't really care if the act is right or wrong at this point, he just wants the pain to go away and will do anything to accomplish that goal. Your goal at this point is to listen, build a trusting relationship and persuade the teen to put his harmful intentions on hold until he has first tried talking with a professional about his problems.

> The hurting adolescent doesn't really care if the act is right or wrong at this point, he just wants the pain to go away and will do anything to accomplish that goal.

Do not give advice when you should be listening. While a potential suicide can be a very frightening scenario and you want to keep a hurting teen from following through with their suicidal plans, you do not help the situation by immediately trying to "fix it" before you listen to the teen's struggle and story. Being a careful listener and offering a sympathetic ear may be all that is needed to help the teen consider other options.

Do not act out "poor me" when the person seems to be rejecting your efforts to help. Yes, you have a great desire to intervene and to save a life. Yes, you probably see the situation more rationally and may have some excellent alternatives for the teen to consider. But if the teen rejects your counsel, this is not the time or place for a "pity party." It is not about you—it is about them and saving a life. Simply and calmly try a different track to connect with them.

Do not become too emotionally involved with the individual or their problem. This does not mean that you don't care or are not concerned about the teen. It means that you must remain circumspect and able to accurately assess the situation and make the right call without your mind being clouded because of overwhelming emotions that you are experiencing.

The Bible and Suicide

Inevitably when discussing suicide, the issue of one's eternal destiny comes up. People want to know whether their loved one who committed suicide is in heaven or hell. We'll look at what the Bible says about suicide and then look at how the church has treated suicide down through the centuries.

There are seven suicides that are mentioned in the Bible:
1. Abimilech (Judges 9:52-55)
2. Samson--Judges 16:30
3. Saul - I Samuel 31:3-6
4. Saul's armor bearer--I Samuel 31:3-6
5. Ahithophel--II Samuel 17:23
6. Zimri--I Kings 16:18-19
7. Judas Iscariot--Matthew 27:3-5

In all of the previous passages, the Bible makes no comment about the suicide other than a description of the method and the circumstances surrounding it. This does *not* mean that God approves of suicide, but only that there was ample opportunity to teach about it if it needed additional warning, teaching, and explanation. Note that in all of these situations, except for Judas, they were battle or war situations, with death or dishonor as their only other choices if they didn't choose suicide. These are not typical of most of the suicides that you will encounter today. Most suicides today seem to arise from despair.

> All of these accounts are straightforward narratives; none offers any particular comment on the act of suicide. In fact, while the Bible condemns murder in general, it nowhere condemns suicide in particular. The strange silence of Scripture on the morality of suicide has led some people to either one of two extremes. Some read far too much into these passages, seeing suicide as the unforgivable sin though it is not so described. Others minimize the acts entirely, arguing that because these suicides are not condemned, suicide is morally neutral or excusable."[115]

While Scripture may not explicitly condemn suicide, it certainly does not commend it. In all of the narratives the person's choice of suicide is presented negatively. "Scriptures silence does not mean tacit approval or indifference. The stories were meant to be instructive to future generations, portraying biblical suicides not as examples to be followed but rather as cautionary warnings of how not to go."[116]

While the Bible casts all acts of suicide in a negative light, this is not to be equated with teaching that suicide always separates the person from the presence of God. Suicide is *not* the unforgiveable sin! If it were then Samson, who chose a suicidal death, would not have been listed among the "faithful" in Hebrews 11. According to Matthew 12:31-32, the only unforgiveable sin is "blasphemy against the Holy Spirit." There is no connection anywhere in Scripture between suicide and a sin that cannot be forgiven.

> **While the Bible casts all acts of suicide in a negative light, this is not to be equated with teaching that suicide always separates the person from the presence of God.**

Still, there have been many in the church who have argued that a person who committed suicide could not go to heaven because he died with unforgiven sin.

> Ethicist and theologian Gilbert Meilaender writes: Contrary to what Christians have often believed, such rational suicide does not necessarily damn one. The suicide dies, so to speak, in the moment of sinning, without opportunity to repent. But then, so may I be killed instantly in a car accident while potting revenge against an enemy of mine. God judges persons, not individual deeds, and the moment in one's life when a sinful deed occurs does not determine one's fate.[117]

"Christian salvation is not dependent on whether a person was able to 'wipe the slate clean' at the moment of death, but rather whether the person was walking in relationship with God in life."[118] If salvation depends upon our ability to die with no unconfessed sin, then that would make salvation a matter of works and not grace.

Preventing Suicide

As people committed to Jesus Christ, and truly reflecting his love and life, we can make a difference in the lives of those who are hurting and lonely and may be considering suicide. Here are some practical things that can be done that will encourage young people to choose life and learn how to cope with suffering, sorrow and disappointment without giving up and seeing suicide as the only answer.

When you encounter a teen who feels lonely and hurt, let him or her know by your actions that *you* care and *you* want to be their friend. Let them know that *God cares* about their suffering and that He has provided Jesus and His church to help comfort those in pain. See: Rom 12:15; 15:5; 2 Cor 1:3-7; Is 61:1-3; Is 42:3; I Thess 5:11.

As a youth leader, you need to be an example who shows young people how to express emotions in a healthy way. Help young people to be comfortable with their emotions, and to see them as a gift from God. Even the emotions that we may consider to be negative, such as anger, need to be expressed in a healthy way. It is not a sin to be angry; Jesus was angry! The Bible says, "Be angry, and sin not." Eph 4:6; See also: John 11:35; Rom 12:9-16; Col 3:12-17.

It is important to communicate to young people that they are *loved unconditionally*! God loves them and wants to help them with their life, and you also will need to love them unconditionally. Even if they are sometimes unlovely, and irritating and hard to put up with, you do not have to like or condone their actions, but you need to love them in spite of them. They need to feel unconditional acceptance. See: Rom 5:5-8; John 3:16; 13:34-35; 15:9-17; I Cor 13:1-13; Rom 12:9-10; Gal 5:13-15; Eph 5:1-2; I Pet 4:8; I John 3:11,14-16; 4:7-21.

As Christians and youth leaders, we need to be the type of people who develop deep and serious relationships, ones where the deep needs and aches of the heart can be expressed. Let us avoid being shallow and only concerned about superficial things. I John 3:18; I Pet 4:9-10; Prov 27:6; 17:17; Ecc 4:9-12; Rom 12:15; 2 Cor 1:3-7.

The Christian's life is one that is characterized by *hope*, rather than hopelessness. Our hope is based upon a powerful, caring, loving God who has promised us eternal life and His everlasting love. When we feel that there is no hope, we need only to call upon God, who gives hope when there seems that there is no hope. Ps 16:9; 31:34; 33:18,22; 43:5; 71:5,14; 146:5; Lam 3:21,24,26; Rom 4:18-21; 5:2-5; 15:4,13; Titus 2:13; I Pet 1:3,13, 21.

As Christians, we need to be burden bearers. The suicidal person feels that they have to deal with their problems all by themselves and the burden feels too heavy to bear. As Christians, we carry each other's burdens and lighten one another's load. Gal 6:2; Rom 15:1; Ecc 4:9-12.

As Christians, we can offer hope because we are assured that we are accepted by God just as we are. We do not have to "earn" or "prove" our worthiness as a person. Being saved by grace means that God takes us just as we are and we do not have to be in competition with anyone else. Eph 2:8; Rom 3:24; 5:8.

For those young people who have no family life, or one that is not healthy, let them know that they are welcome in God's forever family and that each person is respected just as much as another and that all have important duties and gifts to contribute to the family. I Cor 12:12-26; Eph 4:3-7.

Karen Mason, in her book, *Preventing Suicide,* suggests six ways that a pastor, chaplain or youth minister can help prevent suicide:

1. Teaching a theology of life and death, including moral objections to suicide.
2. Teaching theodicy, or how to understand and manage suffering.
3. Directly engaging the issue of suicide—stigma-free—when people become suicidal, attempt suicide or die by suicide.
4. Teaching how to build a life worth living with meaningful purpose and belongingness.
5. Offering community were relationship skills are learned and practiced and where those who need support can get it.
6. Partnering with others in preventing suicide.[119]

Pastoral Care for the Survivors of Suicide

A student once described her cousin's suicide and its continuing effects on his family by saying, "He didn't just take his own life; he took part of theirs too." "Every suicide leaves behind at least six survivors, sometimes ten or more."[120] "Suicide doesn't end pain. It only lays it on the broken shoulders of the survivors."[121]

Survivors of suicide have a variety of initial reactions to the news. Some shut down emotionally. "My world went black" is how Stephanie describes how she felt upon hearing of her mother's suicide. "I felt ice-cold." Others feel physical upheaval, as if punched in the gut. They might be overwhelmed by uncontrollable wails or sobs, or they may experience rage or anger.[122]

Everyone is going to have a slightly different reaction to the suicide of a family member. There is no one "right" or "wrong" way to respond to a suicide. Most people will experience a sense of denial at first, but this soon wears off and other intense emotions will come into play. They will experience all the common emotions associated with the grief process, but this will all be intensified and complicated by the trauma and the stigma of a suicidal death.

> Those of us who experience complicated bereavement are actually grappling with *two* realities, grief *and* trauma. Grief is normal; trauma is not. The combination of circumstances is like a vicious one-two punch. We are grieving the death of our loved one, *and* we are reeling from the trauma of the suicide. The first is difficult enough; the second may seem unbearable.[123]

The grief that one experiences after a suicide in the family does not follow a linear path. There are no neat and clean steps that all can follow that will lead to a quick healing process. It is more of a circuitous path, with one step forward and two steps back.

> Traumatic grief is not a linear process, a straight path mapped out from one starting point to a final destination. Rather, it is a journey filled with twists and turns, unexpected detours and dead ends that force them back over ground they thought they had already covered. Often several different, overlapping emotions may assault them at once, and they find themselves caught in cycles of good days and bad.[124]

There is no absolute time frame for grief. It may take a person between two to five years to experience all of the emotions and the ups and downs of the grief process. The most important thing is to patient and allow oneself a sufficient amount of time to grieve and to process the loss. Some days will seem worse than others. Suicide survivors may feel overwhelmed by their emotions. One of the simplest, yet most helpful things you can do is to encourage the expression of these emotions or to get the person to talk about what they are feeling. Some common emotions experienced in grief are:

Shock	Denial	Pain	Guilt	Anger
Despair	Disbelief	Stress	Hopelessness	Sadness
Anxiety	Rejection	Loneliness	Abandonment	Confusion
Shame	Depression	Helplessness	Self-blame	Numbness[125]

Because of the stigma attached to suicide, the survivors may feel a sense of shame surrounding the death and may not feel comfortable reaching out for help. In times like these, the youth minister must exercise the pastoral initiative and reach out to the family without waiting to be asked.

> When a teenager takes his or her own life, the parents may believe that the suicide confirms their failure in parenting. Not only must they grapple with the sense that their child has rejected them in the worst way possible, they feel as if they have failed. They think, "If only we were better parents, this wouldn't have happened."[126]

Pastoral care calls for you to help the survivors deal with feelings of regret and guilt. Eventually the survivor must realize that the death was not their fault. The person who takes his or her own life by suicide is the one who is ultimately responsible, not the survivor.

There are a number of simple and practical things that you can do to help families who are suicide survivors. These may not seem profound, but sometimes it is the little things that make a difference.

1. Do attend any public services, offer your presence, handshake, hug. Be careful of "rehearsed remarks."
2. Listen without judgment. Let them tell the same story over and over if need be.
3. If you must say something, be especially careful not to assign blame, assume feelings, or rationalize reasons for what has happened.
4. Be careful to avoid inappropriate comments.
5. Accept and love the survivors as they are.
6. Share a positive memory.
7. Do something practical: cook a meal or freeze one for the future, help with babysitting, shopping, phoning, fixing, driving, etc. Don't wait for them to call.
8. Be persistent, but thoughtful and patient. It is hard to accept help, but as months pass they will need you more and more, not less and less.
9. Remember holidays and the anniversaries of important dates with a visit or a call.
10. Perform what you promise.

11. Be aware of suicide self-help groups and offer to go with your friend.

Last of all, it is important that you help the survivors of suicide understand that although suicide may be a part of their history, it doesn't have to be part of their future. One of the most damaging consequences of suicide is the message it seems to send to present and future generations, is that suicide is an acceptable coping mechanism for dealing with life's problems. As believers in Christ, we have the promise that we do not suffer in this world alone. God sees our tears, our pain and has promised to walk with us through the valley of the shadow of death. (See: Ps 23; Isaiah 43:1-5; Hebrews 13:5-6) Suicide should never be seen as a viable option. There is always hope.

Guidelines for Use Of The No Harm Agreement

A No Harm Agreement (NHA) is a conditional promise not to hurt oneself contingent on completion of a specific event or a specified period of time. The following guidelines should be followed when using the NHA in a crisis setting:

1. *Keep it simple!* A person in crisis will have difficulty following, or even understanding, two or three part instructions. Use the "Rule of Fives" as much as possible.
2. *Keep it short!* The greater the crisis, the shorter the time frame. The general range is somewhere between two hours and three days.
3. *Keep up your end*! The NHA is a temporary reprieve from hopelessness. Don't promise follow-through if you can't provide it. Have a "plan B" just in case.
4. *Keep it firm*! Don't allow them to bargain for loopholes or word the agreement ambivalently.
5. *Don't substitute the NHA for therapy*! Problems like depression, substance abuse and schizophrenia can't be cured with a mere promise.

Here is what a sample NHA might look like:

I, _____, will not harm myself or anyone else in any way. If I feel as though I may injure myself or someone else, I will first contact _____ at _____. If I am unable to reach that person, I will then contact _____ at _____. In the event that I am unable to contact either of these people, I promise not to harm myself or anyone else and, I promise to contact the crisis line at _____ immediately.

_____
Signature/Date

_____
Therapist or Witness/Date

Overview of the Counseling Process for Potential Suicide

Connect with the Teen
- They may call you and ask for help – if so, set up a meeting immediately.
- You may hear from others about their possible suicidal situation – if so, take pastoral initiative and go to them or call and set up a meeting.
- Prepare your meeting place and yourself by reviewing how to deal with a potential suicide and don't forget to pray!

Understand the Teen
- Communicate empathy by your posture, position and active listening skills.
- Communicate nonjudgmental, unconditional love and genuineness.
- Ask yourself the empathy question: "How would I feel if I was this student in this situation?"

Explore with the Teen
- Find out what caused the suicidal crisis – what is missing in their life? What is present that is causing the pain? What have they already tried that has not worked to eliminate the pain.
- Explore with them other possibilities – help them to focus in on their strengths and available resources.
- Teach them coping skills.
- You must ask the question: "Are you thinking of suicide?"

Initiate a Plan with the Teen
- If the teen responds "Yes" to the suicide question, then you must persuade them to wait until they have talked with a professional

counselor to help them look for alternative ways of ending the pain.

- Either call the suicide hotline and have them talk to them or take them to the nearest mental health crisis center. If none is available, then take them to the local hospital emergency room.
- Do not let them out of your sight if they have admitted to being suicidal until you can refer them to a mental health professional.
- If they refuse to talk to the crisis hotline or go to a crisis center, then try to utilize the "No Harm Agreement."

Finish with the Teen
- In a potential suicide situation, you are finished when you refer them to a professional crisis team or take them to the emergency room. Only when the student is safe from self-harm have you completed your counseling responsibilities.
- Follow-up is very important. You must maintain your relationship with the student and help them face new challenges as they occur.
- Help them with any shame or embarrassment they may feel as a result of a suicide attempt.
- Be aware of any signs they may be considering a second attempt.

Helpful Resources

The American Association of Suicidology (202) 237-2280
     www.suicidology.org
The American Foundation for Suicide Prevention (888) 333-AFSP (2377)
     www.afsp.org
Compassionate Friends (877) 969-0010 www.compassionatefriends.org
The Link's National Resource Center for Suicide Prevention and Aftercare
     (404) 256-2919 www.thelink.org
SPAN USA — Suicide Prevention Action Network (888) 649-1366
     www.spanusa.org
National Suicide Prevention Lifeline - Call 1-800-273-8255 – 24 hrs a day -
     http://suicidepreventionlifeline.org/

Selected Bibliography

Hsu, Albert Y. *Grieving a Suicide: A Loved One's Search for Comfort, Answers & Hope*. Downers Grove, IL: IVP Books, 2002.

Mason, Karen. *Preventing Suicide: A Handbook for Pastors, Chaplains and Pastoral Counselors*. Downers Grove, IL: IVP Books, 2014.

Quinnett, Paul G. *Suicide: The Forever Decision*. New York, NY: The Crossroad Publishing Company, 2011.

Exercise 5.1 Suicide Intervention Readiness

Rate yourself on possession of the following suicide intervention skills. Use the scale provided: 1 = poor; 2 = below average; 3 = Average; 4 = Above average; 5 = Excellent. Simply check the box that best describes you. Be honest with yourself. Work on the areas that need improvement—it's not an assignment, it's a life that you might save!

Suicide Intervention Skill	1	2	3	4	5
I know the reasons most teens attempt suicide					
I can identify the signs of a possible suicide risk					
I understand the QPR method of intervention					
I am comfortable asking a teen if they are suicidal					
I am familiar with our suicide referral agencies					
I understand and can use SLAP for risk assessment					
I know the behaviors to avoid with teens at risk					
I have worked through the theology of suicide					
I can use a NO HARM agreement					

CHAPTER SIX

DRUG ADDICTION: DETECTION AND INTERVENTION

Parents today do not have the luxury of not worrying about their families being threatened by drugs. Almost every young person experiments with drugs or alcohol, and the statistics for heavy drug use for churched and unchurched kids are almost identical. –Steven Arterburn and Jim Burns— *Drug-Proof Your Kids*[127]

Addiction develops from an unhealthy choice of using drugs as a coping mechanism for dealing with the pain of living. As a society, we have come to believe that having any kind of pain is unacceptable. In reality, pain is a normal and necessary part of life. Pain motivates us to change, to grow, to stay out of trouble. How we learn to deal with pain is most important. The sin of drug addiction is the *loss* of what we have been created to be. – Stephen Van Cleave, Walter Byrd, and Kathy Revell—*Counseling for Substance Abuse and Addiction*[128]

Case Studies

Karl[129] was a good looking, outgoing junior in high school when I met him. He was mature for his age and popular with the girls. His parents were very well off financially and this allowed Karl to dress in the latest trends, have all the cool technological gadgets and drive a fast muscle car. His parents and grandparents attended church regularly, but Karl came only sporadically. Late, on a Friday night, I received a phone call from Karl's mother. She was frantic. Karl had been arrested by the local police and was being held at the police station for possession of LSD. She wanted me to go and visit him and help him with his drug problem.

Caroline was a member of a blended family. There were two siblings from the father's first marriage, two siblings from the mother's first marriage and two from the new marriage. Caroline was the oldest daughter from her mother's first marriage. Caroline attended church every Sunday morning, Sunday night and Wednesday night with her family. The family was very dedicated to the church for all practical purposes. But Caroline was slowly turning more and more rebellious. She was dating a boy in town who was a high school dropout and a known drug user. Caroline was eventually caught with a bottle of wine and some marijuana. Through counseling it was eventually discovered that her alcohol and drug use was a form of self-medication to numb the pain of her sexual abuse by her step-father.

Not only is there a significant number of adolescents who use illicit drugs or alcohol, but there is an alarming trend of minimizing how harmful drugs can be.

It was a strange group—nine boys and one girl. The girl wasn't dating any of the boys and she wasn't having any identity issues. She just liked hanging out with these nine boys because of their common love for drugs. There wasn't necessarily any drug that was preferred by the group—they would take whatever was available and affordable at the time. Alcohol, marijuana, speed, downers, THC, mescaline, LSD and cocaine— it was all fair game.

One Saturday night the group all told their parents they would going camping at the lake. I'm sure the parents pictured the group sitting around a campfire roasting marshmallows and making s'mores while singing Kum By Yah. Little did they know. The group had scored some LSD and they were all going to trip that night. For some reason they decided it would be fun to climb the rock cliffs near the camp site. They were about fifty feet up the side of the cliff when Billy started hallucinating big, green, glowing worms with sharp teeth coming out of the rocks. He screamed and pushed back from the cliff—and fell to the rocks below. He cracked his skull wide open, but didn't die. One of the group drove to a nearby farmhouse and called for an ambulance. Billy ended up being life-flighted to a nearby hospital. He didn't die, but he was never the same. The brain damage was permanent.

None of the parents of this group had a clue that their teens were using drugs until this night. Desperately wanting help, they came and asked me to educate them on teenage drug abuse and what they needed to do as parents to help their teenagers get off the drugs.

Anyone who is involved in youth ministry for any length of time is going to encounter teens who are using, abusing or addicted to drugs. It is imperative that you know how to identify the signs of a user and what to do to help.

Adolescent Drug Use

In 2015, nearly half (48.9%) of U.S. high school seniors admitted to using an illicit drug (not counting alcohol or tobacco) in their lifetime. . . Underage consumption of alcohol and tobacco also poses a significant health risk to adolescents. Within the past year, 21% of eight-grade students reported that they had consumed alcohol, and 8% reported that they had been intoxicated; these numbers skyrocket to 58% and 38%, respectively, for twelfth-grade students.[130]

"By the time they are seniors, almost 70 percent of high school students will have tried alcohol, half will have taken an illegal drug, nearly 40 percent will have smoked a cigarette, and more than 20 percent will have used a prescription drug for a nonmedical purpose."[131]

Not only is there a significant number of adolescents who use illicit drugs or alcohol, but there is an alarming trend of minimizing how harmful drugs can be. "Between 2014 and 2015, the perceived harmfulness of regularly smoking marijuana dropped significantly from 36.1% of high school seniors rating it as a "great risk" to 31.9%. This decline is a continuation of a 10-year trend of decreasing perceived risk (in 2005, 58% of high school seniors rated regular marijuana use as a "great risk").[132]

The good news concerning adolescent drug use is that there are some indications that it is declining. Consider the following from the National Institute on Drug Abuse:

> This year's Monitoring the Future (MTF) survey of drug use and attitudes among American 8th, 10th, and 12th graders continues to show encouraging news, with decreasing use of alcohol, cigarettes, and many illicit drugs over the last 5 years—many to their lowest levels since this survey's inception; no increase in use of marijuana among teens; decreasing use of synthetic drugs; and decreasing misuse of prescription drugs. However, the survey highlighted continuing concerns over the high rate of electronic cigarette (e-cigarette) use and softening of attitudes around some types of drug use, particularly a continued decrease in perceived harm of marijuana use.[133]

Drug abuse is found in all cross-sections of the adolescent subculture.

While we can be encouraged that the use of drugs and alcohol among adolescents is trending downward according to some indicators, there is still a large percentage of teenagers who are going to experiment with drugs and a significant number who will develop an addiction or abuse problem. Any amount of illegal drug and alcohol abuse among adolescents should be a concern for the youth worker. While the specific statistics will vary from year to year and with the organization collecting the data, alcohol is still the substance of choice. Some have estimated that there could be more than four million American alcoholics under the age of eighteen, and the age at which young people begin experimenting with alcohol continues to drop. According to Dr. Les Parrott III, trying alcohol today is already more common among current fifth graders than it was among current eighth graders when they were in the fifth grade.[134]

Drug abuse is found in all cross-sections of the adolescent subculture: rich, poor, black, white, male, female, etc. Children of alcoholics are in the "high risk" category having a 50-60% higher risk. The reason children of alcoholics are more susceptible to drug abuse is because they do not have a concept of "normal" so they turn to chemicals to learn to deal with life.

Why Do Adolescents Abuse Drugs?

You would be surprised at how many adolescents could not explain to you why they first got into drugs, including alcohol, because of their lack of self-awareness and their lack of the various dynamics affecting their lives. A common answer given by a teen would be, "I just tried some one day, and I guess I liked it and then tried it some more." They may not even be aware that it was the peer group that they chose to hang around with that first introduced them to drug use. They were invited to a Friday night party after the football game and even though they didn't go intending on using alcohol or drugs, because everyone else was doing it, the joined in to be an accepted part of the group.

> For a good number of adolescents, experimenting with drugs is simply another adventure.

Curiosity is one factor. Trying drugs is a new experience and this generation of young people is all about experience. They love to push life to the extreme. For a good number of adolescents, experimenting with drugs is simply another adventure. A large number of high school students report having gotten high or drunk at least once or twice. It doesn't always end in addiction, for some they just wanted to try it to see what it was all about. Unfortunately, there is also a significant number who never intended to become addicted, but they did because of what started from giving in to their curiosity.

Closely related to curiosity is the teen that abuses alcohol and drugs *just for kicks*—for the thrill of participating in something that is illegal or dangerous. Some things are more desirable simply because they are forbidden. The apostle Paul wrote: "I would not have known what coveting really was if the law had not said, 'Do not covet.'"[135] Some kids are drawn to the forbidden thrill of drug use and end up addicted in the process.

> Some teens use drugs and alcohol because *it fits the image* they want to portray.

Other teens will use drugs and alcohol in order *to be accepted* in a particular group. Andy Stanley has said that teens don't choose their friends; their friends choose them. By that he is referring to the power of peer pressure and the desire to belong. Teens will adjust their morals in order to be accepted by a particular group. If the group that has embraced them uses drugs and alcohol, the teen will do whatever it takes to remain a part of the group.

Some teens use drugs and alcohol because *it fits the image* they want to portray. They have developed an identity that revolves around rebellion and a devil-may-care attitude. It is a way of asserting their independence.

An obvious reason why teens will get high or drunk that is often overlooked is that getting high or drunk is *a pleasant experience*. It can become a self-rewarding behavior because each time the teen participates in drinking or getting high he has a good time.

Teens will also drink or use drugs to *relieve boredom or frustration*. I don't know how many times I have heard youth ministers from small communities bemoan the fact that so many teens in the town drink and do drugs simply because "there isn't anything else to do."

Some teens will use drugs as a means of *escape*. They simply want to run away from any kind of physical or emotional pain that they are experiencing. Adolescents with a history of physical and/or sexual abuse are more likely to be diagnosed with substance use disorders. It could also be that they want to avoid the pain of a parental divorce or the breakup of a significant relationship. They could be suffering from feelings of inadequacy, fear of the future, pressures of school or unrealistic expectations of their parents. While drug abuse only brings temporary relief, they figure that temporary relief is better than no relief at all.

There are also those who never intended to become addicted to drugs but were first *prescribed a pain medication* after a needed surgery or injury and then became addicted to the pain killer. "After marijuana and alcohol, prescription drugs are the most commonly abused substances by Americans age 14 and older."[136] "Every day in the US, 2,500 youth (12 to 17) abuse a prescription pain reliever for the first time."[137] Teenage boys are more likely to abuse prescription drugs for the "high," while teenage girls will abuse them for weight control or to stay awake in class.

> Research has shown that the key risk periods for drug abuse are during major transitions in children's lives. The first big transition for children is when they leave the security of the family and enter school. Later, when they advance from elementary school to middle school, they often experience now academic and social situations, such as learning to get along with a wider group of peers. It is at this stage—early adolescence—that children are likely to encounter drugs for the first time.

> When they enter high school, adolescents face additional social, emotional, and education challenges. At the same time, they may be exposed to greater availability of drugs, drug abusers, and social activities involving drugs. These challenges can increase the risk that they will abuse alcohol, tobacco, and other substances.[138]

Genetics or familial predispositions can be another contributing factor as to why an adolescent ends up with a drug or alcohol problem. It has been known for decades that the offspring of alcoholics are significantly more likely than other people to become alcoholics themselves. But, genetics cannot be blamed for all addiction problems because "over a third of all alcoholics have no family history of the disorder and only 30-40 percent of the sons of alcoholics have ever become alcoholics themselves."[139]

Drug Categories[140]

Drugs are available in various forms and can be taken a number of ways. They can be swallowed, drank, inhaled, smoked, eaten, and injected. Some drugs are legal and others are not. Drug abuse and misuse can take place with either legal or illegal drugs. It is helpful if you have a basic understanding of the different categories of drugs and the most common drugs used under each category.

Stimulants. These drugs speed up the body's nervous system and create a feeling of energy. The street term for stimulants is "uppers" because of their ability to keep the user very alert and awake. Students will use uppers during finals week when cramming for tests or during an athletic contest in order to be "hypervigilant." When the effects of the drug wear off, the user is typically left with feelings of sickness and a loss of energy. A stimulant is commonly prescribed by a physician to treat ADD and ADHD. Some commonly used simulants would be: cocaine, methamphetamines, amphetamines, Ritalin, and Cylert.

Depressants. Depressants slow down activity in the central nervous system and provide the user with feelings of relaxation. Thus, they are commonly known as "downers." Depressants are available as a prescription drug to relieve anxiety, stress and anger. Some common depressants would be: barbiturates, benzodiazepines, Valium, GHB, Quaaludes, alcohol, PCP and tranquilizers.

Hallucinogens. Hallucinogens affect the person in two main ways. First, they hallucinate objects, colors, and people who are not present in reality and they can distort the visual picture of what is seen by creating altered perceptions. Secondly, hallucinogens can cause intense emotions and emotional switching in the person. Some common hallucinogens are: LSD, Mescaline, Psilocybin, and magic mushrooms.

Opiates. The opiates and morphine derivatives cause drowsiness, confusion, and nausea but also provide feelings of euphoria and pain relief for the user. Common opiates and its derivatives would include: Codeine, Fentanyl, Heroin, Morphine, Opium, Oxycodone, Hydrocodone.

Cannabinoids. These drugs result in feelings of euphoria, cause confusion and memory problems, and affect one's motor skills and reaction times. There can also be alterations in time and space perception, exaggerated laughter and a general sense of well-being—feeling "mellow". Depending on the quality of the marijuana and how much one has taken, hallucinations may also accompany usage. Typical cannabinoids would be: marijuana and hashish.

Inhalants. Inhalants are sniffed or huffed and giver the user immediate feelings of exhilaration and release. Unfortunately, these immediate results can also result in sudden brain damage. Younger teens and pre-teens are most likely to abuse inhalants because they are cheap and readily available. Common inhalants include: glues, paint thinner, gasoline, laughing gas, and aerosol sprays.

Prescription Drugs. Prescription drugs can be very helpful when used properly and when under the guidance of a qualified physician. The drugs are used as aids in surgery, pain relief, treatment of mental conditions such as anxiety and depression, and weight control. However, the misuse and abuse of prescription drugs can be very dangerous. A recent trend among teenagers, which is of great concern to me, is the phenomenon of "pharm parties" or "skittles." This is where students will raid their parents or grandparents medicine cabinet and dump the pills into a large bowl and everyone grabs a handful of pills and washes them down with some alcohol. The types of prescription drugs that are commonly abused are: opioids, such as Codeine, Oxycodone, Morphine; depressants, such as barbiturates and benzodiazepines; and stimulants, such as dextroamphetamine, and methylphenidate.

Anabolic Steroids. Steroids are taken to improve physical performance as well as to enlarge muscles and increase strength. Hostility is a frequent side effect of anabolic steroid abuse. Common steroids are: Anadrol, Oxandrin, Durabolin, Stanozol and Dianbol.

Signs That a Student May Be Abusing Drugs/Alcohol

Incredible as it may seem, parents are often the last ones to know that their teen is using drugs. When their teen begins to exhibit a radical change in friends and activities the parents just chalk it up to typical teenage behavior. Parents and youth workers need to be informed about the signs and symptoms of drug abuse.

If a student exhibits four or five of the following symptoms, this may indicate a problem and the need for referral. Spotting any of these behaviors may be a serious concern. However, be sure to keep your evaluation in context. Every student is unique and just because a student may exhibit several of the key markers, it does not necessarily mean the students is abusing drugs. There could be other issues going on in the student's life that are causing the identified behaviors such as a parental divorce, a breakup with a boyfriend or girlfriend, not making the athletic team, or struggling with depression. But, if you do observe a significant number of these behaviors and it seems out of character for the student and you cannot attribute the behaviors to any other known cause, then you must consider the possibility the student is abusing drugs or alcohol.

Incredible as it may seem, parents are often the last ones to know that their teen is using drugs.

1. A DROP IN GRADES
   - This could be a slow decrease in the past six months to a year, or a sudden decrease.
   - Lower grades/lower achievement
   - Academic failure

- Always behind in class
- Lack of motivation apathy
2. SCHOOL ATTENDANCE
   - Absenteeism
   - Excessive tardies
   - In suspension
   - Frequent schedule changes
   - Frequent visits to counselor
   - Skipping class
   - Sleeping in class
   - Poor performance in class
   - Not doing assignments
3. EXTRA-CURRICULAR ACTIVITIES
   - Loss of eligibility
   - Increasing non-involvement
   - Has dropped out
4. SWITCHING FRIENDS
   - Are you seeing a different set of friends around the school?
   - More friends that you object to?
   - Not meeting any friends?
5. EMOTIONAL HIGHS AND LOWS
   - Easily upset
   - Emotional state changes rapidly
   - Doesn't seem as happy as they used to
6. DEFIANCE TO RULES AND REGULATIONS
   - Pushing limits around the home or school
   - Not doing responsibilities around the home
7. BECOMING MORE SECRETIVE
   - Not sharing any, or very, little of their persona: problems
8. LOSS OF INITIATIVE
   - Less energy
   - Sleeping more than usual.
9. WITHDRAWING FROM FAMILY, CHURCH, SCHOOL FUNCTIONS
   - School activities – athletic games, concerts, plays, recitals
   - Church attendance
   - Meals
10. CHANGE IN PHYSICAL HYGIENE
   - Becoming sloppier, wearing same clothes frequently
   - Hair not combed or washed
   - Not showered or bathed

11. NOT BEING HONEST WITH YOU ABOUT SCHOOL PROBLEMS
    - Not getting assignments in on time
    - Academic probation
    - Academic suspension
12. MANY EXCUSES FOR STAYING OUT LATE
    - Not being back home on time
    - Not coming back home at all but staying out all night
    - Constant excuses when asked of whereabouts
13. ISOLATING THEMSELVES
    - Possibly spending a lot of time in their room
    - Not participating in family activities, i.e. dinner table, recreational outings
14. SUSPICION OF MONEY OR PRESCRIPTION DRUGS MISSING
    - From parents or brothers and sisters
    - Taken from other students in school
15. SELLING POSSESSIONS
    - Clothing, records, gifts, seems to have money but no job
16. FEELING MANIPULATED AND BARGAINED WITH
    - Playing friends against each other
    - Pitting authority against peers (i.e. parents against teachers, etc.)
17. WEIGHT CHANGES
    - Drastic loss or gain.
18. SHORT-TEMPERED
    - Becomes angry often
    - short fuse
19. LEGAL PROBLEMS
    - Driving while intoxicated
    - Curfew violation
    - Attendance at parties that get broken up by police.
20. DEFENSIVE
    - When confronted on behavior or other concerns.
21. COMING BACK HOME DRUNK OR HIGH
    - Smelling of pot or alcohol
    - Seems unusually giddy
    - Slurred speech
    - Red eyes
22. FINDING PARAPHERNALIA
    - Rolling Papers
    - Pipes
    - Roach clips

- Drug residue or capsules
- Bottles

23. ABUSIVE BEHAVIOR
    - Verbally or physically abusive to any parents, teachers, coaches, etc.

24. PHYSICAL SYMPTOMS
    - Staggering or stumbling
    - Breath or clothing smells suspiciously of alcohol or pot
    - Evidence of having vomited
    - Glassy or blood-shot eyes/ dark glasses
    - Erratic coordination
    - Speech seems slurred
    - Bad hygiene
    - Sleeping in class
    - Physical complaints
    - Physical injuries

25. DISRUPTIVE BEHAVIOR
    - Defiant attitude toward rules
    - Irresponsibility/blaming/denying
    - Suspected of fighting
    - Suspected of cheating
    - Suspected of throwing objects
    - Defiant littering
    - Sudden outbursts - verbally abusive
    - Suspected of obscene language, gestures
    - Dramatic attention-seeking
    - Crying
    - Extreme negativism
    - Hyperactivity/nervousness

26. ATYPICAL BEHAVIOR
    - Talks frequently about drug use
    - Avoids contact with others
    - Erratic behavior changes
    - Change of friends (usually negative)
    - Sudden popularity
    - Constant adult contact
    - Older social group contact
    - Hypersensitivity won't be touched
    - Sexual looseness/public intimacy
    - Time disorientation

- Unrealistic goals
- Inappropriate responses
- Depression
- Seeking adult advice without a specific problem
- Defensive
- Withdrawn/a loner

If enough signs are present to cause you to suspect drug or alcohol abuse, then you must gently and compassionately confront the teen with your observations and reasons for concern. Be sure to communicate unconditional love to the teen, but you must also not allow yourself to be "conned" by them and accepting some phony excuse for the behaviors when it is in reality drug or alcohol use. Your next step is to determine which stage of drug use the teen is in and then take appropriate action.

Stages of Drug Use

Not all adolescent drug users are created equal. Some will try it once or twice out of curiosity and decide in the end that it is not for them. Others will only use occasionally if it is available or at a party to fit in. Then there is your "hard core" user who makes drug use their life and is using daily, everything centers around the drug. When you encounter a teenager who admits to using drugs, you must first determine what stage of drug use they are in, so that you know how to appropriate respond.

Stage one. Adolescents don't automatically go from no drug use to addiction. They pass through definite stages that are defined by significant changes in their behavior and the amount of drugs and alcohol that is consumed.

> **It's hard to spot drug use in a Stage One kid because he looks and acts normal.**

In Stage One, kids take drugs only when it's convenient and they're available. They only smoke pot or drink alcohol if someone else has some to share. It's like the person who says he's quit smoking, and he bums cigarettes. What he means is that he quit *buying*, not smoking. In his own mind, he's not a smoker. So it is with a kid on drugs. As long as he's not buying, he can deny to himself that he is doing drugs.

Stage one students smoke or drink on weekends and not
even every weekend.[141]

It's hard to spot drug use in a Stage One kid because he looks and acts normal. The only way you might discover drug use in this period is by catching the student in the act—by accident.

Stage two. This is where the student will begin living a "dual lifestyle." Early in Stage Two the student will keep up the pretense of being a "straight" kid. The student will still go to school, still be involved in sports and other extra-curricular activities. At home this student is still fairly well behaved and obedient. They still care what other significant adults think about them, such as teachers, coaches, scout leaders and youth ministers. So, they will try to maintain an appearance of being a good kid, even though their drug use has elevated to the point where there are distinct signs of change.

The signs to watch for in Stage Two drug use are: passive withdrawn periods that turn into aggressive, angry periods. There is significant time spent alone, in a bedroom with loud rock music blaring that is offset by temper tantrums and abusive language.

Towards the end of Stage Two the student will begin to show signs of disinterest in activities that were once important to them. Involvement in activities such as hobbies, sports, and youth group begins to interfere with the time that they now want to spend in recreational drug use. The student will sometimes get high alone without a party or friends to spur him on. Given the choice of feeling good because he made the soccer team or feeling good from taking drugs, the student already controlled by the chemical learning sequence will opt for drugs. It's easier and faster.

> Given the choice of feeling good because he made the soccer team or feeling good from taking drugs, the student already controlled by the chemical learning sequence will opt for drugs. It's easier and faster.

Stage Three. The student in Stage Three drops all Stage Two pretenses of being straight. Forget the dual lifestyle. The student no longer cares if they are pleasing parents, youth ministers or coaches. The student is only interested in getting high. Regular weekday use has now grown to include use before and during school. Straight friends are dropped from the student's circle of friends and they openly hang out with known druggies. Because of the student's need for an increasing amount of drugs or alcohol, the student may begin stealing money from their parents or becoming involved in crime.

By the time the student reaches this stage, getting high has become the most important thing in his life. He uses drugs to feel good and to avoid bad feelings. He gets high almost every day and either goes to school already high or gets high at school, much like the alcoholic who drinks on the job, first at lunchtime, then on coffee breaks and eventually keeps a bottle in his locker or desk drawer. He is losing his ability to cope with stress, disappointment, fear and other everyday emotional difficulties.[142]

Stage Four. This is the final stage of drug use. Beyond Stage Four is death. The student who has advanced to this stage uses drugs not just on weekends, not just on weeknights, not just weekdays, not just before school and at school, but excessively and compulsively. *All the time!* He no longer uses drugs to feel good. Now he uses drugs to feel normal. Pain is now associated with drugs, but the drug user can't stop. The Stage Four drug user can no longer distinguish between normal and high. Their fellow straight students would derisively call this kid "a burnout." They are wasted all the time. As the need for increased drug use intensifies, so does the crime. By the time a student reaches Stage Four drug use, it will either end with continued physical deterioration and death or by an intervention staged by family and friends.

Defining Addiction and Abuse

The *Diagnostic and Statistical Manual of Mental disorders (DSM-5)* is the "bible" of the mental health profession. It uses a multiaxial system of classification for the identification of the various mental illnesses and addictions that people suffer with. According to the DSM-5, an alcohol use disorder is: "A problematic pattern of alcohol use leading to clinically significant impairment or distress, as manifested by at least two of the following, occurring within a 12-month period:"[143]

1. Alcohol is often taken in larger amounts or over a longer period than was intended.
2. There is a persistent desire or unsuccessful efforts to cut down or control alcohol use.
3. A great deal of time is spent in activities necessary to obtain alcohol, use alcohol, or recover from its effects.

4. Craving, or a strong desire or urge to use alcohol.
5. Recurrent alcohol use resulting in a failure to fulfill major role obligations at work, school, or home.
6. Continued alcohol use despite having persistent or recurrent social or interpersonal problems caused or exacerbated by the effects of alcohol.
7. Important social, occupational, or recreational activities are given up or reduced because of alcohol use.
8. Recurrent alcohol use in situations in which it is physically dangerous.
9. Alcohol use is continued despite knowledge of having a persistent or recurrent physical or psychological problem that is likely to have been caused or exacerbated by alcohol.
10. Tolerance, as defined by either of the following:
    A. A need for markedly increased amounts of the substance to achieve intoxication or desired effect.
    B. Markedly diminished effect with continued use of the same amount of the substance.
11. Withdrawal, as manifested by either of the following:
    A. The characteristic withdrawal syndrome for alcohol
    B. Alcohol (or closely related substance) is taken to relieve or avoid withdrawal symptoms.[144]

While the behaviors listed were specifically for alcohol use disorder, they would easily apply to type of substance abuse. In an earlier version of the DSM, (DSM-IV-TR), there was a distinction made between drug addiction or dependency and drug abuse. The DSM-IV-TR defined psychoactive substance *abuse* as the presence of at least one or more of the following occurring within a 12-month period:

1. Recurrent substance use resulting in a failure to fulfill major role obligations at work, school, or home (e.g., repeated absences or poor work

performance related to substance use; substance-related absences, suspensions, or expulsions from school; neglect of children or household)

2.   Recurrent substance use in situations in which it is physically hazardous (e.g. driving an automobile or operating a machine when impaired by substance use)

3.   Recurrent substance-related legal problems (e.g., arrests for substance-related disorderly conduct)

4.   Continued substance use despite having persistent or recurrent social or interpersonal problems caused or exacerbated by the effects of the substance (e.g., arguments with spouse about consequences of intoxication, physical fights)[145]

Are You Part of the Solution or Part of the Problem?

Many times, when family and friends try to "help" alcoholics or drug addicts, they are actually making it easier for them to continue in the progression of the disease. This baffling phenomenon is called enabling. What is the difference between helping and enabling? Simply, enabling creates an atmosphere in which the alcoholic or drug user can comfortably continue their unacceptable behavior. While enabling is not intentional, it is still like saying, "Here, let me help you hurt yourself!"

Are you an enabler? Here's a few questions that might help determine the difference between helping and enabling an alcoholic/drug addict in your life:

1.   Have you ever "called in sick for the alcoholic/drug addict, lying about his symptoms?

2.   Have you accepted part of the blame for his or her drinking or behavior?

3.   Have you avoided talking about his drinking out of fear of his response?

4.   Have you bailed him out of jail or paid for his legal fees?

5.   Have you paid bills that he was supposed to have paid himself?

6.   Have you loaned him money?

7.   Have you tried drinking/doing drugs with them in hopes of strengthening the relationship?

8.   Have you given them "one more chance" and then

another and another?

9. Have you threatened to leave and didn't?

10. Have you finished a job or project that the alcoholic failed to complete himself?

If you answered "yes" to any of these questions, you at some point in time have enabled the alcoholic/drug addict to avoid his or her own responsibilities. Rather than "help" the alcoholic/drug addict, you have actually made it easier for him or her to get worse.

If you answered "yes" to any of these questions, you at some point in time have enabled the alcoholic/drug addict, you have probably become a major contributor to the growing and continuing problem and chances are have become effected by the disease yourself.

As long as the alcoholic/drug addict has his or her enabling devices in place, it is easy for them to continue to deny they have a problem—since most of their problems are being "solved" by those around them. Only when they are forced to face the consequences of their own actions, will it finally begin to sink in how deep their problem has become. The choice to quit enabling and to force the addict to suffer the consequences of their choices is not easy for the friends and families of alcoholics to make. These kinds of choices are difficult. They require "detachment with love."

Denial and Resistance

If you suspect that a teenager is using or abusing drugs, then a loving confrontation must be made. When that happens, don't expect the teenager to acknowledge your accusation or be thrilled about it. In fact, he or she will most likely deny that there is a problem. Even when you share your observations of key changes that have taken place in the student's life as a result of drug use, such as, dropping out of former favorite activities, lower grades, change in personality, emotional swings and appearance, the student will try to attribute all of those things to some other cause. It's an unfair coach, the stress of school, unreasonable parents or even society itself. It is never, ever the drugs. Even if the student admits to using drugs, he or she will deny that drugs or alcohol are having any harmful effects on his or her life. It is rarely helpful to try and argue the point if the person disagrees with your observations and connections to drug use. However, you must maintain that your observation is reasonable and that you are not going to be persuaded otherwise, easily.

When my work becomes confrontational in this way, I often use the analogy of a lighthouse keeper to illustrate how I view my role. I explain that my job is to shine the light to signal the presence of dangerous rocks. I point out that the student is the "captain" of his or her own life and can "steer the ship" as close to the rock as he or she chooses. What I will not do, however, is allow the student to pretend the rocks are not there.[146]

If you or the student's parents have enough evidence or observations to believe that drugs or alcohol and causing significant problems in the student's life, then an intervention is called for, even if the student continues to deny that there is a problem.

Intervention

The standard operating procedure for dealing with alcoholics and drug addicts used to be for family members and concerned friends to wait until the addict "hit bottom." The theory was that you had to wait until the person's addiction caused them enough pain, (i.e. being fired from their job, involved in drug-related automobile accidents, jail time, bankruptcy, loss of friends and family), before the addict was ready and willing to give up their drugs or alcohol. The good news is that recovery doesn't have to wait until the addict brings these tragedies upon themselves. These destructive consequences of drug addiction can be avoided if the family and significant friends participate in an intervention.

> **The standard operating procedure for dealing with alcoholics and drug addicts used to be for family members and concerned friends to wait until the addict "hit bottom."**

An intervention is a deliberate process by which change is introduced into peoples' thoughts, feelings and behaviors. A formal intervention usually involves several people preparing themselves, approaching a person involved in some self-destructive behavior, and talking to the person in a clear and respectful way about the behavior in question with the immediate objectives being for the person to listen and to accept help.[147]

The first step to planning an intervention is to contact an agency or professional counselor who can provide a professional assessment of the family situation and who can educate the family in the key issues of chemical dependency and who can serve as a step-by-step guide through the intervention process. After the education process is completed the family members will conduct an intervention rehearsal. They will practice saying what they want to communicate to the addict and the interventionist will suggest the possible responses of the addict. Each family member will come up with a "bottom line" which consists of what they will no longer do to enable the addict if the addict refuses help. Some typical bottom lines would be to quit providing the addict with free rent, food, transportation, cell phone, money, and anything else that keeps the addict from experiencing the full consequences of addiction.

The actual intervention takes place with all concerned family members and significant friends present. Each person will read a letter to the addict expressing their love and appreciation for the person and then list detailed accounts of how the person's addiction has changed them and hurt them. It ends with a plea for the addict to accept the help that is offered this day. The family will have arranged for the addict to enter some type of facility that day. If the addict refuses the offer of help that the family makes through the intervention, then all of the "bottom lines" must come into play. The addict will then have to deal with the harsh consequences of their addiction because the family will no longer enable them and make it easy for them to remain addicted.[148]

Because the denial process is so developed in many teenage users, it is important to have a minimum of two and preferably even more people involved in the intervention. Great care must be taken not to overwhelm and create defensiveness (which is already going to be present to some degree) by having too many people bombarding the user with examples. The facilitator must ensure that the climate of the session be one of love, concern, and hope.

The goal of any intervention is to break through the denial process and motivate the teenager to want help. If after an intervention has taken place, the user continues to deny the problem and resists help, then those who participated must enforce the consequences they indicated would happen, (e.g. no more making excuses to employer, no more loaning money, paying bills, etc.) The goal in all of this is to get the addict into treatment.

In-patient Treatment

Teenage drug and alcohol addiction is a very serious problem—one that can be life threatening any day. As such, the best protocol may be to require intensive in-patient treatment by a professionally trained staff in a hospital or clinic setting. These programs usually require six to eight weeks with several months of follow up sometimes requiring the person to live in a half-way house residential setting to help them remain clean and sober for a longer period of time before going back home and facing old friends and past temptations.

Hospitalization should be considered in these cases:

1. Adolescents have unsuccessfully tried to quit or stop abusing drugs several times on their own.
2. They have been unsuccessful in outpatient treatment programs.
3. There has been an overdose, or the potential for one is strong. For example, they are mixing street drugs and alcohol.
4. Medical attention is necessary to control sever withdrawal symptoms.
5. Suicidal thoughts, bad trips, and flashbacks are occurring.
6. Adolescents' behavior is out of control. They are truant, failing school, stealing to obtain drugs, or in denial when confronted with evidence of drug abuse.
7. Family members are emotionally drained from the roller coaster ride of mood swings, social problems, and arguments that accompany drug abuse.[149]

If the family cannot afford a residential or inpatient treatment program, then the family should encourage the addict to begin attending one of the many 12-step recovery programs that are available in every community such as Alcoholics Anonymous or Narcotics Anonymous. Some churches offer 12-step recovery programs that are Christian based such as Celebrate Recovery or Teen Challenge.

Substance addiction is a disease that takes the very best

of effort from those who treat it and a commitment to persevere from those receiving the treatment, if success is to be achieved. What is success in drug treatment? It is drug-free living, responsible living, and being happier drug-free than when addicted. There is no such thing as an addict who is beyond hope. Recovery is *always* possible, because what is impossible with man is possible with God.[150]

When Do I Need to Refer?

When dealing with an adolescent who has drug and alcohol problems, it is important to know your limits. If the student you are working with is only at stage one or stage two of their drug or alcohol involvement, then you may have success in counseling with them and helping the student make better choices concerning the use of drugs or alcohol. But if the student has already reached stage three or four, then it is wisest to refer the student to a professional counselor who specializes in addictions. If you are not sure what stage the student is in, I would advise you to refer if any of the following conditions apply to the student you are working with:

- Withdrawal symptoms are observed or are acknowledged by the student.
- The student admits to having blackouts.
- Tolerance to alcohol or any drug is admitted.
- Alcohol or drugs are being used at school.
- The student has used inhalants.[151]

Overview of the Counseling Process for Drug and Alcohol Abuse

Connect with the Teen
- They may call you and ask for help – if so, set up a meeting giving them instructions on location, time and length of session.
- You may hear from others about their drug and alcohol use – if so, take pastoral initiative and go to them or call and set up a meeting.
- Prepare your meeting place and yourself by reviewing how to deal with drug and alcohol abuse and addiction. Don't forget to pray and ask the Holy Spirit for guidance and insight!

Understand the Teen
- Communicate empathy by your posture, position and active listening skills.
- Communicate nonjudgmental, unconditional love and genuineness.
- Ask yourself the empathy question: "How would I feel if I was this student in this situation?"

Explore with the Teen
- Find out what caused them to begin abusing alcohol or drugs – what is missing in their life? What is present in their life that is causing the pain?
- Explore with them other possibilities to deal with the pain and problem in their life other than abusing drugs or alcohol. Help them focus in on their strengths and available resources.
- Teach them new coping skills that would take the place of the drugs or alcohol.
- Find out which drugs/alcohol the student is using and how much and how often.
- Determine which stage of drug use they are in.
- Be on guard and aware of denial and resistance from the student.
- Discover who and how others are enabling the student.

Initiate a Plan with the Teen
- If the student is resistant or in denial, then you must work with the family and other key people in the student's life to set up an intervention. Referral to a professional drug and alcohol counselor is advised.
- With the help of a professional, determine if an in-patient treatment center is needed or if out-patient treatment will suffice.
- If in-patient treatment is recommended, help the family make this choice.
- Make available any information about out-patient treatment such as Alcoholics Anonymous, Narcotics Anonymous, Celebrate Recovery, etc.
- Support the family's "bottom line" if treatment is rejected.

Finish with the Teen
- Encourage them to complete their 30, 60 or 90-day in-house treatment program.
- Support their continued attendance at AA or Celebrate Recovery.
- Maintain your relationship with the teen and family and help them to develop new friendships and activities as they will probably have to give up their old ones as they were related to their addiction.
- Prepare for a relapse and take appropriate measures if one occurs.

Helpful Resources

Alcoholics Anonymous. http://www.aa.org/ The national web site will direct you to local chapters and offer resources.
Alateen. http://www.al-anon.alateen.org/ This organization helps teens who have alcoholic parents and provides resources and meetings.
Celebrate Recovery. http://www.celebraterecovery.com/ A Christ-centered recovery program.
Hazelden Betty Ford Foundation. Butler Center For Research. http://www.hazeldenbettyford.org/
National Institute on Drug Abuse. https://www.drugabuse.gov/
Teen Challenge. https://www.teenchallengeusa.com/ Started by David Wilkerson of *The Cross and the Switchblade* fame.

Selected Bibliography

Arterburn, Steven and Burns, Jim. *Drug Proof Your Kids*. Ventura, CA: Regal Books, 1995.
Drews, Toby Rice. *Getting Them Sober; A Guide for Those Who Live With an Alcoholic.* South Plainfield, NJ: Bridge Publishing, Inc. 1980.
Klaus, Tom. *Healing Hidden Wounds: Ministering to Teenagers From Alcoholic Families*. Loveland, CO: Group Books, 1989.
Finnigan, Candy. *When Enough Is Enough: A Comprehensive Guide to Successful Intervention.* New York, NY: Avery, 2008.
Polson, Beth and Newton, Miller. *Not My Kid: A Parent's Guide to Kids and Drugs*. New York, NY: Avon Books, 1984.

Exercise 6.1 Drug and Alcohol Intervention and Treatment

Rate yourself on your knowledge and skill concerning the following drug and alcohol intervention and treatment issues. Use the scale provided: 1 = poor; 2 = below average; 3 = Average; 4 = Above average; 5 = Excellent. Simply check the box that best describes you. Be honest with yourself. Work on the areas that need improvement—it's not an assignment, it's a life that you might save!

Drug and Alcohol Intervention Skill	1	2	3	4	5
I understand why teenagers might misuse drugs.					
I have a good understanding of the various categories of drugs that are misused by teens.					
I am familiar with the common signs that a teen may be abusing alcohol or drugs.					
I understand the various stages of drug use.					
I am familiar with the DSM-5 system of defining a person who has an alcohol or drug problem					
I understand the danger and concept of enabling as it relates to addiction.					
I understand the issue of denial and how to deal with it in a resistant adolescent.					
I understand the concept of an "intervention" and know how to set one up.					
I know the signs when hospitalization or inpatient treatment is called for.					
I know the signs that would indicate that I need to refer the teenager and family to a professional.					

CHAPTER SEVEN

CUTTING TO COPE: COUNSELING ADOLESCENTS WHO SELF-INJURE

Psychiatrist Joshua Weiner, who has treated adolescent cutters in metropolitan Washington, says self-injury is "the anorexia and bulimia of the new millennium." And just as Americans were slow to catch on to the problems of anorexia and bulimia 20 years ago, Weiner says, we are just now beginning to understand the nature and depth of this phenomenon. -- Patrick Welsh[152]

Cutting and other forms of mutilation become a coping mechanism . . . a way of dealing with powerful emotions that they don't know how to deal with. It's as if they have a volcano inside, and that has to erupt. Cutting makes them feel calmer. --Kaye Randall[153]

Case Study

Danielle's mother first noticed the marks on Danielle's arm when she was putting on her coat getting ready to leave for school one morning. "What happened to your arm?" she asked. Danielle told her that the family cat had scratched her. Her mother thought that the scratches looked quite deep for cat scratches and it was very puzzling because Fluffy was usually a very docile pet, but she didn't pursue the matter.

Danielle's friends had also noticed something strange as well. Even when the weather was hot, Danielle would still wear long-sleeved shirts. She had become very secretive also, like something was bothering her. But no one actually questioned Danielle directly. If they had, they may have found out that Danielle had made the deep cuts herself. When she was feeling really depressed and sad, Danielle would cut herself with a razor.

The National Center for PTSD estimates that 13-35 percent of students have injured themselves on purpose at some point.

Whether cutting is happening more or whether people are becoming more aware is hard to say. Mental health professionals say a little of both. Research suggests an estimated 2 percent of people, or about 3 million nationwide, purposefully hurt themselves.[154] The behavior often starts in the teenage years but may persist much longer.

The rate increases dramatically for teenage girls, jumping to about 10 percent of that age group. Cutting is so common among young women with eating disorders that it's sometimes called "new-age anorexia."[155]

Though females appear to cut more than males, there is growing evidence that men and boys engage in it more than once believed.

How Prevalent Is Cutting?

When I began my first youth ministry in the early 70s cutting was unheard of—unless it was "cutting" classes! It wasn't until the 90s when Princess Diana went public with her struggle with cutting that the public became aware of this issue. Since then, celebrities like Fiona Apple, Johnny Depp, Angelina Jolie, Courtney Love and Marilyn Manson have all admitted that they have engaged in self-injury at one time or another. Because self-injury is such a private act and those who engage in acts of self-injury usually do not want to be discovered, it is difficult to obtain accurate statistics on how prevalent the problem is.

> Estimates vary widely from 3% to 38% in adolescents and young adults. Studies conducted with university students demonstrated a 17% lifetime prevalence rate in this population, with 13% reporting that they had engaged in self-harm more than once. Studies of high school students indicated prevalence rates of self-harm in this population ranged from 13% to 24%. Onset can occur in children as young as seven years old, but the age of onset is usually between the ages of 12 and 15 years. Self-injury may also begin during the college years, with surveys reporting that 30% to 40% of college students report engaging in self-harm after the age of 17.[156]

A publication by the US National Library of Medicine reported that 1/3 to 1/2 of U.S. adolescents had engaged in some type of self-injury.[157] "A 2014 study conducted by researchers at Queens University found that one in every 10 teenagers has considered self-harming at some point. The National Center for PTSD estimates that 13-35 percent of students have injured themselves on purpose at some point."[158] While accurate statistics on self-injury are difficult to verify, it is known that the average age at which a person engages in self-injury is ". . . at age 14 and continues the practice, usually with increasing severity, into their late 20s."[159]

- Each year, 1 in 5 females and 1 in 7 males engage in self-injury.
- 90 percent of people who engage in self-harm begin during their teen or pre-adolescent years.
- Nearly 50 percent of those who engage in self-injury activities have been sexually abused.
- Females comprise 60 percent of those who engage in self-injurious behavior.
- About 50 percent of those who engage in self-mutilation begin around age 14 and carry on into their 20s.
- Many of those who self-injure report learning how to do so from friends or pro self-injury websites.
- Approximately two million cases are *reported* annually in the U.S.[160]

The problem of self-injury isn't limited to any particular demographic, ethnic or socioeconomic group. Although females hold a slight majority in the percentages of those who engage in self-injury, a significant number of males engage in this practice also.

Self-injury is commonly referred to as "cutting," but there are other forms of self-injury that students engage in as well. The following list shows the estimated percentages of those engaging in the specific self-injurious behavior.

- Cutting: 70-90%
- Skin picking or scratching: 14%
- Burning: 15-35%
- Self-Hitting: 30%
- Wound interference (picking off a scab): 22%
- Biting (e.g. extreme nail biting): 2%
- Head banging: 21-44%
- Bone breaking: 8%
- Hair pulling: 10%[161]

Why Do Adolescents Cut Themselves?

Simply put, cutting is an unhealthy coping mechanism. It is a symptom of something much deeper. The students who engage in self-injurious behavior have not developed healthy ways of dealing with strong emotions, intense pressure, or upsetting relationship problems.

Contrary to what some people may think, teens that cut themselves are not usually suicidal.[162] In fact, it is just the opposite. Instead of trying to die, the teens that cut themselves are trying to feel alive. Strange as it may sound, students who cut themselves do it because it actually makes them feel better. Some use cutting as self-punishment. Others do it to assert control when everything seems to be spiraling out of control. There are two main explanations why cutting seems desirable to some teens.

First, there are a number of teens that have never been allowed or taught how to properly handle or express strong emotions like anger, frustration or depression. Since they are not allowed or don't know what to do with the strong emotions that build up as a natural part of growing up, they simply stuff them. But, these repressed emotions do not simply go away. They build up

> Strange as it may sound, students who cut themselves do it because it actually makes them feel better.

and build up like steam in a pressure cooker. The teen feels like they are going to explode if something isn't done to relieve these strong emotions. The pain of cutting serves as a kind of "release valve" to eliminate the pressure that has built up within from the unexpressed emotions. It is a kind of dysfunctional "catharsis." If the student can concentrate on

> If the student can concentrate on the pain on the outside, then it helps her to forget the pain on the inside.

the pain on the outside, then it helps her to forget the pain on the inside. Open wounds become a distinct expression of emotional pain. One of the reasons why students will cut is so that they can transform internal pain into something more tangible, external and treatable.

People who cut themselves are often full of intense emotional pain, but they have difficulty relieving the tension this causes in the usual ways. They may think that they have to be strong, and so they may not allow themselves to cry. They may have been taught as children that expressing emotions is wrong. But the tension inside their bodies and their minds becomes almost unbearable, and they find that cutting themselves somehow relieves that tension. It's as if the physical pain releases the emotional pain they've been feeling. It actually calms them, at least for a short time. It helps them feel as if they are in control of their situation and their moods.[163]

A second reason why teens may cut or practice self-harm is because of severe physical or sexual abuse that took place when they were very young. Little children cannot physically defend themselves against adults who abuse them. They do not have the cognitive abilities to reason or argue with them. Either they don't know who to call for help or they are too afraid to ask for help because the abuser has threatened them. About the only kind of "defense" against this terrible physical and emotional pain left for the young child is to subconsciously choose to dissociate. The child "compartmentalizes" the pain and shuts it off from the rest of the child's awareness. This way the child no longer feels pain because they have effectively shut down their emotions.

But the problem is, when the child shuts down their emotions so that they no longer feel any pain from the abuse, the child also is kept from feeling any positive emotions as well. In effect, the child becomes "the walking dead"—an emotional zombie. Eventually, feeling dead inside is no longer desirable either, so the student begins to "cut" or to "burn" because when the student feels the pain, it feels good because the student knows that they are alive. At this point, feeling anything is preferable to feeling nothing.

Some students engage in self-injury because they want to punish themselves. They may feel guilty about hurting other people or mistakes they've made. They may feel bad about themselves or how empty their life feels so they take out their anger on themselves.

Others who feel out of control may harm themselves as a way to gain control. Self-injury is a way to have control over your body when you can't control anything else in your life. A lot of people who cut themselves also have an eating disorder which is also often related to control issues.

> **Each time the student cuts, the brain "rewards" the action by producing the painkilling, mood-lifting natural drug.**

In addition to this, you have the added physiological phenomenon of the brain releasing endorphins in response to the physical injury. Endorphins are a natural painkilling drug that the brain produces. Each time the student cuts, the brain "rewards" the action by producing the painkilling, mood-lifting natural drug.

Cutting can be habit forming. It can become a compulsive behavior—meaning the more a person does it, the more he or she feels the need to do it. The brain starts to connect the false sense of relief from bad feelings to the act of cutting, and it craves this relief the next time tension builds. When cutting becomes a compulsive behavior, it can seem impossible to stop. So, cutting can seem almost like an addiction. A behavior that starts as an attempt to feel more in control can end up controlling you.[164]

There are a number of mental health disorders that co-occur with self-injurious behaviors. The most frequently co-occurring, co-morbid mental health disorders may include:

- Major depressive disorder
- Post-traumatic stress disorder
- Generalized anxiety disorder
- Conduct disorder
- Oppositional defiant disorder
- Depersonalization disorder
- Dissociative disorders
- Eating disorders
- Substance use disorders
- Borderline personality disorder
- Autism spectrum disorders
- Bipolar disorder
- Anxiety disorders
- Trauma[165]

Although cutters don't intend to hurt themselves permanently, they are at risk each time they injure themselves. They may misjudge the depth of a cut and require stitches or, in extreme cases, hospitalization. Cuts can become infected because the person uses dirty cutting instruments (a cutter may use razors, scissors, pins, or even the sharp edge of the tab on a can of soda). If two people who are self-injurers cut themselves and share the cutting instrument, they risk spreading illnesses such as HIV disease and hepatitis.

Signs of a Cutter

Parents are usually taken by surprise and completely shocked when they find out their teen is engaging in self-injurious behavior. This doesn't mean the parent has been negligent because most teens who self-injure try very hard to keep it a secret. If you suspect a student may be a cutter, but the student has not confided in you that they are using self-injury as a coping mechanism, the following are guidelines for you to make an assessment. Remember, not all students who exhibit *some* of these signs are cutters, but the more of them you observe the higher the likelihood the student is involved in cutting.

- The student wears long sleeves and long pants even when the weather is hot in order to hide her scars.
- When the student changes clothes at camp or a retreat, she always changes alone so that no one can see the scars.
- There are unusual marks on the student's arms, legs, or other parts of the body.
- The student has a lot of Band-Aids on her arms or legs a lot of the time.
- The student seems to buy a lot of bandages, vitamin E oil and/or triple antibiotic.
- When asked about the scars, the student will make up wild stories about how she got them or seem flustered or highly embarrassed and not know how to answer.
- The student asks to be excused to use the bathroom a lot, or retreats from uncomfortable or emotionally tense situations.
- The student has a history of sexual abuse or trauma.
- The student has a fascination with knives and other sharp objects.
- The student finds blood appealing.
- The student creates dark art and poetry using images of blood, death, etc. and the colors red, black, and gray.
- The student refuses to go swimming and/or wear a bathing suit.
- The student is very insecure about her body and dislikes being touched.
- The student has sharp objects such as razors, scissors, safety pins, etc. in her purse/backpack.
- Chronic interpersonal challenges leading to social withdrawal and isolation.
- Impulse control difficulties.
- Feeling helpless, hopeless, or worthless.
- Internalized hostility.[166]

Besides these specific behavioral signs of a typical adolescent who cuts, there are also a number of social and psychological characteristics that are common to those who self-injure as well. These signs would include:

- Strongly dislike/invalidate themselves.
- Hypersensitive to rejection.
- Chronically angry (usually at themselves).
- Tend to suppress their anger.
- High levels of aggressive feelings, which they disapprove of strongly and often suppress or direct inward.
- Impulsive and lacking impulse control.
- Tend to act in accordance to their emotions.
- Depressed and suicidal/self-destructive
- Suffer chronic anxiety.
- Tend to be irritable.
- Do not see themselves as skilled at coping.
- Lack coping skills.
- Do not feel like they have much control over how to cope with life.
- Tend to be avoidant.
- See themselves as lacking.[167]

When you observe enough of the behavioral or psychological characteristics displayed in a student's life to give you concern, then your concern should be expressed. If the student is cutting, the problem won't go away by itself. The longer cutting goes on in a student's life, the harder it will be to help them stop. You must intervene.

Intervention for Someone Who Self-Injures

It is important for the concerned youth worker to realize that if you know that a student is cutting themselves you cannot force them to stop. You cannot take responsibility for the student's life. What you can do is let them know that you are there to help. You must remain calm while listening to the student tell their story of pain even if it is very upsetting to listen to them talk about the various times and ways that the teen has chosen to cut. Reaffirm your concern and commitment to the student. The teen needs to know that you do not think less of them because they have chosen to self-injure. You don't think they are a bad person for doing this. Avoid panic and overreaction. Don't show shock or revulsion at what they've done. That only closes up people emotionally and shames them.

Anything that you can suggest that would be a healthy way of dealing with intense emotions would be helpful. You can encourage the student to journal and to write down all of their deepest pains and darkest secrets. You might encourage the student to spend time in vigorous exercise to help sublimate some of the energy that goes into cutting. Other healthy ways of dealing with stress are relaxation and breathing techniques, meditation or art therapy. I know of one counselor who recommends teaching students to place their hands and wrists in ice-cold water until the desire to injure subsides.

You can suggest that the student try something physical and violent, but something not directed at a living thing such as:

- Slash an empty plastic soda bottle or a piece of heavy cardboard or an old shirt or sock.
- Make a soft cloth doll to represent the things you are angry at. Cut and tear it instead of yourself.
- Flatten aluminum cans for recycling, seeing how fast you can go.
- Hit a punching bag.
- Use a pillow to hit a wall, pillow-fight style.
- Rip up an old newspaper or phone book.
- On a sketch or photo of yourself, mark in red ink (non-toxic) what you want to do. Cut and tear the picture.
- Make Play-Doh or Sculpey or other clay models and cut or smash them.
- Throw ice into the bathtub or against a brick wall hard enough to shatter it.
- Break sticks.
- Crank up the music and dance.
- Clean your room (or your whole house).
- Go for a walk/jog/run.
- Stomp around in heavy shoes.
- Play handball or tennis.
- Sad, Soft, Melancholy, Depressed, Unhappy
  Do something slow and soothing:
- Take a hot bath with bath oil or bubbles
- Curl up under a comforter with hot cocoa and a good book, babying yourself somehow.
- Light sweet-smelling incense.
- Listen to soothing music.
- Smooth nice body lotion into the parts or yourself you want to hurt.
- Call a friend and just talk about things that you like.

130

- Make a tray of special treats and tuck yourself into bed with it and watch TV or read.
- Visit a friend.
- Do whatever makes you feel taken care of and comforted.[168]

> Don't confuse the symptom with the real problem. Cutting is not the problem. It is merely the visible outworking of much deeper issues. Kids cut for a reason, and we need to find out what that reason is. Hiding the knives or removing sharp objects from the house is not only impractical and next to impossible, but it doesn't work. Kids will always find a way to cut, whether it is with their fingernails, staples, straws or other common household items.[169]

Ultimately, if the problem is severe or long lasting, the youth worker will need to make a referral to a professional counselor or therapist who specializes in treating this particular disorder. The therapist will come up with a treatment plan that is best suited for the student's needs. It may be a combination of behavioral therapy and medication.

> There is no single therapeutic approach that works with all self-injurers, since the roots of the disorder are so varied. Acute symptoms need to be brought under control with medication or behavior modification in order for the patient to be able to tolerate exploring the deeper issues. If the underlying trauma is not resolved, the patient will likely relapse into cutting or replace it with some other destructive coping behavior. Other self-destructive behaviors that go hand in hand with cutting must also be treated, such as alcohol and drug abuse, eating disorders, and sex and relationship addictions. Successful treatment generally involves a combination of medication, psychotherapy, and cognitive-behavioral techniques, staged and individualized to the patient's particular needs.[170]

Although cutting can be difficult to stop, it is possible. Once the student gets help in solving the problems that are at the root of the behavior, chances are good that she'll be able to stop hurting herself and lead a healthier, happier life.

Overview of the Counseling Process for Cutting and Other Forms of Self-Injury

Connect with the Teen
- They may call you and ask for help – if so, set up a meeting giving them instructions on location, time and length of session.
- You may hear from others about their self-injury or seen the evidence of self-injury yourself – if so, take pastoral initiative and go to them or call and set up a meeting.
- Prepare your meeting place and yourself by reviewing how to deal with cutting and self-injury. Don't forget to pray and ask the Holy Spirit for guidance and insight!

Understand the Teen
- Communicate empathy by your posture, position and active listening skills.
- Communicate nonjudgmental, unconditional love and genuineness. This is especially important with those who self-injure. They tend to be very secretive and are sensitive to critical statements and judgmental attitudes towards them.
- Ask yourself the empathy question: "How would I feel if I was this student in this situation?"
- Remember that cutting is not an act of suicide but of wanting to feel alive.
- Understand that cutting often releases the strong emotional tension that has built up.

Explore with the Teen
- Find out when the cutting began – what is missing in their life? What is present that is causing the pain?
- Explore with them other possibilities for relieving the stress and tension in their life. Help them come up with alternatives to cutting.
- Listen for other self-destructive behaviors that may accompany cutting.

Initiate a Plan With the Teen
- Explore healthy ways to deal with intense emotions.
- Teach them coping skills.

- If the teen has accidentally cut too far or severed an artery, then they must be taken to the emergency room immediately.
- If they have developed an infection from the cuts or sharing implements they need to see a physician.
- if the problem is severe or long lasting, the youth worker will need to make a referral to a professional counselor or therapist who specializes in treating this particular disorder.

Finish with the Teen
- Maintain a good relationship with the teen outside of the counseling session.
- Continue to offer a "safe place" if the student needs to process more.
- Watch for any relapse and take appropriate action.

Helpful Resources

S.A.F.E. Alternatives: Self-Abuse Finally Ends – 1-800-DON'T CUT (366-8288) http://www.selfinjury.com/ Email:info@selfinjury.com
HelpGuide.org.
http://www.helpguide.org/articles/anxiety/cutting-and-self-harm.htm
Kids Health. "Helping Teens Who Cut."
http://kidshealth.org/en/parents/help-cutting.html?WT.ac=ctg#
The Adolescent Self-Injury Foundation, Inc. (ASIF)
http://www.adolescentselfinjuryfoundation.com/

Selected Bibliography

Levenkron, Steven. *Cutting: Understanding and Overcoming Self-Mutilation.* New York, NY: W. W. Norton and Company, 1998.
Penner, Marv. *Hope and Healing for Kids Who Cut.* Grand Rapids, MI: Zondervan Publishing, 2009.
Strong, Marilee. *A Bright Red Scream: Self-Mutilation and the Language of Pain.* New York, NY: Penguin Books, 1998.

Exercise 7.1 - Understanding and Treating Self-Injury

Rate yourself on your knowledge and skill concerning self-injury. Use the scale provided: 1 = poor; 2 = below average; 3 = Average; 4 = Above average; 5 = Excellent. Simply check the box that best describes you. Be honest with yourself. Work on the areas that need improvement—it's not an assignment, it's a life that you might save!

Understanding and Treating Self-Injury	1	2	3	4	5
I understand and am knowledgeable about the different forms of self-injury.					
I understand the different reasons why students self-injure.					
I know the common signs of someone who is engaged in self-injury.					
I am familiar with the social and psychological characteristics that are common to those who self-injure.					
I have a number of alternative behaviors to offer the one who self-injures.					
I realize that cutting is not the problem, but only a symptom of a greater, deeper problem.					
I understand the referral is the best action to take when I have a student who is engaged in self-injury.					

CHAPTER EIGHT

SWALLOWING YOUR FEELINGS: DEALING WITH EATING DISORDERS

Eating disorders have become a major health problem, especially among young women. Most large churches, and many that are smaller, have families who struggle over the erratic eating habits of a family member. – Raymond E. Vath, *Counseling Those with Eating Disorders*[171]

Eating disorders are not merely problems with food. They are psychological disorders, many aspects of which are not apparent to an outside observer. –Michele Siegel, Judith Brisman and Margot Weinshel. *Surviving an Eating Disorder*[172]

The Pervasive Problem Within Our Culture

Our culture is obsessed with thinness. Teens are especially vulnerable and susceptible to distorted views of body image because they struggle so much with self-esteem issues. Because of an over-emphasis on body image a great number of teens and young adults have developed an eating disorder. National surveys show:[173]

- About 7 million women and 1 million men in America suffer from an eating disorder.
- 50% of adolescent females and 20% of males report dieting to control their weight.
- 13.4% of girls and 7.1% of boys have engaged in disordered eating patterns.
- 27% of adolescent girls who rate themselves as being at the "right weight" are still trying to lose weight.
- 30-67% of normal weight adolescent girls and college females believe they are overweight.
- 44% of individuals treated for anorexia recover completely.
- 28% show some weight gain but remain underweight.
- 24% have a poor prognosis.
- 2/3rds continue to have weight and body image preoccupations and up to 40% have bulimic symptoms.
- Rates of eating disorders are high among Hispanic American and Native American females and increasing among immigrant Asian females.

- Although African American women are less likely than white women to have eating disorders, the rates are increasing.
- The mortality rate for those with anorexia nervosa is the highest of any major psychiatric disorder, with many deaths occurring suddenly, usually from ventricular arrhythmias.
- One long-term follow-up study on those suffering from anorexia found a mortality rate as high as 20%.
- 41 U.S. states have obesity rates higher than 20%.

It is obvious from these statistics that eating disorders are at epidemic levels and those of us who are involved in the mental, social, emotional and spiritual care of adolescents need to be cognizant of them and have a plan to help.

Two Case Studies

Kasey was a typical teenage girl from a Christian home growing up in the big city. She loved athletics and made the varsity volleyball team when she was just a sophomore in high school. She had a bright future ahead of her as an athlete and may have received some scholarship offers until she developed an eating disorder her junior year of high school.

> Her physical change in appearance was so pronounced that her teammates nicknamed her "Holly"—short for "holocaust" because she looked just like a holocaust victim to them.

Kasey developed anorexia. She went from a healthy 5'9" and 140 pounds to just 100 pounds. She had reduced herself to just skin and bones. She continued to try and play volleyball but in her weakened and deteriorated condition she couldn't even make the junior varsity squad her senior year. Her physical change in appearance was so pronounced that her teammates nicknamed her "Holly"—short for "holocaust" because she looked just like a holocaust victim to them. Instead of being appalled by her nickname, Kasey took pride in it because it proved that her control over her eating was successful!

Kasey may have died if it wasn't for the intervention of her church small group leader. She confronted Kasey about her eating disorder and contacted her parents. Incredibly, her parents didn't have a clue that Kasey had a problem and for a short while tried to deny it, in spite of the evidence and concern of others. With some encouragement, Kasey's parents placed her in counseling and Kasey eventually made a full recovery.

136

Sandy battled bulimia for about ten years before seeking help through counseling. She would purge at least three times a day and was obsessed with exercising, also. She would exercise up to two hours a day.

Sandy did such a good job of keeping her eating disorder a secret that her husband never suspected there was a problem. When he would take her out on a date to a nice restaurant, Sandy would look over the menu and order the item she thought would be the easiest to throw up. She wouldn't even wait until she returned home to purge; she would excuse herself to the lady's restroom and force herself to throw up before she left the restaurant.

> **Sandy would look over the menu and order the item she thought would be the easiest to throw up.**

Eating disorders gained public attention in 1983 when pop singer Karen Carpenter died from heart failure at the age of thirty-two. She had struggled with anorexia for over twelve years. In 1994, Christy Henrich, an Olympic gymnast, died from complications of anorexia nervosa. Since that time, there have been a number of models, actresses, athletes and singers who have gone public with their struggle with eating disorders.

Eating disorders are not just a "fad"—they are a matter of life and death. "Eating disorders may damage the brain, heart, bones, kidneys and liver."[174] The complications of anorexia and bulimia are so serious that up to 20% of those who are diagnosed *and receive professional help* still succumb to the effects of the disorder. It is imperative that youth workers are educated about the various eating disorders, and are able to spot the signs of a teen that is struggling with an eating disorder and know how to intervene in a healthy way.

Risk Factors for Developing an Eating Disorder

> **Eating disorders are complex conditions that can arise from a combination of long-standing behavioral, biological, emotional, psychological, interpersonal, and social factors.**

There is no consensus in the mental health field as to the root cause of eating disorders. "Eating disorders are complex conditions that can arise from a combination of long-standing behavioral, biological, emotional, psychological, interpersonal, and social factors. Once started, however, they can create a self-perpetuating cycle of physical and emotional destruction."[175]

Obviously, the media, and especially the fashion industry with its emphasis on thinness, may contribute to the development of an eating disorder. The universal practice of photo-shopping all the Hollywood stars and musical entertainers' pictures in all the popular magazines presents an unrealistic ideal that many teens will try to match. Our society associates thinness with positive qualities like attractiveness, health, success and love.

Having friends and family who diet for weight loss and express high body image concerns can place a student at risk. When a student is in an environment in which key people express body image concerns and model weight loss behaviors, they are more likely to develop body dissatisfaction themselves regardless of actual appearance or weight.

Participation in activities that value thinness, such as modeling, ballet and gymnastics, can increase the risk of teen eating disorders. Boys who are trying to reach a certain weight class in wrestling may develop unhealthy attitudes and behaviors about eating and weight loss.

> Many teenagers report that the onset of their eating disorder involved comments or teasing by peers, usually about appearance. Whether done in the context of an innocent family nickname or in a malicious bullying event, these instances of feeling shame, or being shamed, based on size or physical appearance are powerful contributors to a teenager developing an eating disorder. The tendency for females, specifically, to 'bond' around 'fat talk' and negative body discussions have also been associated with the development of an eating disorder.[176]

Mental health workers are still gathering data on the factors that can contribute to the development of an eating disorder. However, they have identified a number of risk factors that you should be aware of.[177]

Psychological Risk Factors
- Perfectionism
- Anxiety
- Depression
- Difficulties regulating emotion
- Obsessive-compulsive behaviors
- Rigid thinking style (only one right way to do things, etc.)

Sociocultural Risk Factors
- Cultural promotion of the thin ideal
- Size and weight prejudice
- Emphasis on dieting
- "Ideal bodies" include only a narrow range of shapes and sizes

Biological Risk Factors
- Having a close family member with an eating disorder
- Family history of depression, anxiety, and/or addiction
- Personal history of depression, anxiety, and/or addiction
- Presence of food allergies that contribute to picky or restrictive eating (e.g. celiac disease)
- Presence of Type 1 Diabetes

If you suspect that one of the teens in your care has an eating disorder, you should consider the risk factors and combine them with your observations of the emotional, behavioral and physical signs of someone who is struggling with an eating disorder in order to come up with a reasonable assessment of the student's condition.

Emotional, Behavioral and Physical Signs of an Eating Disorder

Those struggling with an eating disorder may have some, but not necessarily all, of the following emotional, behavioral and physical signs. The more signs that are present the greater the possibility that they may be struggling with an eating disorder and is cause for serious concern and you should take appropriate action to make sure they are directed to the appropriate help.

Emotional Signs[178]
- Intense fear of gaining weight
- Negative or distorted self-image
- Frequent checking in the mirror for perceived flaws
- Self-worth and self-esteem dependent on body shape and weight
- Fear of eating in public or with others
- Preoccupation with food
- Little concern over extreme weight loss
- Social withdrawal
- Flat mood or lack of emotion
- Irritability

- Mood swings

Behavioral Signs[179]
- Eating tiny portions or refusing to eat
- Avoiding eating with others
- Hoarding and hiding food
- Eating in secret
- Disappearing after eating—often to the bathroom
- Obsessive interest in cooking shows on television and collecting recipes
- Unusual food rituals (cutting food into small pieces, chewing each bite an unusually large number of times, eating very slowly)
- Any new practice with food or fad diets, including cutting out entire food groups (no sugar, no carbs, no dairy, vegetarianism/veganism)
- Consumption of only "safe" or "healthy" foods
- Making excuses for not eating
- Cooking elaborate meals for others, but refusing to eat them themselves
- Eating strange combinations of foods
- Elaborate food rituals
- Hiding weight loss by wearing bulky clothes
- Hyperactivity and restlessness (unable to sit down, etc.)
- Rigidity in behaviors and routines, and experience of extreme anxiety if these are interrupted
- Excessive exercising
- Exercising even when ill or injured, or for the sole purpose of burning calories

Physical Signs[180]
- Noticeable fluctuations in weight, both up and down
- Stomach cramps, other non-specific gastrointestinal complaints (constipation, acid reflux, etc.)
- Menstrual irregularities—missing periods or only having a period while on hormonal contraceptives (this is not considered a "true" period)
- Difficulties concentrating
- Abnormal laboratory findings (anemia, low thyroid and hormone levels, low potassium, low blood cell counts, slow heart rate)
- Dizziness

- Fainting/syncope
- Feeling cold all the time
- Sleep problems
- Cuts and calluses across the top of finger joints (a result of inducing vomiting) Dental problems, such as enamel erosion, cavities, and tooth sensitivity
- Dry skin
- Dry and brittle nails
- Swelling around area of salivary glands
- Fine hair on body
- Thinning of hair on head, dry and brittle hair (lanugo)
- Cavities, or discoloration of teeth, from vomiting
- Muscle weakness
- Yellow skin (in context of eating large amounts of carrots)
- Cold, mottled hands and feet or swelling of feet
- Poor wound healing
- Impaired immune functioning

Identifying the Various Eating Disorders

"*Anorexia nervosa* literally means 'nervous loss of appetite.' In actuality, the anorexic generally suffers extreme hunger pains, but refrains from eating in order to achieve thinness."[181] The American Anorexia Nervosa Association defines anorexia as a "serious illness of deliberate self-starvation with profound psychiatric and physical components."[182]

The primary characteristics of a student who is suffering from anorexia would include the following:

1. A refusal to maintain a body weight above the minimum normal weight for one's age and height (e.g., weight loss leading to maintenance of body weight less than 85% of that expected; or failure to make expected weight gain during period of growth, leading to body weight less than 85% of that expected).
2. An intense fear of becoming obese, which does not diminish with weight loss.
3. Body image distortion. For example, victims may claim to "feel fat" even when emaciated, or believe

that one area of the body is "too fat" even when they are obviously underweight.

4. In females, the absence of at least three consecutive menstrual cycles when they are otherwise expected to occur. This is known as amenorrhea.

5. There is no other known reason or physical cause for the weight loss.[183]

> Students who suffer from anorexia often have low self-esteem and/or a tremendous need to control their surroundings and emotions.

It is not easy to understand a student who is suffering from anorexia. Students who suffer from anorexia often have low self-esteem and/or a tremendous need to control their surroundings and emotions. The eating disorder may be a unique reaction to a variety of external and internal influences and conflicts. The student suffering from anorexia may have an unrealistic fear of becoming fat and losing control over the amount of food they eat. The control of their daily food intake may be a symbolic way of regaining control over their life. Some students do not feel they deserve the pleasures of life so they will deprive themselves of situations offering pleasure which includes eating.

Bulimia nervosa is an eating disorder characterized by recurrent episodes of binge eating (the rapid consumption of large quantities of good) at least twice a week for three months, during which the person loses control over eating."[184] There are two subtypes of this particular eating disorder. The first, and most common, is the purging type in which the individual regularly forces themselves to vomit or use laxatives, diuretics or enemas to rid themselves of the food and calories consumed. The second, is the nonpurging type, in which excessive exercise or fasting is used in an attempt to compensate for the binges. The DSM-5 criteria for bulimia nervosa is as follows:

A. Recurrent episodes of binge eating
   1. Eating, in a discrete period of time, an amount of food that is definitely larger than most people would eat during a similar period of time and under similar circumstances.
   2. A sense of lack of control over eating during the episode.

142

B. Recurrent inappropriate compensatory behavior in order to prevent weight gain, such as self-induced vomiting; misuse of laxatives, diuretics, or other medications; fasting; or excessive exercise.

C. At least once a week for 3 months.

D. Self-evaluation is unduly influenced by body shape and weight.[185]

Students who suffer from bulimia also have a negative self-image, feelings of inadequacy, dissatisfaction with their bodies, and a tendency to perceive events as more stressful than most people would.

Students with bulimia know that their eating habits are not normal and they are frustrated by that knowledge. They become disgusted and ashamed of their eating and try to hide it from others. When they binge, they almost always do it in private.

While a student with advanced anorexia is relatively easy to identify because of their emaciated body, a teen that struggles with bulimia is harder to spot because their weight is usually within the normal range. One physical side effect of continued purging that is noticeable is the erosion of tooth enamel from stomach acid.

Binge-eating disorder is similar to bulimia nervosa in that they both involve the consumption of large amounts of food over a short period of time, an accompanying feeling of loss of control, and marked distress over eating during the episodes."[186] The difference between bulimia and binge-eating disorder is that in binge-eating disorder the episodes are not followed by vomiting, excessive exercise or fasting. There are a number of reasons why a student would binge eat. The student uses compulsive eating to hide from their emotions, to fill a void they feel inside and to cope with daily stresses and problems in their life.

Here are some common eating disorder warning signs:[187]

- Preoccupation with body or weight
- Obsession with calories, food, or nutrition
- Constant dieting, even when thin
- Rapid, unexplained weight loss or weight gain
- Taking laxatives or diet pills
- Compulsive exercising
- Making excuses to get out of eating

- Avoiding social situations that involve food
- Going to the bathroom right after meals
- Eating alone, at night, or in secret
- Hoarding high-calorie food

Intervention

The first and most obvious place to start is to confront the student with your observations and suspicions. This must be done without judgment and in a spirit of genuine concern and gentleness. You must understand that eating disorders are a very serious illness and they are difficult to treat because they have developed over a lifetime and are deeply ingrained. Don't expect a quick and easy cure.

One of the first things you must do with the student you suspect has an eating disorder is to try and assess the intensity of the student's eating disorder. You also want to know how long it has gone on. There are some self-scoring tests available that will help you in your assessment.[188]

If possible, monitor the student's on-line activity. There are a number of web sites that actually promote eating disorders. Content on these sites, sometimes called "pro-ED," "pro-ana" (referring to anorexia), or "pro-mia" (bulimia) sites, often includes message boards, chat rooms, weight-loss tips, and pictures of emaciated women (called "thinspiration"). These sites promote eating disorders as a lifestyle choice, not an illness.

If the student admits to having an eating problem, the family should be informed and encouraged to take appropriate action. One of the first steps would be to make an appointment with the family physician to check for medical problems that are commonly related to starvation and malnutrition. A common problem with both anorexia and bulimia is an electrolyte imbalance that may cause the heart to stop.

It may be if the problem is severe enough that the physician will recommend an in-house treatment center. If the illness is in its early stages and hospitalization is not needed, then consultation with a dietitian would be helpful along with participation in a self-help group for those suffering from eating disorders.

It is of great importance that the student be invited to participate in all the decisions regarding treatment because eating disorders are often a manifestation of the need for control. If the one area in the student's life that they feel some control is taken away, it may exacerbate the problem.

Help the student develop healthy strategies to deal with stress and pressure. Increase their comfort in expressing their feelings to peers, family members and significant others.

If the student's health is in imminent danger, you must intervene. Teens with eating disorders can die from starvation or excessive vomiting. Call a doctor or take the student to the emergency room if you see signs of real trouble and the student will not cooperate with you on taking the initiative to get help. The longer an eating disorder remains undiagnosed and untreated, the harder it is on the body and the more difficult to overcome, so urge the teen to see a doctor right away.

Because eating disorders are potentially life-threatening, this is one of those areas where referral to a professional is a must. As the youth pastor, you should stay involved in the teen's life and be supportive of the teen and family. However, the counseling needs to be done by a mental health professional in conjunction with the oversight of the family physician or treatment team.

> **If the student's health is in imminent danger, you must intervene. Teens with eating disorders can die from starvation or excessive vomiting.**

Overview of the Counseling Process for Eating Disorders

<u>Connect with the Teen</u>
- They may call you and ask for help – if so, set up a meeting giving them instructions on location, time and length of session.
- You may hear from others about their eating disorder – if so, take pastoral initiative and go to them or call and set up a meeting.
- Prepare your meeting place and yourself by reviewing how to deal with an eating disorder. Don't forget to pray and ask the Holy Spirit for guidance and insight!
- Know the signs of someone with an eating disorder.

<u>Understand the Teen</u>
- Communicate empathy by your posture, position and active listening skills.
- Communicate nonjudgmental, unconditional love and genuineness.
- Ask yourself the empathy question: "How would I feel if I was this student in this situation?"

Explore with the Teen

- Find out what caused them to develop an eating disorder – what is missing in their life? What is present in their life that is causing the pain?
- Explore control issues with the teen as one of the underlying issues of an eating disorder is control.
- Teach them new coping skills that would take the place of the eating disorder.
- Determine which eating disorder they struggle with—anorexia or bulimia.
- Be on guard and aware of denial and resistance from the student concerning their eating disorder.
- Explore inaccurate perceptions of body image.

Initiate a Plan with the Teen

- If the student is anorectic and in serious physical health, medical attention is called for.
- If the student is resistant or in denial, then you must work with the family and other key people in the student's life to set up an intervention. Referral to an in-patient treatment center may be necessary.
- If in-patient treatment is recommended, help the family make this choice.

Finish with the Teen

- Encourage them to complete their in-house treatment program.
- Support their continued attendance at support groups after leaving treatment.
- Help them develop a biblical sense of self-esteem—one that is not based upon physical appearance.
- Prepare for a relapse and take appropriate measures if one occurs.

Helpful Resources

Eating Disorder Hope. https://www.eatingdisorderhope.com/ 1-888-253-4827.

National Eating Disorders Association. "Parent Toolkit." This is a 76-page manual to help parents understand eating disorders and to know how to best support a child who is dealing with an eating disorder. This is a free pdf download from the website.

https://www.nationaleatingdisorders.org/sites/default/files/Toolk
its/ParentToolkit.pdf

The Healthy Teen Project. 1-844-845-5510 info@healthyteenproject.com
http://www.healthyteenproject.com/adolescent-eating-
disorders-ca

Selected Bibliography

Le Grance, Daniel and Lock, James. *Treating Bulimia in Adolescents: A Family-Based Approach*. New York, NY: The Guilford Press, 2007.

Jantz, Gregory L. with McMurray, Ann. *Hope, Help & Healing for Eating Disorders*. Colorado Springs, CO: Waterbrook Press, 1995.

Vath, Raymond E. *Counseling Those with Eating Disorders*. Waco, TX: Word Books, 1986.

Exercise 8.1 - Understanding Eating Disorders

Rate yourself on your knowledge and understanding about eating disorders. Use the scale provided: 1 = poor; 2 = below average; 3 = Average; 4 = Above average; 5 = Excellent. Simply check the box that best describes you. Be honest with yourself. Work on the areas that need improvement—it's not an assignment, it's a life that you might save!

Understanding Eating Disorders	1	2	3	4	5
I understand the psychological, sociocultural and biological risk factors that contribute to developing an eating disorder.					
I can identify the emotional signs of someone who has an eating disorder.					
I can identify the behavioral signs of someone who has an eating disorder.					
I can identify the physical signs of someone who has an eating disorder.					
I can identify the signs that a teen struggles with anorexia.					
I can identify the signs that a teen struggles with bulimia.					
I can identify the signs that a teen struggles with binge eating disorder.					
I know how to do an intervention and make a referral for a teen who has an eating disorder.					

CHAPTER NINE

HELPING VICTIMS OF SEXUAL ABUSE

Some sources indicate that every two minutes in the United States a child is sexually abused, but that less than 2% of molestations are ever reported. —Lynn Heitritter & Jeanette Vought, *Helping Victims of Sexual Abuse*[189]

Date and acquaintance rapes account for 60% to 80% of all reported rapes, but the true numbers are much higher than we known, since these victims are the least likely to report (for fear of being blamed). Also, 50% of the offenders in rapes of females under the age of eighteen are their boyfriends. —Kay Scott, *Sexual Assault: Will I Ever Feel Okay Again?*[190]

Case Study

For all practical purposes the family seemed very normal and healthy from the outside looking in. They were faithful attenders at church coming to Sunday School, morning worship, Sunday night worship and Wednesday night prayer meeting and Bible study. The teens and children attended youth group, vacation Bible school and went to church camp in the summer. It was a blended family of six children—three boys and three girls. Two were from the husband's first marriage, two from the wife's first marriage and two from their blended marriage. Cassandra was the third oldest, the daughter of her mother's first marriage. I was her youth minister for three years before she worked up the nerve to tell me her horrible secret: her step-father had been making her sleep with him since she was eleven years old. He would demand sex from her on a regular basis and if she ever wanted to do anything special, like go to a concert or a retreat, she had to "pay" for the privilege.

Upon learning of the abuse, I immediately contacted the authorities. An investigation took place and the step-father was arrested and placed in jail over the weekend. Cassandra was removed from the home and placed in foster care for her protection. To my horror and shock, even though the step-father admitted to the abuse, the entire rest of the family turned against Cassandra and sided with the step-father. They blamed her for the situation. (I later learned that this was the rule and not the exception in cases of incest.)

She ended up with feelings of rejection, shame, guilt and very low self-esteem. She needed professional Christian counseling to help her deal with the strong emotions, false guilt and to rebuild her self-esteem. Healing was not going to happen overnight, but would take place through commitment and perseverance, even when the process was painful.

Shocking Statistics Regarding Sexual Abuse

> **Youth workers must not bury their heads in the sand with respect to this issue, but become knowledgeable about the signs of sexual abuse and know how to bring about healing and wholeness.**

For a number of reasons, people don't like to talk about or acknowledge the amount of sexual abuse that takes place in today's society. But this is a serious issue that affects a significant number of students. Youth workers must not bury their heads in the sand with respect to this issue, but become knowledgeable about the signs of sexual abuse and know how to bring about healing and wholeness. Part of your pastoral ministry is to take responsibility for providing a safe place within the church where teenagers can share their pain and begin the journey toward healing. Consider the following statistics regarding various issues concerning sexual assault and abuse:

- A victim of one incident of teen sexual abuse is likely to experience further sexual abuse.
- Teenagers account for 51% of all reported sexual abuse
- Teenagers between the ages of 16 and 19 are 3.5 times more likely than the general public to be victims of sexual abuse.
- 69% of the incidences of teen sexual abuse occur in a residence.
- 23% of all sexual offenders are under the age of 18
- Female victims of teen sexual abuse while in grades 9 through 12 are more likely than others to experience eating disorders, suicidal behavior, pregnancy and risky sexual behaviors.[191]
- In most cases, sexual abuse is not an event that occurs out of the blue, suddenly and capriciously by someone who lurks in the bushes and waits for an unsuspecting child to walk into his lair. In fact, only 11% of all sexual abuse is perpetrated by a stranger. The vast majority of sexually abusive events occur in relationship with a family member (29%) or with someone else known by the victim (60%).[192]

Sexual abuse would be any form of sexual contact or conversation in which a child or teen is sexually exploited for the purpose of bringing sexual gratification to the exploiter.

While female teenagers are more likely to be sexually abused that male teenagers, cultural, racial and economic factors do not seem to have an effect on the likelihood of becoming a victim of teen sexual abuse. Here are some sexual abuse statistics from the CDC (Center for Disease Control):

- 20 people are victims of physical violence by an intimate partner every minute in the US.
- 1 in 2 women (50%) are sexually abused in their lifetime.
- 1 in 5 men (20%) are sexually abused in their lifetime
- 79% of female rape victims report that the rape occurred before age 25.
- 28% of male rape victims say they were first raped by the age of 10.
- 42.2% of female rape victims were first raped before age 18.
- 86% of female rape victims know their abuser as an intimate partner, family member, or acquaintance.
- 52.4% of male rape victims report their perpetrator was as acquaintance.[193]

Only about 31% of teen sexual abuse incidents are reported. Social stigma, fear of retribution and the trauma of not being believed stymie reports of teen sexual abuse. Additionally, the low probability of an arrest or substantial prison sentence for the perpetrator can cause reluctance on the part of teen sexual abuse victims to report. Here are teen sexual abuse reporting and prosecution statistics:

- When sexual abuse is reported, the probability that an arrest will be made is 50.8%.
- When teen sexual abuse does occur, the overall probability that the perpetrator will be sent to prison is 16.3%. – The average sentence for the perpetrator of a teen sexual abuse crime is 128 days.
- Of men incarcerated for rape, a form of sexual abuse, 80% of them reported that their victims were under the age of 18.[194]

What Is Considered Sexual Abuse?

Contrary to what a person might think, from a legal standpoint, sexual abuse encompasses a much wider range of activities than only forced participation in oral, anal or vaginal sex. Sexual abuse would be any form of sexual contact or conversation in which a child or teen is sexually exploited for the purpose of bringing sexual gratification to the exploiter. The following would all be considered forms of sexual abuse:

- An adult showing a child his or her genitals.
- An adult asking a child to undress to be looked at or fondled.
- An adult touch a child's genitals.
- An adult having a child touch his or her genitals.
- Oral-genital contact.
- Forced masturbation.
- Penetration of the anus or vagina with fingers or another object.
- Anal penetration.
- Vaginal intercourse.
- Use of children for the production of pornographic materials.[195]

What Does the Victim of Sexual Abuse Feel and Experience?

The first thing the victim of sexual abuse feels is *confusion*.[196] They want to know: "What is going on?" "What is happening to me?" "Is this right or wrong?" "Will it happen again?" "Should I tell someone?" This is especially true of young victims of incest, but even in cases of adolescent date rate the victim may experience feelings of confusion.

The next thing they feel is *guilt*. Almost universally, the victim feels responsible and guilty for the abuse. Children believe the abuse was their fault for a number of reasons: 1) they didn't try to stop the abuse; 2) the abuse was sometimes pleasurable; 3) they received special favors or rewards; 4) they feel they have done something to cause the abuse; or 5) they believe they are so bad they deserve the abuse.

Very closely related to feelings of guilt are feelings of *shame*. It is not uncommon for victims of sexual abuse to describe themselves with such words as, "dirty," "unclean," "disgusting," and "bad." Because of these strong emotions, the first response a victim feels after a rape is to want to shower and rid themselves from memories of the violation and the feelings of uncleanness. But this urge must be repressed until after the victim has been to the hospital or personal physician and had a rape examination done and evidence collected. This is very important if the victim wants to be able to press charges against the perpetrator at a later date.

Abuse victims also feel a great deal of *fear*. They fear they have been physically damaged in some way. They fear that others will find out the abuse. They fear the family will break up as a result of the abuse. They fear rejection by both the offender and the others in the family.

It is understandable that victims of sexual assault will also feel *anger*. They will be angry with the abuser for what has been done. They will be angry with themselves for not trying to stop the abuse or for enjoying parts of it. In the case of incest, the victim will be angry with the non-abusing parent for not being protective or for not stopping the abuse. The victim will also feel angry with God for allowing it to happen.

In the case of incest victims, there is also a *loss of trust*, especially in authority figures. The very person who was supposed to protect them ended up being the one who abused them.

> Men don't commit rape to satisfy a sexual urge any more than an alcoholic drinks because he is thirsty. The rapist's motivation is a desire to dominate, humiliate, or get even. Rape is a violent act of aggression. It is on person overpowering and controlling another. It is devastatingly fearsome and horribly traumatic. Just because it happens on a date does not make it any less terrifying. In fact, a date rape may be even more terrifying because the rapist is someone the victim trusted, chose to be with, and possibly cared about or loved.[197]

While the physical effects of rape are traumatic, the emotional wounds and scars such an act of violence leaves are often more horrible and more difficult to overcome.

"While the physical effects of rape are traumatic, the emotional wounds and scars such an act of violence leaves are often more horrible and more difficult to overcome.'[198]

Factors Affecting the Impact of Sexual Abuse on The Victim

There are a number of factors that affect the impact of the sexual abuse upon the victim. The first is the *age and developmental level* of the victim.[199] A younger child may simply be confused by the molestation, whereas a young teen knows that it is wrong and not only feels violated, but somehow responsible for the act.

The child's *relationship with the offender* also affects the impact upon them. Usually the sexual crime committed by a stranger has less impact than the same crime committed by a trusted parent or someone with whom the victim has a dating relationship.

The *duration of the abuse* is another key factor. Usually, the longer the abuse has continued, the greater the impact.

The *type of sexual activity* affects the overall impact of the abuse on the victim. It is often assumed that touching and fondling is less traumatic than full penetration. Not only is this assumption untrue, but other forms of non-touching sexual abuse can be equally devastating from the child's viewpoint. Often one type of abuse will set the victim up to be repeatedly victimized in other ways.

The *parental reaction* to the abuse can either make the impact greater or lesser on the victim. More than any other variable, the reaction of the parents or others who are important to the child can have the greatest impact. Experts agree that this is the single most important factor in preventing the abuse from becoming a life-destroying event.

Why Are the Abused Victims Silent for So Long? Why Don't They Tell?

People often are confused as to why students keep silent about the abuse and don't ask for help sooner. One reason is that they *fear* that they will be yelled at and *blamed*. They also feel guilty for their participation in the act.

They also fear that they won't be *believed*. Many of the abusers are respected members of the community. They are lawyers, bankers, businessmen and pastors. Who is going to believe a child's word against theirs?

> Many of the abusers are respected members of the community. They are lawyers, bankers, businessmen and pastors. Who is going to believe a child's word against theirs?

Childhood victims will often keep silent about the abuse because they fear that they will be *removed* from the home. Indeed, it used to be standard procedure to remove the child and place them in foster care when there was suspicion of abuse in the home.

Students fear that if they say anything somehow their peers and the "public" will *find out*. The potential embarrassment of everyone knowing what has happened seems worse to the victim that continuing to "put up" with the abuse.

Students fear that if they tell it will break up the *family*, their father will go to jail and their siblings will end up in foster homes. Along with this they fear that their mother won't be able to handle it emotionally and will "crack-up" or "go crazy."

> **Victims may feel guilt over their participation and not feel that they are deserving of any help.**

Some victims believe that if they submit to the abuse it will keep the father from abusing the *other siblings*. This is almost never the case as in reality the other siblings are also likely to end up abused.

Victims may feel guilt over their participation and not feel that they are deserving of any help.

What are the Signs or Symptoms of Abuse?

Early detection of abuse is very important. There are a number of signs and symptoms that are indications that sexual abuse has taken place. Some of the most obvious are *physical signs* such as: venereal disease, vaginitis, bladder infections or pain in urinating or defecating. Any time a child has physical complaints in one of these areas the possibility of abuse should be considered.

There are *behavioral signs* that are also indications of the presence of abuse. If a child suddenly no longer wants to participate in a once enjoyable activity this should be a "red flag," especially if the child expressed fear toward the activity. An example would be if a child no longer wants to go to the church nursery or Sunday School class and throws a tantrum when the parents try to force participation. If a child shows fear towards a particular person, especially if the child used to enjoy being left with this person, the reason for this new-found fear should be carefully examined.

> Sometimes a child acts out the stress of the abuse by self-injurious behaviors such as biting themselves or others, cutting themselves, or by destructive, continuous masturbation. Perhaps a child will reveal the trauma of abuse by drawing pictures of adults' or children's genitals especially with details like pubic hair.[200]

Precocious sexuality is another indicator of the presence of sexual abuse. When children use dolls and other toys and act out intimate

154

sexual acts with them, this is a sign that the child has knowledge of information that is not age appropriate. The most obvious place the child has learned it is through personal experience.

Teenagers will add some additional indicators of abuse. Sometimes *eating disorders* such as anorexia or bulimia are the response to abuse in their life. Because of the guilt and emotional damage that is done by sexual abuse, some victims withdraw and isolate themselves. *Running away* can also be a sign that there is abuse in the home. Because of the anger that has been repressed related to the abuse, many teens will "act out" by being rebellious against all authority figures and engage in other unlawful activities such as: arson, stealing, drug and alcohol abuse, cruelty to animals, vandalism and promiscuity.

"Abused individuals are at high risk for anxiety, depression, substance abuse, physical illnesses, and problems at school or work. It is very important that teenagers who are survivors of abuse are identified as soon as possible to minimize the potential long-term consequences of abuse."[201]

What are the effects of rape? Victims of sexual assault are:

- 3 times more likely to suffer from depression.
- 6 times more likely to suffer from post-traumatic stress disorder.
- 13 times more likely to abuse alcohol.
- 26 times more likely to abuse drugs.
- 4 times more likely to contemplate suicide.[202]

> **The youth minister needs to be aware of his or her legal obligations in situations involving abuse.**

What Should I Do If I Know That Abuse Is Taking Place?

You may be the first one to hear about the abuse. It's important that you take seriously what the student is saying, and commend the student for coming forward and talking to you about it. Survivors of abuse often keep secrets in order to get through it all. Telling an adult takes a tremendous amount of courage. If the student has been or is being abused by someone in his or her family, the student may feel guilty about telling someone. The student may also fear that the abuser will further abuse him or her for exposing the secret.[203]

The youth minister needs to be aware of his or her legal obligations in situations involving abuse. If a student reveals to you that they are being sexually abused, you are required to report it to the proper authorities. Normally this would be an agency like Child Protection Services or the Department of Health and Human Resources. The hotline calls are usually kept anonymous, but some states require the name of the reporter. Even if your state does not require your name if you report the abuse, you should keep a record of the date and time that you made the call. If you are a school teacher, medical doctor, professional counselor or pastor, this reporting is mandatory. Each state has its own reporting laws so it is important to be familiar with your legal obligations for the state you live in.

You need to provide security and affirmation. You provide security by helping them find a safe place where they will no longer be abused. Sometimes you will work in conjunction with the state caseworker in finding a safe haven for the student. Other times you help by providing names of Christian people who will provide foster care. You affirm the victim's decision to reveal to you that they are being abused is the right decision. You need to affirm that the student is loveable and deserving of care regardless of what has taken place in his or her life. You must reassure the victim repeatedly that the abuse was not their fault. The student is not to blame nor is the student "bad" because the abuse happened.

The student who has been abused needs for the youth worker to provide a sense of intimacy and touch in appropriate and healthy ways. The student needs a friendship that is not exploitive. You need to try and help them try to keep a positive, hopeful attitude about their life, family and future.

The victim may feel guilty about their involvement in the sexual activity or about disclosing it to you and the disruption to the family that followed. The concerned youth worker will help the victim express any guilty feelings that may be present. You must help the victim and family members to realize the student is not responsible for the sexual abuse. Reassure the child or student that they have a right to expect protection from the abuser. Reaffirm the child/student that the decision to disclose the abuse was the correct decision.

A student may feel depressed after disclosing the details of the abuse. It is imperative that the youth worker keeps a careful watch on the student and look for signs of depression or suicidal intent. You should help the child or student vent his or her feelings of anger, betrayal and hurt.

The child or student will probably suffer from a low self-esteem because of the abuse. The student may feel unwanted or undeserving of anyone's love because they see themselves as "damaged goods." Affirm their identity as a child of God and a unique and special creation. Communicate God's unconditional love for them.

It is important that you encourage the student to find and participate in a support group where the student can connect with other students their age who have experienced similar abuse. By sharing their story, the student will find healing as they let go of the burden of shame about what has happened.

> **The student may feel unwanted or undeserving of anyone's love because they see themselves as "damaged goods."**

Above all, because of the intense nature of the issue, and how deeply it affects the victim, it's essential that you refer the abused student to a licensed Christian professional. The youth pastor should maintain a supportive role with the victim throughout the entire process, but the counseling must be done by a professional.

Overview of the Counseling Process for Victims of Sexual Abuse

Connect with the Teen
- They may call you and ask for help – if so, set up a meeting giving them instructions on location, time and length of session.
- You may hear from others about their abuse – if so, take pastoral initiative and go to them or call and set up a meeting.
- Prepare your meeting place and yourself by reviewing how to deal with sexual abuse. Don't forget to pray and ask the Holy Spirit for guidance and insight!
- Know the signs of someone who has been sexually abused.
- Explain to the teen that you are mandated by law to report any physical or sexual abuse to the authorities. Reassure them that you will not abandon them but will walk with them through the entire process.
- Compliment the teen for the courage to share their story.
- Be sensitive and don't push for unnecessary details. Be respectful of their pain.

Understand the Teen

- Know the behavioral, emotional and relational signs of someone who has been or is being sexually abused.
- Communicate empathy by your posture, position and active listening skills.
- Communicate nonjudgmental, unconditional love and genuineness.
- Ask yourself the empathy question: "How would I feel if I was this student in this situation?"

Explore with the Teen

- Learn what type of abuse the student has experienced.
- Discover when it first began and how long it has been going on.
- Communicate to the teen that the abuse is *not* their fault!
- Relieve them of any false guilt they may feel.

Initiate a Plan with the Teen

- Provide security and affirmation.
- Contact the appropriate authorities with the pertinent information.
- Work with the authorities to provide a safe place for the abused teen.
- Placement in foster care or a Christian family may be required. Prepare them for this option.
- Guide them to understand that the responsibility for the abuse is on the perpetrator and not on them in any way.
- Assure the teen that healing can and will take place, but that it may be a long and slow process.

Finish with the Teen

- It is very important that you maintain a relationship with the teen through the entire process.
- Support them through the legal proceedings.
- Encourage them to find a professional Christian counselor to help them through the healing process. Help them through the referral process.
- Provide them with self-help resources and support groups.

Helpful Resources

Child Welfare Information Gateway. "Mandatory Reporters of Child Abuse
and Neglect"
https://www.childwelfare.gov/topics/systemwide/laws-
policies/statutes/manda/
Pandora's Project: Support and Resources for Survivors of Rape and
Sexual Abuse.
http://www.pandys.org/index.html
RAINN (Rape, Abuse & Incest National Network) 800-656-HOPE
https://www.rainn.org/index.php

Selected Bibliography

Allender, Dan B. *The Wounded Heart: Hope for Adult Victims of Childhood Sexual Abuse*. Colorado Springs, CO: NavPress, 1990, revised edition 2008.

Heitritter, Lynn and Vought, Jeanette. *Helping Victims of Sexual Abuse: A Sensitive Biblical Guide for Counselors, Victims, and Families*. Minneapolis, MN: Bethany House, 1989, revised edition 2006.

Christa Sands, *Learning to Trust Again: A Young Woman's Journey of Healing from Sexual Abuse*. Grand Rapids, MI: Discovery House, 1999.

Exercise 9.1 - Understanding Sexual Abuse

Rate yourself on your knowledge and understanding about sexual abuse. Use the scale provided: 1 = poor; 2 = below average; 3 = Average; 4 = Above average; 5 = Excellent. Simply check the box that best describes you. Be honest with yourself. Work on the areas that need improvement—it's not an assignment, it's a life that you might save!

Understanding Sexual Abuse	1	2	3	4	5
I understand how widespread the problem of sexual abuse is for both females and males.					
I can list and define the various behaviors which are considered sexual abuse from a legal and psychological standpoint.					
I can list and define the various feelings that most victims of sexual abuse experience.					
I understand the various factors that determine the					

severity of impact upon the victim of sexual abuse.				
I understand the various reasons why victims of sexual abuse stay silent and do not tell others about their abuse.				
I can identify the behavioral and emotional signs of a victim of sexual abuse.				
I am familiar with my state's requirements for mandatory reporting.				
I understand how I can be supportive and helpful to a victim of sexual abuse.				

CHAPTER TEN

HELPING TEENS WHO STRUGGLE WITH DEPRESSION

Depression becomes such a normal part of the growing-up process that detecting severe depression in adolescents becomes difficult. –G. Wade Rowatt, *Adolescents in Crisis.*[204]

Depression, the "common cold of psychopathology," touches everyone's life. Whether it be as a temporary mood or as a suicidal psychosis, no one is exempt—especially adolescents. –Les Parrott III, *Helping the Struggling Adolescent: A Guide to Thirty Common Problems for Parents, Counselors, & Youth Workers.*[205]

Case Study: Seventeen-year-old Melissa

Seventeen-year-old Melissa had been dating Brian for eight months when he broke up with her—through a text message! The following Monday Melissa sat where she and Brian had eaten lunch together since last September. Her friends sat with her.

"I say you're better off without him," Amy said.

"Yeah," agreed Crystal. "You guys fought all the time anyway."

"I hear Joy and Nathan just broke up," offered Julie with an excited smile. "You've always had a crush on him, haven't you?"

Melissa didn't answer. She lifted her tray and left her friends without a word.

They don't understand, she thought. They've all had lots of boyfriends. But Brian was her first real boyfriend, and she had entertained fantasies about marrying him ever since they started dating. When they first started going out, Melissa had made up her mind to be everything Brian wanted. She'd lost a little weight and begun dressing with him in mind. She tried so hard to please him; if he showed the slightest pleasure in something she did or said, she would work to do more of the same.

When their relationship became more physically intimate, she determined to give Brian anything, everything; they began having sex after six months as a couple.

When Brian broke up with her, Melissa couldn't believe it. She cried and begged him not to leave her. She told him she'd change; she'd do anything he wanted. But he refused. Her first reaction was anger. After all I've done to make him happy, she thought. Then her anger turned inward. I did everything I know how to do, and it still wasn't enough. I must be totally worthless. I'll never have a man love me. I don't deserve to have a man love me.

Over the next few weeks, Melissa started spending more time alone in her room. She seldom went out with her friends, preferring instead to stay home, listen to music and stare at the bedroom walls. She found it difficult to eat, and after a few weeks of having trouble getting to sleep, she began to sleep most of the day, both in class and at home. She began to miss school frequently, and her grades plummeted. When her parents confronted her about her conduct, she shrugged, "I don't care" was her only response.

"I don't understand," her mother told the pastor of their church. "She seems like she's a totally different girl than she was."[206]

Everybody feels discouraged and down at times. Life has its struggles and frustrations. Certainly, the adolescent years present some specific challenges that can push teens to the limit. There are many physical, emotional, psychological and social changes that accompany this stage of life. Sadness and discouragement are a normal part of life. But how do you determine when normal sadness crosses the line into depression? The goal of this chapter is to provide you with some specific tools that will aid you in determining if an adolescent you are working with is struggling with a major depression and how to best help them.

> **How do you determine when normal sadness crosses the line into depression?**

162

Statistics on Adolescent Depression

The 2014 statistics from the National Institute of Mental Health (NIMH) show the following numbers for teens that had at least one major depressive episode in the previous 12 months:

- 17.3% of adolescents that had a major depressive episode in 2014 were female.
- 5.7% of adolescents that had a major depressive episode in 2014 were male.
- 5.7% were 12 years old.
- 8.7% were 13 years old.
- 10.7% were 14 years old.
- 13.0% were 15 years old.
- 14.1% were 16 years old.
- 15.1% were 17 years old.[207]

General Teen Depression Statistics

- Depression is the most common mental health disorder in the United States among teens and adults.
- 2.8 million youth age 12-17 had at least one major depressive episode in 2014.
- Between 10 to 15 percent of teenagers have some symptoms of teen depression at any one time.
- About 5 percent of teens are suffering from major depression at any one time
- As many as 8.3 percent of teens suffer depression for at least a year at a time, compared to about 5.3 percent of the general population.
- Most teens with depression will suffer from more than one episode. 20 to 40 percent will have more than one episode within two years and 70 percent will have more than one episode before adulthood. Episodes of teen depression generally last about 8 months.
- Dysthymia, a type of mild, long-lasting depression, affects about 2 percent of teens, and about the same percentage of teens develop bipolar disorder in their late teenage years. 15 percent of teens with depression eventually develop bipolar disorder.

- A small percent of teens also suffer from seasonal depression, usually during the winter months in higher latitudes.[208]

> While depression is very common, often referred to as the "common cold" of psychological problems, that does not mean that it should dismissed lightly.

Teens suffering from depression are at higher risk:

- Teenagers with depression are likely to have a smaller social circle and take advantage of fewer opportunities for education or careers.
- Depressed teens are more likely to have trouble at school and in jobs, and to struggle with relationships.
- Teens with depression seem to catch physical illnesses more often than other teens.[209]

While depression is very common, often referred to as the "common cold" of psychological problems, that does not mean that it should dismissed lightly. Untreated depression is a very serious problem. 30 percent of teens with depression also develop a substance abuse problem. Teens who do not receive treatment are more likely to engage in risky sexual behaviors, leading to higher rates of pregnancy and sexually transmitted diseases. Of greater concern, untreated depression can make a teen as much as 12 times more likely to attempt suicide. Untreated depression is the number one cause of suicide, the third leading cause of death among teenagers. The sad truth is that less than 33 percent of teens with depression get help, yet 80 percent of teens with depression can be successfully treated! Because of the high risk for suicide, it is imperative that the youth worker be able to identify the signs of a student struggling with depression and know how to intervene.

> The sad truth is that less than 33 percent of teens with depression get help, yet 80 percent of teens with depression can be successfully treated!

Note: Depression is not something that a teen can just choose to "snap out of." It is not a matter of lack of faith on the teen's part, nor is it a character flaw. It is a multi-faceted mental health issue that can have serious ramifications and the concerned and compassionate youth pastor will give it the attention that it deserves.

Identifying the Signs of Depression

According to the DSM-5, in order for a person to be diagnosed with a major depressive disorder (clinical depression), five or more of the following symptoms must have been present during the same two-week period and represent a change from previous functioning. At least one of the symptoms must be either a depressed mood or a loss of interest in pleasure. Also, the symptoms must not be able to be attributed to any other medical condition. The symptoms are:

1. Depressed mood most of the day, nearly every day, as indicated by either subjective report (e.g., feels sad, empty, hopeless) or observation made by others (e.g., appears tearful). (Note: in children and adolescents, can be irritable mood.)
2. Markedly diminished interest or pleasure in all, or almost all, activities most of the day, nearly every day (as indicated by either subjective account or observation).
3. Significant weight loss when not dieting or weight gain (e.g., a change of more than 5% of body weight in a month), or decrease or increase in appetite nearly every day. (Note: in children, consider failure to make expected weight gain.)
4. Insomnia or hypersomnia nearly every day.
5. Psychomotor agitation or retardation nearly every day (observable by others, not merely subjective feelings of restlessness or being slowed down).
6. Fatigue or loss of energy nearly every day.
7. Feelings of worthlessness or excessive or inappropriate guilt (which may be delusional) nearly every day (not merely self-reproach or guilt about being sick).
8. Diminished ability to think or concentrate, or indecisiveness, nearly every day (either by subjective account or as observed by others).
9. Recurrent thoughts of death (not just fear of dying), recurrent suicidal ideation without a specific plan, or a suicide attempt or a specific plan for committing suicide.

The symptoms cause clinically significant distress or impairment in social, occupational, other important areas of functioning.

The episode is not attributable to the physiological effects of a substance or to another medical condition.[210]

In addition to the clinical diagnosis, there are affective, cognitive and behavioral symptoms that one should be aware of which are indicative of a major depression. The affective symptoms include: depressed mood, sadness, dejection, excessive and prolonged mourning, feelings of worthlessness, lost joy, irritability, weeping and anxiety.

Cognitive symptoms would include: general feelings of futility, loss of perspective, frequent self-criticism, impaired memory, self-blame, worry, emptiness, hopelessness, pessimism, guilt, inability to concentrate, negative thinking, loss of interest and motivation, and suicidal thoughts. Depression may be reflected in faulty thinking. A cognitive triad develops with negative views of the self, of the outside world, and of the future.

Behavioral symptoms would include: crying spells, withdrawal from others, neglect of responsibilities, loss of interest in personal appearance, loss of motivation, sleeping too much or too little, overeating or loss of appetite, and the use of alcohol or drugs.

A summary or overview of what to look for in a teen suspected of suffering from a major depressive disorder would encompass the following symptoms:

- Sadness or hopelessness
- Irritability, anger or hostility
- Tearfulness or frequent crying
- Withdrawal from friends and family
- Loss of interest or enjoyment in favorite activities, surroundings
- Restlessness and agitation
- Feelings of worthlessness and guilt
- Lack of enthusiasm and motivation
- Fatigue or lack of energy
- Difficulty concentrating or making decisions
- Changes in sleeping habits, either insomnia or sleeping all the time
- Moving more slowly or sometimes becoming agitated and unable to settle
- Loss of interest in food or sometimes eating too much

- Self-neglect
- Physical complaints
- Various acting out behaviors
  Defiant
  Running away
  Substance abuse
  School problems
- Thoughts of death or suicide[211]

What are the Different Types of Depression?

All depression is not created equal. There are a number of different types of depression listed in the DSM-5. While a clinical depression or major depressive disorder is the most common, and that is what this chapter is mainly concerned with, it is important to be aware of the other types of depression?

A teen struggling with bipolar disorder (previously called manic depression) will experience extreme mood swings. They will have periods of depression, periods of mania, and long periods of normal mood in between. The time between these different episodes will vary from teen to teen. When the teen is in the mania phase, they will experience an elevated mood, have unending energy, have no or less need to sleep, will be very talkative and share unrealistic and overly optimistic ideas on how to make a million dollars, cure cancer or bring about world peace. The teen may also make impulsive decisions with respect to sexual activity, drugs or alcohol and gambling.

Some teens are more sensitive to the changing seasons and the decreased amount of light during the fall and winter months. This depression is commonly referred to as SAD (seasonal affective disorder). It is believed that SAD is related to the production of serotonin which is tied to exposure to the light. This depression generally lifts during the spring and summer months.

Dysthymia, or now more commonly referred to as persistent depressive disorder, is like a low-grade depression. It is characterized by fatigue, low energy, low self-esteem, and changes in appetite or sleep. This mood disorder tends to be less severe than a major depression. However, persistent depressive disorder is chronic, in that despite potential brief periods of normal mood, symptoms last at least two years at a time in adults and more than one year at a time in children and adolescents.

Situational depression takes place when a teen is overcome with stress due to uncontrollable events in their life. They may have experienced a natural disaster such as a tornado or flood, their parent's divorce, grandparent's death or the breakup of a boyfriend or girlfriend. If they do not have effective coping strategies to deal with the stress from these issues, then depression may be the result.

One should always be aware of any prescribed medication that the teen is taking as depression can be one of the side-effects. Other physiological problems can also contribute to a depressed mood such as a thyroid imbalance or other endocrine problem. Some women struggle with premenstrual dysphoric disorder which means that they will have many depressive symptoms at the start of their period.

What are the Causes of Depression in Teens?

> **The formation of a major depressive disorder cannot be attributed to just one factor.**

The formation of a major depressive disorder cannot be attributed to just one factor. There are a number of issues which contribute to the development of a clinical depression. Many of these will depend upon the individual. Something that will make one adolescent depressed may not affect another in the same way or to the same degree. The following are all common factors which may lead to the development of a major depressive disorder. The more of these issues that are present in the teen's life, the greater the likelihood that depression may develop.

Biological Factors: lack of sleep, insufficient exercise, side effects of drugs, physical illness, improper diet, hormonal imbalance, neurochemical malfunctioning, brain tumors, or glandular disorders all can cause depression. While depression is not inherited, there are some researchers who believe that people can inherit a predisposition to depression.

Ambivalence: the sense of being trapped, unable to remedy an intolerable situation, and learned helplessness contribute towards depression because it causes the student to believe they have no control over their life. They do not believe that anything they do will make a difference, so they just give up and become depressed.

Unrealistic Expectations: when teens grow up with parents who set their expectations and standards beyond the ability of the teen, failure is inevitable and depression results. The unmet expectations can be in the realm of academics, athletics, the arts or social popularity.

Parental Rejection and/or Abandonment: associated with both depression and low self-esteem, teens who experience a sense of rejection from their parents are more likely to experience depression. This rejection can be the result of unmet expectations on the part of the parents or through a parental divorce and the sense of abandonment that follows.

Abuse: especially physical and sexual abuse—the severity of abuse is a high predictor of depression.

Negative Thinking: when teens have a negative view of the world, themselves, the future. Faulty logic is also an issue for depressed teens. They will ruminate on the one criticism they received and ignore the nine affirmations. They will blow up a single failure in one area and see themselves as a failure in every area. This creates a downward spiral of depression.

Life stress: when the teen encounters stressful events that feel over-powering or threatening, i.e., breakup of an intense relationship, family discord, parental separation, divorce or death of a parent, unwanted pregnancy, any event that lowers a teen's self-esteem

> **When teens have a negative view of the world, themselves, and the future—depression may be the result.**

Anger: any adolescent who has not learned or devised ways of effectively handling and expressing anger is more likely to struggle with depression.

Guilt: guilt and depression often occur together. When a young person believes that he or she has failed or has done something wrong, guilt is the result and along with it comes self-condemnation. Perhaps they have done something wrong and have been denied forgiveness.

> **Depression isn't always negative! Depression may be the healthiest response to what the teen is experiencing in his or her life.**

Social Rewards: some teens *choose* to be depressed because they like the special attention they receive from those who care about them. "The sympathy and concern they receive reinforces their depression."[212] When the well-meaning youth pastor shows lots of attention and concern in trying to help a depressed young girl, she may not want to risk the loss of attention by overcoming her depression.

A Warning Sign: depression isn't always negative! Depression may be the healthiest response to what a person is experiencing in their life. It may be your body's way of trying to tell you that important areas of your life are out of balance and that you need to make some healthy adjustments.

> In many cases depression is the healthiest response to what a person is doing to his life. Depression is a normal reaction to what is happening to him psychologically and physically. Depression is a scream, a message to him that he has neglected some area of his life. He should listen to his depression, for it is telling him something that he needs to know. *Depression is a signal that something in his life is not right;* he ought to respond to the message.[213]

Who Is Likely to Get Depressed?

Depression can affect anyone and everyone. No one is immune. Depression can be found among all ages, all races, male or female, rich or poor, educated or uneducated, successful or not successful. While it can affect anyone, there are some types of people who may be more vulnerable to experiencing depression.

The "Charlie Browns" or "born losers" may find themselves at risk for experiencing depression. These are the people who just can't get a break in life. They live out Murphy's Law every day of their life. Because nothing ever seems to work out right for them, they develop a pattern of hopelessness towards life. Nothing ever seems to make a difference, so why try? They find themselves in a continual downward spiral.

Believe or not, the opposite of the born loser is also at risk—the highly successful person. This is the teen who always makes the starting lineup on the athletic team, gets straight A's on their report card, is first chair in band and is wildly popular. Since this person has experienced nothing but success all of their life, the first time there is a setback or they taste defeat it can be devastating. Plus, the pressure to stay "on top of one's game" can lead to depression.

Teens who cannot communicate may find themselves struggling with depression. These are teens who, for whatever reason, have never been allowed or taught how to express strong emotions in a proper way or in a safe environment. They keep everything bottled up inside of them and it eats away at them. Sigmund Freud defined

> Sigmund Freud defined depression as "anger turned inward."

depression as "anger turned inward." Sometimes just allowing a teen to vent is all that is needed to help them deal with the depression.

Depression may find its way into the lives of adolescents who cannot compete. These are young men and women who have grown up with "helicopter parents" who have protected them from every challenge or from experiencing the consequences of bad choices. In so doing, the parents have prevented the teens from establishing a sense of resiliency and have actually contributed to the teens developing a sense of inadequacy or fear towards life's challenges. This leads to depression.

Because getting into a college of your choice is becoming more and more competitive, there are a number of teens who feel overwhelmed with too much to do. They are on the football or basketball team, taking advanced placement courses, playing in the band, have a position in student council, a part-time job at McDonalds after school, involved in community projects and the church youth group. Trying to accomplish it all, they live on four or five hours of sleep and push themselves to the point of exhaustion. Physically, mentally and emotionally they just break down. Depression is the result.

> **Teens with unrealistic expectations set themselves up to struggle with feelings of depression.**

Having seen that those with too much to do get discouraged and depressed, you may be surprised to learn that those with nothing to do are also at risk for depression. These are the students who lack a sense of purpose or direction in their lives. Boredom gives birth to depression.

Teens who find themselves in drastic circumstances are also at risk for depression. This can be a serious illness such as cancer or being involved in an automobile accident with the resulting loss of a limb or paralysis. It may be a house fire that left the student horribly scarred. The teen may find themselves in the middle of the parent's nasty divorce and have to move with a resulting downturn in economic status. Any kind of serious loss for the teen may lead to depression.

Having a low self-esteem places the developing adolescent at risk for depression. They feel like they can't do anything right, they don't look good, and nobody likes them. This causes them to fall into the depressive triad of a negative view of themselves, a negative view of the world and a negative view of the future.

> **It is important to differentiate between realistic and unrealistic guilt with teens.**

Teens with unrealistic expectations set themselves up to struggle with feelings of depression. It is good to have standards and goals, but when they are unrealistic the teen is only setting themselves up for failure. These expectations can be in the area of academics, athletics, fine arts, leadership or popularity.

Teens who struggle with a lot of guilt may also struggle with depression. It is important to differentiate between realistic and unrealistic guilt with teens. Some teens will feel guilty because they couldn't meet their unrealistic expectations. They wanted straight A's in all of their advance placement courses and to be on the starting lineup of the athletic team. When they get a "B" on a report card or don't make the starting lineup they feel guilty. This is unrealistic guilt and the youth pastor should help them see this and replace it with a more realistic expectation.

On the other hand, if a student is engaging in premarital sex with their girlfriend or boyfriend, guilt is the proper response. Confession and repentance is needed in order for the depression to go away. (See: Psalm 32:1-5; 51:1-12. These psalms are David's prayers of repentance after his adultery with Bathsheba)

What are the Effects of Teen Depression?

The negative effects of teenage depression go far beyond a melancholy mood. It can cause problems at school. Depression can cause low energy and concentration difficulties. At school, this may lead to poor attendance, a drop in their grades, or frustration with schoolwork in a formerly good student.

Some teens see running away as a solution. A depressed teen may run away from home or talk about running away. Such attempts are usually a cry for help.

> **Teens are not always aware of or open about their struggle with depression.**

Substance abuse is often a by-product of teenage depression. Teens may use alcohol or drugs in an attempt to "self-medicate" their depression. Unfortunately, substance abuse only makes things worse.

Having low self-esteem may contribute to the development of depression, but it can also be a by-product of depression. Depression can trigger and intensify feelings of ugliness, shame, failure and unworthiness.

Eating disorders may be a symptom of depression. The teen may feel out of control because of the depression and controlling their food intake becomes a symbolic way of taking back control of one's life. Anorexia, bulimia, binge eating, and yo-yo dieting are often signs of unrecognized depression.

Teens are not always aware of or open about their struggle with depression. There is such a thing as masked depression; these are reactions or behaviors such as angry temper outbursts, impulsive behavior, accident proneness, and compulsive work. These can all be signs of depression that is not expressed in the usual way.

Cutting or other types of non-suicidal self-injury are almost always associated with depression. This can be cutting, burning, scratching, bruising, pulling out hair or breaking bones. These behaviors are all unhealthy and dysfunctional ways of expressing or releasing strong emotions.

To deal with feelings of depression, some teens will develop an internet addiction. They go online to escape from their problems. But excessive computer use only increases their isolation and makes them more depressed.

Reckless behavior may be a form of masked depression. Depressed teens may engage in dangerous or high-risk behaviors, such as reckless driving, out-of-control drinking, and unsafe sex in order to deal with the intense emotions that accompany depression.

Depression in some teens, usually boys, may express itself in acts of violence. Some depressed teens (usually boys who are the victims of bullying) become violent. As in the case of the Columbine school massacre, self-hatred and a wish to die can erupt into violence and homicidal rage.

It is not uncommon for teenagers who are struggling with depression to withdraw from family and friends. They spend more and more time isolated in their bedrooms or dorm rooms. This isolation only intensifies their feelings of loneliness and unworthiness.

> **The most serious concern for teens who are experiencing depression is thoughts of suicide.**

The most serious concern for teens who are experiencing depression is thoughts of suicide. Teens who are seriously depressed often think, speak, or make "attention-getting" attempts at suicide. Suicidal thoughts or behaviors should always be taken very seriously. "Of the people who complete suicide, 43 percent had a mood disorder."[214] The teen may feel so overwhelmed and helpless about life events that the future seems hopeless. They may believe that suicide is the only way out.

173

Tips for Helping a Depressed Teen

The first thing you should do is offer support. Let depressed teenagers know that you are there for them, fully and unconditionally. Hold back from asking a lot of questions (teenagers don't like to feel patronized or crowded), but make it clear that you're ready and willing to provide whatever support they need.

Be gentle but persistent in your involvement with the teen. Don't give up if the student shuts you out at first. Talking about depression can be very tough for teens. Be respectful of your student's comfort level while still emphasizing your concern and willingness to listen.

You must practice good active listening techniques. Listen without lecturing. Resist any urge to criticize or pass judgment once the student begins to talk. The important thing is that the student is communicating. Avoid offering unsolicited advice or ultimatums as well.

> **Be gentle but persistent in your involvement with the teen. Don't give up if the student shuts you out at first.**

As you listen, try to validate their feelings. Don't try to talk the student out of their depression, even if their feelings or concerns appear silly or irrational to you. Simply acknowledge the pain and sadness they are feeling. If you don't they will feel like you don't take their emotions seriously. It is important that you validate their feelings, but do not support or encourage negative behaviors. Gently and compassionately try to encourage them to choose behaviors that will help them out of their depression and not reinforce it or make it worse.

Above all, be understanding. Being a mentor and counselor with a depressed teenager can be difficult and draining. At times, the youth minister may experience exhaustion, rejection, despair, aggravation, or any other number of negative emotions. During this trying time, it is important to remember that the student is not being difficult on purpose. The student is suffering, so do your best to be patient and understanding.

A helping suggestion you might make is to encourage physical activity; encourage the student to stay active. Exercise can go a long way toward relieving the symptoms of depression because it stimulates the production of serotonin, so find ways to incorporate it into the student's day. Something as simple as walking the dog or going on a bike ride can be beneficial.

Encourage social activity. Isolation only makes depression worse, so encourage the student to engage with other friends and praise efforts to socialize. Suggest social activities that might be of interest such as sports, after-school clubs or an art class.

Provide community. Teens struggling with depression often feel they are the only ones who have ever suffered as they have. It is a feeling of being alone. A concerned group of friends or youth group can do much to melt the ice of loneliness and instill hope.

Accentuate the positive in their life. Since depression is a conviction of one's own helplessness, one step to relieve this feeling is to find some area where the student is proficient and engage in that activity. Music? Art? Athletics? Writing? The prime need that a depressed teen has during depression is a feeling of self-worth. Whatever you can do to help lift their value in their own eyes is good.

Help them get organized. Part of a teen's depression may be caused by an overwhelming number of unfinished tasks that are facing them. Help them organize. Re-evaluate priorities and commitments. Talk them into enlisting some help.

Help the teen get their priorities in order. Some activities will just have to go. The depressed teen must learn to say "No!" Don't allow others to manipulate them into accepting jobs or responsibilities that they don't have the time or the desire to do.

> **Accentuate the positive in their life. Since depression is a conviction of one's own helplessness, one step to relieve this feeling is to find some area where the student is proficient and engage in that activity.**

Because of the high potential for danger, you must evaluate the teen for the risk of suicide. Since depressed teens often contemplate suicide, you must be alert to its signals: self-injurious talk, feelings of hopelessness, sudden and unexplained shifts to a cheerful mood, knowledge about the most effective suicide methods, a history of prior suicide attempts, etc. The issue of suicide should be addressed directly with any teen who is depressed. Do not hesitate to ask, "Do you ever have thoughts of harming yourself?" If the teen responds positively, then it is imperative that you assist them in calling or going to the local crisis intervention center and allowing the professionals to take over. If you are unsure of where to direct your teen or you live in an area with limited resources, you can always call

> **Since depressed teens often contemplate suicide, you must be alert to its signals.**

the National Suicide Hotline which is available 24 hours a day, 7 days a week, 365 days of the year at: 1.800.273.8255.

Even if the student has not given any behavioral or verbal hints that they are suicidal, if the depression has persisted for a long time it is still best to refer them to a professional because of the potential for suicide. A clinical depression is a serious mental health issue and one that requires a referral to mental health professional.

Overview of the Counseling Process for Depression

Connect with the Teen
- They may call you and ask for help – if so, set up a meeting giving them instructions on location, time and length of session.
- You may hear from concerned parents or their peers about their depression – if so, take pastoral initiative and go to them or call and set up a meeting.
- Prepare your meeting place and yourself by reviewing how to counsel someone who is struggling with depression. Don't forget to pray and ask the Holy Spirit for guidance and insight!
- Know the signs and symptoms of someone struggling with depression.

Understand the Teen
- Communicate empathy by your posture, position and active listening skills.
- Communicate nonjudgmental, unconditional love and genuineness.
- Ask yourself the empathy question: "How would I feel if I was this student in this situation?"
- Be patient and let the teen set the pace for the counseling session.
- Encourage the teen to express their feelings and validate them.

Explore with the Teen
- Work with the teen to try and discover what caused them to develop the depression—what is missing in their life? What is present in their life that is causing the pain?
- Through active listening and asking pertinent questions, try and determine the type of depression the teen is struggling with. Is it situational, manic-depression (bi-polar), seasonal affective disorder, dysthymia, etc.?

- Teach them new coping skills through cognitive restructuring that will help to eliminate negative thinking and irrational beliefs which may contribute to the depression.

Initiate a Plan with the Teen

- Encourage physical activity. Start with something easy and attainable and then work up to something more vigorous and for a longer period of time.
- Encourage socialization. Do not let them isolate themselves.
- Help them discover and accentuate the positive in their life.
- Help them set priorities and get organized.
- If nothing seems to help, encourage them to see their primary care physician for a complete physical and possible medication to help with the depression.
- Because of the high potential for danger, you must evaluate the teen for the risk of suicide.

Finish with the Teen

- If the depression continues, refer them to a professional Christian counselor.
- Maintain regular contact with the teen and offer continued support.

Helpful Resources

HelpGuide.Org. "Parent's Guide to Teen Depression." Accessed: December 6, 2016.
> http://www.helpguide.org/articles/depression/teen-depression-signs-help.htm

Mayo Clinic. "Teen Depression. Accessed: December 6, 2016.
> http://www.mayoclinic.org/diseases-conditions/teen-depression/home/ovc-20164553

WebMD. "Teen Depression." Accessed: December 6, 2016.
> http://www.webmd.com/depression/guide/teen-depression#1

Selected Bibliography

Bakalar, Nicholas. *Understanding Teenage Depression: A Guide to Diagnosis, Treatment and Management.* New York, NY: Holt, 2001.

Hart, Archibald. *Counseling the Depressed*. Dallas, TX: Word Publishing, 1987.

Schab, Lisa M. *Beyond the Blues: A Workbook to Help Teens Overcome Depression (Teen Instant Help)*. Bel Air, CA: Instant Help, 2008.

Tan, Siang-Yang and Ortberg, John. *Coping With Depression*. Revised and Expanded. Grand Rapids, MI: Baker Books, 2004.

Exercise 10.1 - Understanding Adolescent Depression

Rate yourself on your knowledge and understanding of adolescent Depression. Use the scale provided: 1 = poor; 2 = below average; 3 = Average; 4 = Above average; 5 = Excellent. Simply check the box that best describes you. Be honest with yourself. Work on the areas that need improvement—it's not an assignment, it's a life that you might save!

Understanding Adolescent Depression	1	2	3	4	5
I understand how widespread the problem of adolescent depression is.					
I can list and identify the signs of a teenager who is struggling with a major depression.					
I can list and define the different types of depression that a teen may experience.					
I understand the major causes of depression in adolescents.					
I understand the student who is most likely to become depressed.					
I understand and can list the different effects of depression on a teen's life.					
I am familiar and comfortable with the various ways that I can come alongside and help a teen struggling with depression.					
I know my limits when it comes to helping a teen struggling with depression and know how and when to make a referral to a mental health professional.					

CHAPTER ELEVEN

PASTORAL CARE FOR AN UNPLANNED TEEN PREGNANCY

A seventeen-year follow-up study of pregnant adolescents found that three factors most critical in successfully adjusting to life after having delivered a child as a teenager were continuing with education, being able to limit births of subsequent children, and achieving a stable marriage at a later point in life. –G. Wade Rowatt Jr. *Adolescents in Crisis: A Guide for Parents, Teachers, Ministers, and Counselors*[215]

My pastor's wife was encouraging. She showed me Scripture verses that related to sin, forgiveness and God's love for me. She also helped me see that my being pregnant was not a sin but a consequence of my sinful actions. –Linda I. Shands. *What Now? Help for Pregnant Teens*[216]

A Case Study

Fifteen-year-old Stephanie had told her boyfriend in a quivering voice over the phone that she had something important to tell him. She had insisted on telling him in person. Now, as she faced Brent in the front seat of his car, she struggled to control her emotions. A nervous smile stretched across her lips.

"I have some really great news to tell you," she said, her wide eyes looking into his with a mixture of fear and hope.

Brent's forehead furrowed. He didn't smile. "Yeah?" he said, wondering what this was all about and knowing only that it felt weird.

"I'm—" she stopped herself, almost losing control. But quickly wrestling her emotions like a cowboy roping a calf, she started again. "We're going to have a baby!" She smiled again as broadly as she could and watched his face closely.

Brent's mouth opened, and he peered hard into her face. He had not yet smiled. "You're pregnant?" he asked, his voice squeaking like a choirboy whose voice has just begun to change.

Stephanie nodded vigorously and swallowed before speaking. "Aren't you happy?"

"Well, yeah." He licked his lips. "Are you?"

"Yes," Stephanie blurted, desperately wanting to convince Brent—and herself—of the answer. She threw her arms around his shoulders and pressed her face against his neck. "Aren't you? She asked, her voice barely audible.

Brent slowly wrapped his arms around Stephanie and began to pat her gently as if she were a baby. "Yeah, sure I am. If you're happy about it, then I'm happy too."

Stephanie closed her eyes against the tears that welled inside. She was scared. Scared of being pregnant. Scared of telling her parents. And scared of what Brent was thinking.[217]

This is a very typical response to an unplanned teenage pregnancy. The girl is frightened of what her parents will say when they find out, unsure of her boyfriend's response and not at all confident about how to proceed. She feels lost in a sea of conflicting feelings.

> **The pregnant teenager requires wise counsel, support and resources in order to decide how to best deal with this situation.**

The pregnant teenager requires wise counsel, support and resources in order to decide how to best deal with this situation. It is further complicated because of all the people directly involved—the father of the child, her parents, his parents, siblings and grandparents. The youth pastor will need to first gain the trust of the pregnant teenager and help support her in deciding her future and the future of her baby. At some point in the counseling, the other family members need to be brought in on the process and decision.

Statistics

In 2014, almost 250,000 babies were born to women aged 15–19 years, for a birth rate of 24.2 per 1,000 women in this age group. This is a historic low, and a drop of 9% from 2013. Birth rates fell 11% for women aged 15–17 years, and 7% for women aged 18–19 years. While reasons for the declines are not clear, teens seem to be less sexually active, and more of those who are sexually active seem to be using birth control than in previous years.[218]

- About 750,000 teens become pregnant each year.
- Almost one-third of teen girls will become pregnant.

- Among industrial or developed nations, the United States has the highest rate of teen pregnancy, teen parenthood, and teen abortions.
- About half of U.S. teens are sexually active. Of those who are sexually active, more are having sex at a younger age, which increases the risk of teen pregnancy and sexually transmitted disease.
- More teens are waiting until they are older or until they are married to have sex.
- More than half of teen pregnancies occur in older teens, age 18 or 19. The number of younger teens having babies is declining more than that of older teens.
- About a quarter of teen mothers have a second baby within two years of the first.
- Teens who choose to have teen sex are more likely to use a condom than in the 1980s, and less likely to use less effective methods of birth control and STD protection.
- Most teens who use birth control pills do not use any other method of protection, and many teens are inconsistent in their use of the pill.
- A teenager who is having unprotected sex has a 90 percent chance of becoming pregnant within a year.[219]

Teen pregnancy and childbearing bring substantial social and economic costs through immediate and long-term impacts on teen parents and their children.

- Teen pregnancy accounts for more than $9 billion per year in costs to U.S. taxpayers for increased health care and foster care, increased incarceration rates among children of teen parents, and lost tax revenue because of lower educational attainment and income among teen mothers.
- Pregnancy and birth are significant contributors to high school dropout rates among girls. Only about 50% of teen mothers receive a high school diploma by age 22, versus nearly 90% of women who had not given birth during adolescence.
- The children of teenage mothers are more likely to have lower school achievement and drop out of high school, have more health problems, be incarcerated at some time during adolescence, give birth as a teenager, and face unemployment as a young adult.

- These effects remain for the teen mother and her child even after adjusting for those factors that increased the teenager's risk for pregnancy; such as, growing up in poverty, having parents with low levels of education, growing up in a single-parent family, and having low attachment to and performance in school.[220]
- Only about one third of teenage mothers go on to receive a high school diploma.[221]
- Over half of all mothers on welfare had their first baby while they were still adolescents.[222]

Because of the significant consequences to the pregnant teenager, her child and society it is imperative that great care is taken in deciding what is going to be the best course of action for all involved. This chapter will help the youth pastor understand the girl's situation and the serious ramifications that her decision about the pregnancy will have on her, her unborn child, her family and the father's life and family. Wise counsel is called for and appropriate resources need to be made available, such as prenatal care, adoption information and any other appropriate agencies that may be needed.

The Causes of Unplanned Teenage Pregnancy

> Adolescence is characterized by new and intense sensations, unpredictable moods, overpowering emotions, and conflicting demands and expectations.

Adolescence is characterized by new and intense sensations, unpredictable moods, overpowering emotions, and conflicting demands and expectations. There are a number of different factors which contribute to the problem of teenage pregnancy (other than the obvious physiological).

Lack of Sex Education at Home – There is no substitute for a home in which sex is approached in a frank and sensitive way, in which questions are greeted in an open manner, in which the beauty of sex within marriage and the dangers of sex outside marriage is discussed in a biblical context, and in which an adolescent is calmly prepared for the onset of puberty and the first stirrings of sexual drives and impulses.

Unfortunately, many children don't grow up in a positive environment for sexual education. In their homes the topic of sex is forbidden, either explicitly or implicitly. The parents seem embarrassed or afraid to approach the subject.

Even if a child has been educated about the "technical" aspects of sexual behavior, i.e., the reproductive system, the mechanics of sex, methods of birth control; a child may still be reluctant to discuss sexual questions with the parents.

Psychological Issues – Teenage girls who feel insecure about their bodies, uncomfortable with the physical changes they're experiencing, or uncertain about who they are or where they fit in may turn to sexual involvement and pregnancy as a way of convincing others, and themselves, that they are capable of being wanted and loved.

Pregnancy may also seem, to an insecure adolescent mind, as a way to hold on to a boyfriend or to force a boyfriend into marriage. Others, who come from cold and harsh homes see a baby as a guarantee that someone will love them unconditionally.

Girls who had absent or distant fathers are particularly vulnerable to early sexual involvement. They crave the attention of a significant male and unfortunately sexual involvement seems to be the easiest way to get it.

Alcohol or Drug Influence – A factor that is a high contributor to teenage pregnancy is alcohol and drug abuse. When a young adolescent girl is trying to figure out the "relationship" thing and finds herself at a party where alcohol and drugs are available it is easy for her to make an unwise decision about sexual involvement. This is especially true when considering her own raging hormones and an insistent boyfriend. If she fears that she will lose the boyfriend if she doesn't "put out" then she will soon find herself crossing a line she had not intended to cross. Date rape drugs[223] are often placed unknowingly in a girl's drink at a party and she ends up a victim of sexual assault.

Studies have found that "Christian" teens are more likely to engage in premarital sex without using contraceptives because it seems less of a sin to them.

Contraceptive Failure – Even with all the public and private sexual education campaigns advising the use of contraceptives to prevent pregnancy and disease, many adolescents still engage in sexual behavior without the so-called "protection" afforded by such devices. Studies have found that "Christian" teens are more likely to engage in premarital sex without using contraceptives because it seems less of a sin to them. To use a contraceptive involves planning ahead which seems much more than simply being "overwhelmed" by the passion of the moment.

Many adolescents who do use contraceptive devises only use them part of the time and often incorrectly. According to data collected by Planned Parenthood a teenager expecting to prevent pregnancy with a condom is still taking an 18.4% chance of becoming pregnant.

Rebellion – For some teenage girls, pregnancy is the ultimate expression of rebellion against parental authority. Most girls may not fully understand their own actions or the motivations behind such actions, but (consciously or unconsciously) their sexual activity and resulting pregnancy become a means of communication.

In the mind of an adolescent girl, her pregnancy may be a means of communicating to her parents, "You can't control me," or "I don't have to do what you say." It may also communicate, "I'm grown up; why can't you see that?" Or it may be a cry for help, simply, "Pay attention to me!"

A Desire for Freedom – Most adults are baffled by a teenager's choice to become pregnant. They say, "Why would you give up for freedom and future like that?"

But for many adolescent girls, they think it is just the opposite. To them a pregnancy and parenthood will bring them freedom. It will force their parents to accept them as adults. It will enable them to control their own lives. It will get them out of the drudgery of school. It will allow them to make decisions for themselves.

Intellectual Confusion – Some girls end up pregnant because they simply do not have the ability to say "no" to a boyfriend's need to prove his manhood. Some Christian teens believe that since they prayed that they won't get pregnant that God wouldn't let it happen. Others have a fantasy that marriage and homemaking will bring them happiness and stability in an otherwise confusing and demanding world. Some girls believe that the responsibility for preventing pregnancy rests with the boy and it is up to him to take "precautions."

> **Teens who begin dating at age 12 have a 91 percent chance of being sexually active as teens, and teens who begin dating at 13 have a 56 percent chance of teen sexual activity.**

Risk factors – The risk factors for sexual activity teens and teen pregnancy include:

- Dating at a young age. Teens who begin dating at age 12 have a 91 percent chance of being sexually active as teens, and teens who begin dating at 13 have a 56 percent chance of teen sexual activity.
- Lack of self-discipline, which is required to reach goals, delay gratification, and make choices like waiting to have sex or using a condom
- Using alcohol, drugs, or tobacco
- Dropping out of school, or not having a commitment to education

- Having little social support, such as caring family or friends
- Not feeling involved with family, school, or community
- Feeling like they have no opportunities, or not recognizing their own potential
- Being in an environment where teen pregnancy is common
- Living in poverty
- Being a victim of sexual abuse
- Being the child of a teen mother
- Suffering from depression or other mental health problems
- Lack of positive role models in their family or their life[224]

Being involved in dating or sexual activity at a young age is a major risk factor for unprotected sex and the potential pregnancies and STDs that go with that choice. The younger a teen is when he or she first has sex the more likely he or she is to have unprotected sex resulting in a pregnancy or STD.

The Effects of an Unplanned Pregnancy

Socioeconomic Consequences – A teen pregnancy usually means a decreased likelihood of high school graduation, a greater likelihood of divorce, single parenthood (and all the economic hardships that come with that), unemployment and welfare dependency.

> **Denial is common among pregnant teens, even when the pregnancy was not wholly unintentional.**

Denial – Denial is common among pregnant teens, even when the pregnancy was not wholly unintentional. Even after the signs of pregnancy would seem incontrovertible to an objective observer, many young women continue to delay seeking a diagnosis and important prenatal care hoping that ignoring it will make it go away.

Fear - A teenage girl who discovers she is pregnant may fear how her boyfriend will react. She may fear her parents' anger and retaliation. She may be afraid of the changes that will happen in her body or the pain of labor. She may fear judgment from her teachers, neighbors, and church.

Guilt – In some cases the guilt becomes so intense that she can barely focus her mind on anything except finding relief for the guilt that afflicts her and that will soon be apparent to all. Such a desperate feeling will sometimes prompt a teen to seek an abortion, attempt a self-inflicted abortion, run away, or attempt suicide.

Shame – Few girls want to be known as *one of those kinds of girls*. Though they may be sexually active, they still want a reputation as a "good girl," a worthwhile, valued, loved, respected human being. For many pregnancy represents the end of that "illusion" as a pregnancy invariable publicizes a girl's sexual activity.

> **Teens may not be able to fully comprehend that some actions cannot be undone, some consequences are irrevocable.**

Regret – Teenagers have an imperfect understanding of the irrevocability of certain actions or events. Teens may not be able to fully comprehend that some actions cannot be undone, some consequences are irrevocable. As a result, a pregnant teen may be overcome with regret. She may feel that she has ruined her life or her boyfriend's life. She may think she has shattered her parents' reputation in the church or community. She may for the first time feel the pain of facing the consequences for an action which cannot be undone.

A Biblical Perspective on Unplanned Pregnancy

God's design for sex is that it is only to take place within the bonds of marriage. Anything other than this is sin. Sex outside of marriage is sin, and pregnancy outside of marriage is often a visible token of that sin. (1 Cor 6: 13-20; Gal 5:19; Eph 5: 3; Col 3:5; 1 Thess 4:3-8; Hebrews 13:4; Rev 21:8)

Premarital sex is *not* the unforgivable sin, however. (Matt 12:31-32). Repentance is appropriate and forgiveness is possible. (Psalm 32, 51)

Regardless of how a pregnancy occurs, the life that grows inside a woman's womb is known to God and is precious to Him. God's word clearly emphasizes the value the Creator places on each human life. Ps 139:13-16 teaches us that God has a great concern and plan for us even in the prenatal state.

While premarital sex is sin that should be repented, the biblical response will also involve concern for the young woman who is pregnant, the boy who has fathered the child, and the unborn child. All three are precious in God's sight. All three should be afforded the best possible protection, counsel, and care in the days to come.

Response to an Unplanned Pregnancy

When a teenage girl first sees the results of a home pregnancy test or hears the doctor's words, "You're pregnant," she will probably experience some form of shock or denial. "This can't be happening to me," she thinks. After the initial shock of the news wears off, she must then decide how she is going to cope with this unplanned pregnancy. There are unhealthy ways and there are healthy ways to cope in this situation.

Here are some common unhealthy ways of coping with an unplanned pregnancy:

- Deny that a problem exists. (I'll wear a tight binding girdle until I can't and then only wear baggy and loose fitting clothes.)
- Refusing to seek or accept help. (I'll handle it myself.)
- Run away from it. (I'll get high to escape and forget.)
- Fail to explore alternatives. (I've made up my mind already.)
- Blame others. (It's all *his* fault.)
- Turn away from friends and family. (Everyone just leave me alone!)[225]

> There are unhealthy ways and there are healthy ways to cope with an unplanned pregnancy.

Here are some healthy ways of coping with an unplanned pregnancy:

- Face the problem.
- Gain a better perspective of it.
- Work through bad feelings.
- Accept responsibility for coping with the problem.
- Explore alternative ways to handle the crisis.
- Distinguish between what can and cannot be changed.
- Be open to communication with people ready to support her.
- Take steps, however small, to handle the crisis positively.[226]

> Even with the positive benefits of an adoption, such a decision can still be emotionally traumatic.

As soon as the teenage girl suspects or gets affirmation that she is pregnant, she must see a physician. This can be the family doctor, or if she is embarrassed to use the family doctor, she can make an appointment through a crisis pregnancy center. This is important because studies have shown that mothers who have early, regular prenatal care are more likely to have healthy babies than women who have little or no care. "Teenage pregnancy is a high-risk situation; nearly half of young pregnant women receive no prenatal care in their first trimester."[227]

The pregnant teenager must make a choice about the future. What is she going to do with this baby? She should definitely involve her parents in this decision. The father, along with his family, should also have some input, but in the end, it is the pregnant teenager who has the last say in this matter. The father should not be allowed to pressure her into a decision against her will. There are basically four options to consider at this point.

Adoption is an option that is too often neglected today because of the easy availability of abortion. Adoption allows a girl to be responsible to her unborn baby without being strapped with the burden of parenthood before she is mature enough or economically able to handle it. Adoptions can be arranged through the girl's doctor, through an adoption agency, or through friends and relatives with the help of a lawyer. Even with the positive benefits of an adoption, such a decision can still be emotionally traumatic.

However, societal changes have made adoption a much more palatable solution because the people involved have more choices than before. In the past, birth parents had few rights. Today birth parents can develop a plan with which they are comfortable. Birth parents can now participate in selecting an adoptive couple from written, picture or video profiles. They can meet the potential adoptive parents before or after the birth. The birth parents can negotiate the amount of contact that takes place after the adoption is finalized.

Marriage is another consideration. This is a good choice if both are mature and deeply love each other. Married adolescents sometimes live with one of their families through it is usually preferred for them to be able to have an apartment on their own, even if they require some temporary financial support. This gives them the privacy required for successfully transitioning from being single teenagers to being a young married couple. The major problems with this choice revolve around their relative immaturity, need to finish school, and the severe impact on their peer relationships.

> There was a time when couples involved in premarital sex were forced to marry, especially when a baby was involved. But pregnancy should never be the main reason for marriage. Nothing cools a hot love faster than a pile of unpaid bills, a screaming infant and an exhausted wife. There are few young men mature enough to sacrifice

their dreams and take up the cross of marital and parental responsibility.[228]

These negative impacts become greater with younger teenagers. While marriage is an option, a pregnant teen must not feel that she *has* to get married. Most teen marriages that begin because of an unplanned pregnancy do not end up "happily ever after." "Currently between 70-75% of teen marriages end in divorce, and when pregnancy is *the* reason for the marriage, the failure rate is nearly 90%."[229]

> **Currently between 70-75% of teen marriages end in divorce, and when pregnancy is *the* reason for the marriage, the failure rate is nearly 90%.**

The mother, along with her parents, may decide that single parenthood is the best choice. A growing number of teen mothers decide to keep their babies and raise them alone. Most do so with the assistance of their parents, though some go to live with other relatives and some even attempt to set up housekeeping on their own. Single parenthood can be an extremely difficult route and will necessitate further discussion about completion of school, day care, job, etc. Many teens are caught up in a fantasy about how wonderful single parenting will be. They need to be informed of the facts.

Fantasy	Fact
Parenting will be fun.	Parenting is sometimes fun. More often it is hard, unrewarding, repetitive work. Ask any parent.
I can work, go to school, be a single parent and still have time for a social life.	You will work at home, at school, at a part-time job and be too exhausted for a social life. Ask any single parent.
My friends will be around all the time after the baby is born. Nothing will change.	Your friends will be busy with sports and boys. Your world will revolve around your child.[230]

There are a lot of expenses to consider if choosing to keep the baby. There are the medical bills for prenatal care, delivery and the hospital. If there are complications or if the baby has special needs the medical expenses will soar. After the baby is born there will be immunizations against childhood diseases, well-baby checkups, ear infections, bronchitis and prescriptions to fill. Besides the medical costs there are the one-time purchases of a baby crib, mattress pad, crib sheets, car seat, high chair, bottles, baby eating utensils, pacifier, toys, teething ring, blankets and baby clothes. In addition to the one-time purchases, there are the weekly or monthly needs for diapers, lotion, baby cereal, diaper rash ointment, baby shampoo and formula. If the mother is working and the grandparents are not available or willing, then the single mother has the additional burden of paying for child-care.

Another issue to think through if the mother decides to keep the baby is how involved is the father going to be? Is he willing and able to provide financial help? If the father's name is on the birth certificate the mother may have the legal right to pursue child support, but it may also give the father and his family custody and visiting rights unless otherwise worked out in court.

Unfortunately, because of the liberal political climate and the government supported Planned Parenthood, abortion is often the choice the pregnant teen makes. "Out of all teenage pregnancies, 26% are terminated by abortion, down from 29% over a decade ago."[231]

> **Abortion is not only a biblically abhorrent option, it also has very negative emotional, psychosocial, and physical effects on all those involved.**

Abortion is not only a biblically abhorrent option, it also has very negative emotional, psychosocial, and physical effects on all those involved. After an abortion, especially if the girl felt the baby move within her, she is likely to feel murderous and need counseling to help her resolve these feelings. Some girls annually remember the date of their abortion with renewed guilt, remorse and grieving. As the billboard proclaims: "Abortion doesn't make you unpregnant, it makes you the mother of a dead baby." "There are no psychological indications for abortion; there are only psychosocial justifications."[232] Christian counselors need to help girls deal effectively with the spiritual aspects of abortion. They need to work sensitively, fully accepting her and communicating no sense of judgment toward her while, at the same time, confronting her with the reality of what abortion really is.

With all the negative aspects to abortion, why would a pregnant teenage girl even consider having one? It is because an unplanned pregnancy represents many threats, such as:

- Threat of the loss of a future college education
- Threat of rejection by parents or boyfriend
- Threat of financial insecurity
- Threat of the loss of a lifestyle she has known

- Threat of the loss of respect and reputation if the pregnancy was known.[233]

With the issue of abortion, one must also consider the spiritual warfare that is taking place. Satan wants to deceive and destroy. Jesus said of Satan: "He was a murderer from the beginning, not holding to the truth, for there is no truth in him. When he lies, he speaks his native language, for he is a liar and the father of lies."[234] Satan lies to the family and tries to convince them that abortion is the best choice.

Satan's Lie to the Mother	Satan's Lie to the Father	Satan's Life to Parents (as grandparents considering abortion)
My life will be ruined.	No one will know.	What will people think of you now as a parent?
No one will know.	This will have no effect on me.	You can get rid of this embarrassment--no one will know.
This will have no effect on me.	This isn't a baby—it is tissue.	You have failed.
This isn't a baby—it is tissue.		Think of the shame when people find out.[235]

If the pregnant teenager, her boyfriend, and their parents believe the lies that Satan is trying to convince them of, and act upon them and follow through with an abortion, then Satan will return as the accuser and torment them will guilt and condemnation.

The Mother's Guilt	The Father's Guilt	The Parent's Guilt
You are a Christian and killed your baby.	You are a Christian and took your girlfriend to kill your baby.	How could you have allowed your grandchild to be aborted?
There is no way God can forgive you.	You failed to protect your baby.	God will never forgive or forget.
You are a murderer.	You are a bad person.	You are a horrible parent.[236]

Some women feel temporary relief after the abortion because the perceived threats to their life are now resolved. However, these feelings are frequently followed by a period of emotional paralysis or a type of post-abortion numbness. Not unlike soldiers returning from the battlefield, these women experience a type of shell shock and are unable to express or even feel their own emotions. A psychological price is paid when a woman terminates a pregnancy. "One study found that one out of every three teenagers who aborted showed signs of emotional aftermath. Another study reported that less than one-fourth of teens who aborted were able to cope with the aftermath of their abortion in a nondestructive manner."[237]

The emotional fallout from the decision to have an abortion will require compassionate and sensitive individual counseling. It is also highly recommended that the woman be directed to a support group sponsored by a local crisis pregnancy center to find a place to express her feelings and to know that others understand because they have been through what she is experiencing.

Overview of the Counseling Process for An Unplanned Teenage Pregnancy

<u>Connect with the Teen</u>
- They may call you and ask for help – if so, set up a meeting giving them instructions on location, time and length of session.
- You may hear from her parents or peers about the pregnancy--if so, take pastoral initiative and go to them or call and set up a meeting.
- Prepare your meeting place and yourself by reviewing how to deal with an unplanned teenage pregnancy. Don't forget to pray and ask the Holy Spirit for guidance and insight!
- Have the information about local resources for unplanned pregnancy available, such as Life Choices, Birthright, etc.

<u>Understand the Teen</u>
- Communicate empathy by your posture, position and active listening skills.
- Communicate nonjudgmental, unconditional love and genuineness.
- Ask yourself the empathy question: "How would I feel if I was this student in this situation?"
- Help the teen deal with the fear, guilt and shame associated with a pregnancy out of wedlock.
- Assure her of God's forgiveness.

Explore with the Teen
- The first priority is to verify the pregnancy. This can be done through a home pregnancy test or a doctor's visit.
- Talk with teen about the father's involvement.
- Talk about the need to involve both sets of parents with the issue.
- Legal proceedings may need to be initiated to guarantee and enforce child support.

Initiate a Plan with the Teen
- With the involvement of the parents, come up with a plan on how to proceed with the pregnancy—choosing either adoption, single parenthood or marriage. Help them explore the pros and cons of each choice.
- Encourage the teen and family to make appointments for regular pre-natal care and checkups.
- Educate the teen on healthy choices while pregnant, such as no smoking or alcohol, etc.
- Decide how much involvement, if any, the father and his family will have.

Finish with the Teen
- Offer continued support and contact through the pregnancy to the birth of the child.
- Support the girl and her family in how they choose to deal with the pregnancy, either adoption, single parenthood or marriage.
- If the girl decides to keep the child, provide information on childcare and parenting.
- Provide a caring and supportive community through the church.

Helpful Resources

Bethany Christian Services – 1-800-238-4269 – Provides pregnancy counseling, temporary foster care, adoption services and more
Birthright – 1-800-550-4900 – Provides free and confidential pregnancy testing and more.
Single Mother Help. https://www.singlemotherhelp.org/top-10-non-profit-organizations-that-help-mothers.html

Selected Bibliography

Schooler, Jayne E. *"Mom, Dad. . . I'm Pregnant." When Your Daughter or Son Face an Unplanned Pregnancy*. Colorado Springs, CO: NavPress, 2004.

Shands, Linda I. *What Now? Help for Pregnant Teens*. Downers Grove, IL: InterVarsity Press, 1997.

Exercise 11.1 - Understanding Unplanned Teenage Pregnancy

Rate yourself on your knowledge and understanding of unplanned teenage pregnancy. Use the scale provided: 1 = poor; 2 = below average; 3 = Average; 4 = Above average; 5 = Excellent. Simply check the box that best describes you. Be honest with yourself. Work on the areas that need improvement—it's not an assignment, it's a life that you might save!

Understanding Unplanned Teenage Pregnancy	1	2	3	4	5
I understand how widespread the problem of unplanned teenage pregnancy is.					
I understand the forces that contribute to an unplanned teenage pregnancy.					
I understand the various risk factors surrounding an unplanned teenage pregnancy.					
I understand the effects of an unplanned teenage pregnancy on the girl, the father, the parents and society.					
I understand the biblical perspective of an unplanned teenage pregnancy.					
I am familiar with the four choices that the mother must make concerning her unplanned teenage pregnancy.					
I am familiar with the resources in my area to help with an unplanned teenage pregnancy.					
I know when and where to refer a teenager who is pregnant to a professional counselor.					

CHAPTER TWELVE

LIVES OF QUIET TURBULENCE: COUNSELING CHILDREN OF DIVORCE

A critical challenge facing the church today is the need for Christian communities to be hospitable, healing, and supportive havens for teenagers and parents in transition. Many families are isolated, overwhelmed, and lacking in support as they face the challenges of divorce.[238] –Les Parrott III

Growing up as a child of divorce is hard. For me it has been the definition of pain, a death that continues dying. But even this can be overcome, and its long-lasting effects can be softened to the point of nonexistence. Remember, the same Lord who brought Lazarus back from the dead is able to bring your spirit, or at least the parts that have been crushed, back to life as well.[239] –Jeromy Diebler

A Case Study

Rick grew up in a very conservative evangelical family. Both of his parents served as professors at a small Bible College. His mother taught Music and Worship and his father taught in the Bible Department. His father was also an associate pastor at a local church and his mother lead the choir and played the piano for worship services.

For all practical appearances, this was a model Christian family. They believed in the authority of the Bible, went to church regularly, the two boys participated in Sunday School, VBS, and church camp. But that all changed in one weekend.

Both Rick and his brother had left the home. Sid, his older brother, had married his high school sweet-heart and was living in another state. Rick had received a music scholarship from a Christian College and was living in the dorm half-way across the States. His father came home from school on a Friday afternoon to find the house completely empty of furniture, pictures and furnishings. The only thing that was left was a black trash bag with his father's clothes in it placed in the middle of the bedroom floor. In the kitchen, there was a small table, one chair, one plate, one glass and one knife, spoon and fork. Everything else was gone. His father was served divorce papers the next week.

In the months that followed, not only did his father lose his job as a Professor at the Bible College, but he was relieved of his position as a pastor, also. His life was crushed. He eventually found work at a local business in town and years later remarried. But the scars remained.

For Rick, the tragedy didn't end with his parent's divorce. His brother's wife left him for an old boyfriend that she hooked up with on social media. Sid couldn't stand the pain of losing his family after seeing what his father had went through so he chose to end his life by suicide.

When I reconnected with Rick he was in his late twenties or early thirties. He came to me for counseling because every serious relationship he previously had with a woman, ended in a break-up when things started to get serious. He was reaching out to try and figure out what he was doing wrong. Through a three-generational look at his family, Rick realized for the first time how much his parent's and his brother's divorce had affected him. He had severe intimacy issues because he was afraid of commitment. He couldn't bear the thought of another marriage failure so when the relationships became serious, he would bail out of fear of failure.

The good news is that Rick worked through his intimacy issues and fear of commitment and has been married for over twenty years and has a wonderful, loving and close family. But it was difficult and painful to work through all the baggage that he carried with him from his parent's and his brother's divorce. While children of divorce are not necessarily doomed to unhappy lives or futures, there are serious issues that must be confronted and worked through. These must not be ignored.

> **41% of first marriages end in divorce.**
> **60% of second marriages end in divorce.**
> **73% of third marriages end in divorce.**

The purpose of this chapter is to acquaint the reader with the main emotional, psychological, behavioral and spiritual issues that confront children of divorce at the various stages of growth and to provide insight on how to best support them through this painful process.

Statistics on Divorce

- 41 percent of first marriages end in divorce.
- 60 percent of second marriages end in divorce.
- 73 percent of third marriages end in divorce.
- The average length of a marriage that ends in divorce is eight years.
- People wait an average of three years after a divorce to remarry (if they remarry at all).
- The average age for couples going through their first divorce is 30 years old.

- 79.6 six percent of custodial mothers receive a support award, while only 29.6 percent of custodial fathers receive a support award.
- 46.9 percent of non-custodial mothers totally default on support, while only 26.9 percent of non-custodial fathers totally default on support.[240]

Statistics on the Likelihood of Divorce

- If your parents are happily married, your risk of divorce decreases by 14 percent.
- People who wait to marry until they are over the age of 25 are 24 percent less likely to get divorced.
- Living together prior to getting married can increase the chance of getting divorced by as much as 40 percent.
- If you've attended college, your risk of divorce decreases by 13 percent.[241]

Divorce and Children Statistics

- The divorce rate among couples with children is 40 percent lower than couples without children.
- Forty-three percent of children growing up in America today are being raised without their fathers.
- Seventy-five percent of children with divorced parents live with their mother.
- Twenty-eight percent of children living with a divorced parent live in a household with an income below the poverty line.
- Half of all American children will witness the breakup of a parent's marriage. Of these children, close to half will also see the breakup of a parent's second marriage.[242]

Concerns of Children Who Are Experiencing a Divorce

You should never make promises that you cannot keep or give false assurance to a young child.

Young children have an especially difficult time with divorce because they do not have the intellectual or developmental maturity to understand everything that is involved with this decision. It seems very confusing for them and they have a number of questions that run through their heads, such as:

- Why are you getting a divorce?
- Did I cause the divorce? Maybe if I had been good it wouldn't happen.
- Can I fix the problem? If I'm real good, will they get back together?
- Is it permanent?
- Who will take care of me?
- Will I be abandoned? If dad left, will mom leave too?
- Will I have to move?
- Is my grandmother still my grandmother if my dad is gone?
- Why is God letting mom and dad divorce?
- Will mom and dad stop loving me, too?
- Can I still love both my mom and dad if they don't love one another?
- Will I have to take my dad's/mom's place?
- If I pray, will God bring mom and dad back together again?
- Will I always feel this bad?
- How can divorce happen to people who were in love?[243]

The job of the counselor is to listen to the concerns and to do your best to answer them honestly and openly. Some of their fears are unfounded, but others may play out exactly how they feared. Remember that you cannot change the situation. You should never make promises that you cannot keep or give false assurance to a young child. Just because they are young and don't understand all the ramifications of divorce, that doesn't mean they don't experience the emotional devastation brought on by divorce. Consider the depth of insight about divorce written in a poem by a ten-year-old Chicago girl.

> **It is safe to assume, whether a child seems resilient or not, that the divorce will have some damaging effect on him or her.**

Divorce shakes you off the ground.
Divorce whirls you all around.
Divorce makes you all confused.
Divorce forces you to choose.

Divorce makes you feel all sad.
Divorce pushes you to be mad.
Divorce makes you wonder who cares.
Divorce leaves you thoroughly scared.

Divorce makes a silent home.
Divorce leaves you all alone.
Divorce is supposed to be an answer.
Divorce, in fact, is emotional cancer.[244]

The Effect of Divorce on Children

It is true that some children can go through a divorce with little noticeable effect on their later life. They exhibit strong and healthy egos, and utilize adequate coping measures. They have a healthy sense of identity and self-esteem built from the earlier part of the marriage, before the relationship deteriorated.

> But it is a mistake to assume that resilient children are the ones who show no pain, or who act continually strong and courageous during or after the divorce! It is not necessarily a bad sign for children to cry a lot, or to act weak and upset. . . It is safe to assume, whether a child seems resilient or not, that the divorce will have some damaging effect on him or her.[245]

> Adults often assume from a child's silence that the child has adjusted to the divorce and accepts it. Although it's easier to understand that "bad" or aggressive behavior might be a cry for help, don't be fooled into thinking that "good" behavior signals that the child needs no guidance. All children of divorce need to express what's on their minds.[246]

The age and sex of a child greatly affects how they will respond to the divorce. Every child and every situation is unique and so the reactions will fit the child and their particular situation. But generally speaking, boys are usually harder hit. Girls are allowed to vent their hurt by crying and expressing their painful emotions. Boys are not allowed that needed release, so they try to hold it in, but this adversely affects them in other areas.

"After a divorce, children, teens, and adults alike sometimes go through stages of grief much as they would after the death of a loved one."[247] This cycle takes the child from grief to recovery and the acceptance and reconstruction of a new lifestyle. This cycle usually takes from one to two years to complete.

The Crisis Cycle[248]

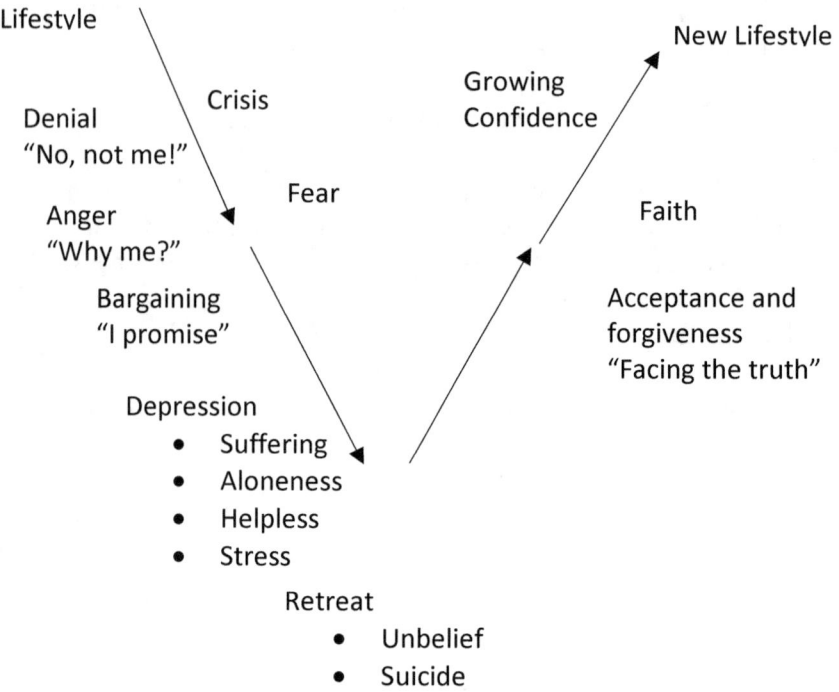

Lifestyle

Crisis

Denial
"No, not me!"

Anger
"Why me?"

Fear

Bargaining
"I promise"

Depression
- Suffering
- Aloneness
- Helpless
- Stress

Retreat
- Unbelief
- Suicide

New Lifestyle

Growing
Confidence

Faith

Acceptance and
forgiveness
"Facing the truth"

It is helpful to look at how divorce affects children at the different developmental stages because it will impact them in different ways at the different ages. In order to know how to best counsel and help those going through divorce, it is imperative that the youth pastor be familiar with the major issues of divorce at these various developmental stages.

The Pre-Schooler (3-5 years)

At this stage, there is a lot of basic anger and sadness. Boys tend to become noisier, angrier and more restless. They do not play as well with friends and tend to sit alone. They will disrupt group activities with other children. Girls will also exhibit some anger, but they are more likely to become "little adults." They are overly concerned with being neat, and good, and lecture other kids on their "bad" behavior.

Children at this age who are going through a divorce will often regress to a more dependent level demanding to be fed instead of feeding themselves and even reverting to diapers and soiling their clothes. They are extra sensitive to stress and anxiety. While they cannot articulate what is going on, they do have a sense that something is happening and that it is "wrong." It is not uncommon for a number of them to suffer from fears and frightening dreams.

School Age (6-12 years)

> **Children of the middle-age group may submerge their feelings only to have them come out in the teen years as rebellion and other destructive behaviors.**

The spiritual development of the child is most likely to be damaged at this age. There is a great deal of sadness, and they tend to blame themselves for the divorce. Children at this age carry a sense of guilt and frustration, abandonment and rejection because of the divorce. Boys tend to be more upset by the separation than girls. There are several possibilities for this: 1) boys are not encouraged to share their feelings like girls are in society so the boys feel like they have one less avenue with which to deal with their pain and; 2) a young boy's identity is wrapped up in his father. How is he going to know how to act, walk and talk like a man when his main role model is now absent? Boys will complain of missing their fathers and yet at the same time, may reject their father's visitation attempts. Children at this age will express more anger over the divorce and it becomes harder for mothers to discipline their boys. School performance declines. Both boys and girls may have problems getting along with peers. There may be a lack of appetite, complaints of stomach aches, sad facial affect, muscle weakness or physical exhaustion. There is usually anger directed at the parent who initiated the divorce. These students may become cynical, sarcastic, extremely critical of peers, and distrustful of all authority figures. Competition in sports or academics may become fierce and compulsive. Children of the middle-age group may submerge their feelings only to have them come out in the teen years as rebellion and other destructive behaviors. Many feel this is the most critical age for children of divorce and unfortunately, it is also the one with the largest number of children affected.

Teenage (13-19)

Teenagers whose parents decide to divorce end up feeling very self-conscious and think that they are different from other students their age. Adolescents will also be filled with guilt and believe that they are somehow responsible for what has happened. The divorce affects the adolescent's attitude toward all adults. They think: "My parents let me down, therefore adults cannot be trusted." It also affects their view of having a successful marriage in the future. "Because my parents divorced, my chances of having a happy marriage are pretty slim."

The teens are greatly affected by custody choices. Since the mother usually gets custody of the children, that means that there will be limited financial resources due to lower income and the cost of maintaining two households. As a direct result of the divorce, the teen usually has to shoulder additional responsibilities due to the absent parent. This means helping take care of younger siblings by getting them up and dressed for school. It may also mean that the teen has to make the evening meals because of the mother's work schedule.

There are usually new rules and roles in the home resulting from the absence of one parent. This can be especially confusing for teenagers who were raised in conservative Christian homes because since the divorce, the rules for what is right and wrong behavior for mom and dad have completely changed. The very foundation for what is acceptable behavior seems to have become undone.

The teens will usually feel one parent is more at fault than the other. When parents date again, the teens respond with either intense jealousy, feeling threatened, or fear another disruption to their lives. Many teens will "act out" their anger and frustration by rebellious and destructive behavior; i.e. promiscuity, drugs, alcohol, etc.

Some will rally to support the parent with whom they live or who has been abandoned. They don't feel the "blame" as much as younger children do, but feel the "loyalty dilemma" much more. Teens usually cope with divorce by distancing themselves from the parental relationship by becoming more involved in their own interests and future. Many feel "betrayed" and will distance themselves out of anger. Here is a typical post from an adolescent whose parents are divorcing: "I'm going to smile like nothing's wrong, talk like everything is perfect, act like it's all a dream, and pretend like it's not hurting me."

> "I'm going to smile like nothing's wrong, talk like everything is perfect, act like it's all a dream, and pretend like it's not hurting me."

General Overall Effects

In Hart's book, *Children & Divorce*, he explains how some experts believe that experiencing the trauma of a parental divorce is second only to death. "Children sense a deep loss and feel they are suddenly vulnerable to forces beyond their control."[249] Rabbi Earl Grollman believes that divorce is *worse* on children than a death. "The big difference is, death has closure; it's over. But with divorce, it's never over."[250] Hart offers some of the more important reasons why he believes divorce is damaging to children:

- It signals the collapse of the family structure--the child feels alone and very frightened. The loneliness can by acute and long remembered.

> **Rabbi Earl Grollman believes that divorce is *worse* on children than a death. "The big difference is, death has closure; it's over. But with divorce, it's never over."**

- Parents have a diminished capacity to parent. They are preoccupied with their own emotions and survival during the critical months (or years) of the divorce.
- The divorce creates conflicts of loyalty in the children. Whose side do they take? Often children feel pulled by love and loyalty in both directions.
- Uncertainty about the future causes deep-seated insecurity. Being dependent mainly on one parent creates a great deal of anxiety.
- The anger and resentment between the parents, which is so prevalent in most divorces, creates intense fear in the child. The younger the child, the more damaging this climate of anger can be.
- The children take upon themselves much anxiety over their parents. They worry intensely about their mother in particular, with the departure of the father (or the mother, in those rarer cases where it is the wife who leaves) being a terrifying event.
- If the family moves, a child may lose an at-home parent, a home, a school, neighborhood, church, and friends. Divorce represents a loss of so many things that a deep depression is almost unavoidable in children. Most parents fail to recognize this depression.[251]

Children who grow up in single-parent or stepparent families are less successful as adults, particularly in the two domains of life--love and work--that are most essential to happiness. Needless to say, not all children experience such negative effects. However, research shows that many children from disrupted families have a harder time achieving intimacy in a relationship, forming a stable marriage, or even holding a steady job.[252]

What is the long-term effect of single-parenting and divorce on the children who suffer through it? For many years, psychologists, therapists and lawyers tried to convince the public that the kids "would get over it." "Children," they said, "bounce back after the initial pain of the breakup of the family." This is proven to be only wishful thinking. The evidence shows that many problems persist even on into adulthood. Barbara Whitehead has produced one of the finest research articles on the long-term effects of divorce and single parenting on children to date. It is all well documented, thorough in its coverage, convincing and a challenge to politically correct assumptions about career, family and parenthood.

> Five years after divorce more than a third of the children experienced moderate or severe depression. At ten years, a significant number of the now young men and women appeared to be troubled, drifting, and under-achieving. At fifteen years, many of the thirtyish adults were struggling to establish strong love relationships of their own. In short, far from recovering from their parent's divorce, a significant percentage of these grownups were still suffering from its effects. In fact, according to Wallerstein, the long-term effects of divorce emerge at a time when young adults are trying to make their own decisions about love, marriage, and family.[253]

This is why it is imperative that positive pastoral counseling be made available to the children and teens and soon as possible following the break-up of the family. The sooner key issues can be worked through, the greater the chances that a teen will be able to go on and mature to a healthy adulthood and be able to establish strong personal relationships.

Encouraging Parents on How to Best Support Their Children Through a Divorce

Most parents want to help their children cope with the trauma of divorce in the best way that they can. However, parents often find themselves limited by their own emotional needs and the demands of keeping up two households. They are struggling with trying to find their own path through this change and don't feel like they have any great answers to offer their children. Plus, they often feel a lot of guilt, especially if they were the one who initiated the divorce. The following is practical advice that you can offer to the parents who want to do the best they can at helping their children navigate the daily problems that arise from the divorce.

Although the stigma of divorce stings less these days, partly because it is so common, children almost never think it is as good an idea as the parents who seek it.

- Become aware of the child's feelings, hurts, changes, etc.
- Be honest. Explain things. Clarify issues. Try to do this without going into unnecessary detail and without malice towards the other spouse.
- Comfort children by word or touch.
- Encourage the children. They need positive input liberally.
- Don't reveal all your emotions. Don't dump everything on your children and create a role reversal.
- Don't destroy the other parent. Speak the truth when necessary, but do not give more details than necessary and avoid slander.
- Allow children time to heal. One to two years.
- Keep the faith. Don't blame God for your divorce or quit attending church services and activities.
- Measure responsibility and keep discipline consistent
- Advice from divorced children to children who are going through it.
  1. Try to make the best of the situation, stay positive and hopeful.
  2. Share your feelings honestly with a close friend, preacher.
  3. Don't take your anger and hurt out on your parents.
  4. Don't blame one parent for the divorce.
  5. Learn to accept the fact that they will probably not get back together again.

Although the stigma of divorce stings less these days, partly because it is so common, children almost never think it is as good an idea as the parents who seek it. Don't insult them by trying to talk them into agreeing with your point of view about its benefits or its hazards. Children, especially the young ones, <u>love</u> having their families together and often feel anxious, angry and saddened when they begin to come apart.[254]

What Can the Church Do to Minister to Children of Divorce?

The apostle Paul wrote in 1 Corinthians 12:12-26 that as Christians we are all part of the body of Christ and if one part of the body hurts, then the whole body hurts. We have an obligation to minister to one another and to lift one another up in times of need. This is especially true concerning the trauma of divorce.

First of all, the church must be proactive. "The church must clearly and unhesitantly teach the biblical condemnation of easy divorce as the moral equivalent of adultery. But it must also learn to forgive and to minister to the fallen."[255] Caution needs to be taken to ensure that the church's position of condemnation for divorce does not get transferred to a condemnation of the children of divorce. Sometimes the welcome mat is subtly removed. If the children of divorce do not find acceptance and support in the body of Christ, they will seek it elsewhere.

The church needs to be aware of and consider the needs of those families within the congregation that are not "traditional families." Scholarships for church camp and other youth conferences should be made available to those of less economic means. This also helps the children of divorce to not have to feel "left out" or angry at the custodial parent because there isn't enough money to allow them to participate in the programs that their peers are involved in.

> "A number of studies on the effects of trauma on children indicate that the presence of one caring, supportive adult in the life of a traumatized child can make a huge difference in decreasing the impact of the trauma."

Intact families should invite the children and parent of a divorced family into their home to share quality time with them. Give them the much-needed emotional support. Be especially sensitive to significant times like holidays when the separation is keenly felt. Include single families in special activities such as picnics, camping, ball games, holidays.

Have men and women in the church look for children in single parent families who need a significant male or female role model. Invite them to spend time that allows for a significant relationship to develop. The time does not have to be spent in formal teaching or training. Nor does it have to be doing activities that are expensive. Just working together on a home project, fishing or attending a local ball game allows for significant life to life transference to take place. This can help fill the gaps that an absent parent has left. "A number of studies on the effects of trauma on children indicate that the presence of one caring, supportive adult in the life of a traumatized child can make a huge difference in decreasing the impact of the trauma."[256]

Above all, simply be a good listener. Single parents and children of divorce need to share frustrations, anger, fears, hopes, and victories. The church needs to be a safe place where grace is offered to all as a healing balm. From a very practical standpoint, offering regular "Divorce Recovery" seminars and singles support groups will go a long way in helping those who struggle with divorce recover.

While the church should be a place of healing for all, sadly it has not lived up to its calling with the issue of divorce and ministering to the children of divorce. In a survey of children who experienced a divorce only 8% said that someone in the church was helpful to them while the divorce was occurring. But, 60% wished that the church would have helped or expressed anger toward the church leaders and members who did not know how to help or just chose not to.

As a youth pastor or youth leader, it is your responsibility to help kids realize that it's not God's fault that their parents decided to get a divorce. Rather, it is God's desire that all marriages remain firm and together; it's man's sinful nature that causes the breakups. Also, you must be sure to let the child or teen know that they are in no way responsible or to blame for the parent's divorce.

While the church can provide a supportive environment for healing, most families will still benefit from professional counseling as well. "Parents should not assume an easy adjustment and acceptance of the divorce by their children, even when no emotional or behavioral problems are evident."[257]

> It is imperative to refer teenagers for professional help if their responses to family changes begin to interfere with school, social relationships, or behavior. Statistics on children of divorce suggest that increased behavioral and emotional problems are common. The importance of counseling increases proportionately to the degree of ongoing conflict between divorcing parents, since conflict with interfere with cooperative parenting and with parental support of children through the divorce process.[258]

Overview of the Counseling Process for Teens Whose Parents Are Divorcing

Connect with the Teen
- They may call you and ask for help--if so, set up a meeting giving them instructions on location, time and length of session.
- You may hear from the parents or their peers about the impending divorce—if so, take pastoral initiative and go to them or call and set up a meeting.
- Prepare your meeting place and yourself by reviewing how to deal with the break-up of the family. Don't forget to pray and ask the Holy Spirit for guidance and insight!

Understand the Teen
- Communicate empathy by your posture, position and active listening skills.
- Communicate nonjudgmental, unconditional love and genuineness.
- Ask yourself the empathy question: "How would I feel if I was this student in this situation?"
- Understand the concerns and fears of a child or teen whose parents are divorcing. Encourage them to express these fears and concerns.
- Understand how divorce affects children and teens in different ways at the different ages.

Explore with the Teen
- Help the child and teen to understand that the divorce is *not* their fault.
- Encourage them to express their anger, fears and frustrations.
- Help them to see that they are only responsible for their own choices. They cannot make choices for their parents.
- Encourage them to be respectful of their parents, even if they do not agree with their decision to divorce.

Initiate a Plan with the Teen
- Help them to cope and adjust to a two-home situation with new rules, etc.
- Eventually they may have to adjust to a blended family situation with step-brothers and step-sisters. Prepare them for this possibility.

Finish with the Teen
- Refer the teen to a professional Christian counselor if warranted.
- Support the teen with your continued presence and availability.
- Provide information about divorce support groups for children and teens.

Helpful Resources

Barbara Dafoe Whitehead. "Dan Quayle Was Right." *The Atlantic Monthly*, April 1993, pp. 47-84.

Divorce Magazine.com. "Children and Divorce." Accessed: January 6, 2017. http://www.divorcemag.com/articles?category=children-and-divorce

DivorceCare for Kids. DC4K. Accessed: January 6, 2017. https://www.dc4k.org/

Judith S. Wallerstein. "Children After Divorce." *The New York Times*, January 22, 1989. Accessed: January 6, 2017. http://www.nytimes.com/1989/01/22/magazine/children-after-divorce.html?pagewanted=all

Selected Bibliography

Hart. Archibald D. *Children & Divorce: What to Expect. How to Help*. Waco, TX: Word Books, 1982.

Nystrom, Carolyn. *Mike's Lonely Summer: A Child's Guide Through Divorce*. Belleville, MI: Lion Publishing, 1986.

Teyber, Edward. *Helping Your Children With Divorce: A Compassionate Guide for Parents*. New York, NY: Pocket Books, 1985.

Exercise 12.1 - Understanding the Trauma of Divorce on Children and Teens

Rate yourself on your knowledge and understanding the trauma of divorce on children and teens. Use the scale provided: 1 = poor; 2 = below average; 3 = Average; 4 = Above average; 5 = Excellent. Simply check the box that best describes you. Be honest with yourself. Work on the areas that need improvement—it's not an assignment, it's a life that you might save!

Understanding the Trauma of Divorce	1	2	3	4	5
I am knowledgeable with the percent of marriages that end in divorce for first, second and third marriages.					
I am familiar with the main concerns and questions that children have concerning divorce.					
I understand that whether a child seems resilient or not, a divorce will have some damaging effect on him or her.					
I am familiar with the divorce grief cycle and can confidently walk a young person through it.					
I understand the different ways that divorce affects a child or teen at the various developmental stages.					
I understand the serious long-term effects that divorce can have on a child and therefore, the need for counseling as soon as possible.					
I am familiar with the various ways that parents can help their children best navigate the changes that divorce brings to their lives.					
I know what the church can do to support families who are experiencing the pain of divorce.					

CHAPTER THIRTEEN

SAME-SEX ATTRACTION

Few topics trigger more emotional reaction and controversy today than homosexuality. The issue ignites heated debates in virtually every aspect of society: schools, local elections, the military, the courts, sports, science, professional societies, the entertainment world, business and industry, the media, and especially the church.[259] –Les Parrott III

If the same-sex struggler feeds on the petty, miserable, dark same-sex identity, desire, and sin, there will be no change. But if he sees Jesus— spends time with him, falls in love with him, and learns from him— transformation will most certainly happen. . . This does not mean that a same-sex struggler will no longer have same-sex feelings; it means that those feelings will get swallowed up in the greater affection he has for God.[260] –Adam T. Barr and Ron Citlau

A Case Study

From childhood Bryan felt different from other boys. He would get teased on the playground and called "sissy." He was told that he ran and threw the ball like a girl. He was frequently bullied by the other boys in his school and began avoiding them as much as possible, hanging out with the girls.

In high school, Bryan tried out for the school musical and finally felt like he had found a place to fit in. He began hanging out with the other students in theater and found that many of them had similar stories of rejection so they all began to hang out and support one another. When Steve told Bryan that he was sexually attracted to other boys the two of them were soon involved in a homosexual relationship. This was very confusing for Bryan because he craved the attention and affection that he received, but he also felt guilty about the sexual involvement.

Bryan had been raised in the church and had heard the sermons and Sunday School lessons on how much God hated homosexuals. He had prayed earnestly over the years for God to take away his feelings for other boys. But no matter how hard he prayed, those feelings were still there. He wondered why God would make him this way, only to condemn him. Eventually he heard that there were churches that welcomed gays and lesbians and taught that homosexuality was not condemned by God. Yet, when he read his Bible, it seemed clear to him that God did not approve of homosexuality.

Desperate for help, Bryan sought out a Christian counselor who was skilled in working with those who struggle with same-sex attractions. The counselor told Bryan that their work together would result in one of three things: 1) Bryan would experience a significant reduction in his same-sex attractions and eventually feel greater heterosexual attraction; 2) Bryan would find his same-sex attraction reduced in intensity, but not necessarily experience heterosexual attraction; or 3) he would not find his same-sex attraction significantly reduced and not feel any heterosexual attraction. In which case, he would learn how to live celibately.

Stanton Jones, provost and professor psychology at Wheaton College, conducted a study of people seeking change in sexual orientation. The span of the study was six to seven years. His results showed:

> Of the 61 subjects, 53 percent were categorized as successful outcomes . . . Specifically, 23 percent of the subjects reported success in the form of "conversion" to heterosexual orientation and functioning, while an additional 30 percent reported stable behavioral chastity with substantive disidentification with homosexual orientation. On the other hand, 20 percent of the subjects reported giving up on the change process and fully embracing gay identity.[261]

Statistics

Homosexuality is not nearly as widely practiced as once believed. The Kinsey report of the 1950's claimed that 10% of the population was homosexual. Several new studies have shown that figure to be greatly inflated. A study conducted by the French scientific community revealed that only 1.1% of the males surveyed and only .3% of the females surveyed reported homosexual relationships within the past 12 months.[262] In a survey of 3,321 men by the Alan Guttmacher Institute it was found that only 2.3% of U.S. men ages 20-39 say they have had same-sex experiences in the past 10 years. Only 1.1% indicate that they are exclusively gay.[263] "In the first large-scale government survey measuring Americans' sexual orientation, the National Health Interview Survey reported in July 2014 that 1.6 percent of Americans identify as gay or lesbian, and 0.7 percent identify as bisexual."[264]

> Several other surveys, governmental and non-governmental, have over the years measured sexual

orientation, but the largest such study by far has been the Gallup Daily tracking measure instituted in June 2012. In this ongoing study, respondents are asked "Do you, personally, identify as lesbian, gay, bisexual or transgender?" with 3.8% being the most recent result, obtained from more than 58,000 interviews conducted in the first four months of this year.[265]

While the percentages will vary slightly depending upon the survey, it is now proven that Kinsey greatly exaggerated the percentage of the population that was homosexual. And yet, the average American estimates that 23%-25% of the population is gay or lesbian![266] Why the discrepancy? It is largely a sign of the success of the militant LGBTQ push for gay rights and acceptance in society and

> **The National Health Interview Survey reported in July 2014 that 1.6 percent of Americans identify as gay or lesbian, and 0.7 percent identify as bisexual.**

the media's portrayal of gays and lesbians through popular sitcoms and dramas.

The percent of the population that struggles with same-sex attraction may not be as large as popularly portrayed by the media or political groups, but that doesn't make the issue any less important to the young man or women in your youth group who is in desperate need of counsel because of their fears and confusion.

Homosexuality and The Bible

Students who struggle with same-sex attraction will google the topic and search the web for answers to their questions. Unfortunately, many do not have the discernment or tools to know when an argument is factually true or not. This is especially the case when it comes to searching what the Bible says about homosexuality. There are many sites that apply post-modern hermeneutics or simply ignore good exegetical process to determine the author's intended meaning. The Christian counselor or youth pastor must be familiar with what the Bible actually teaches on the subject in order to respond to the student's questions or errant beliefs. I would highly recommend Kevin DeYoung's book, *What Does the Bible Really Teach About Homosexuality?* and *Homosexuality and the Christian* by Mark A. Yarhouse for those who would like a more detailed response.

Genesis 1-3 - One must consider the "norm" before looking at "deviation." When considering the issue of homosexuality, it is important that one does not limit himself to *only studying* the passages that specifically mention homosexuality. If one does that, he fails to take into account the broader view of sexuality as God created it. As Tim Stafford said in an article entitled "Issue of the Year" in *Christianity Today*: "To look only at passages that deal with deviant behavior and to neglect those passages which set the norm. . . is a little like writing a theology of stealing without mentioning the principle of honesty."[267]

> **When considering the issue of homosexuality, one must consider the "norm" before looking at "deviation."**

The first passage dealing with the issue of homosexuality must be Genesis 1-3. Here it is seen that sexuality is the direct result of God's creative work. He created woman to meet the physical, psychological, and spiritual needs of the first man. The ability to reproduce is built into this relationship. Since homosexuality cannot reproduce it leads one to suspect that this inability is a result of an improper ground. Man is designed to live together as male and female, nothing else fulfills God's will. That is why it is Adam and Eve, and not Adam and Steve.

Genesis 19 and Judges 19 - In the deliverance of Lot from Sodom and Gomorrah, the Bible says in Genesis 19:4-5: "Before they had gone to bed, all the men from every part of the city of Sodom, both young and old, surrounded the house. They called to Lot, 'Where are the men who came to you tonight? Bring them out to us so that we can have sex with them.'" NIV

Lot resists their request and offers his two virgin daughters instead. The angels of God intervene to save Lot and his family and lead them out of the city as God's destruction falls upon the people.

Advocates of homosexuality will try to rationalize this event away. One explanation that is offered is to refer to Ezekiel 16:49-50 which reads: "Now this was the sin of your sister Sodom: She and her daughters were arrogant, overfed and unconcerned; they did not help the poor and needy. They were haughty and did detestable things before me. Therefore, I did away with them as you have seen." NIV

They will also refer to Isaiah 1:9-10 and 3:9 and connect it with blatant indulgence in all kinds of iniquity and also Jeremiah 23:14 with lying and adultery in conjunction with the sins of Ezekiel. Gay advocates argue from these passages that Sodom was not condemned for its homosexuality but for its pride, inhospitality and neglect and abuse of the poor.

But rather than negate the condemnation of homosexuality in the Genesis passage, these other verses go to show that sexual sins are only part of a larger pattern of sin and corruption in the pagan world. Sodom was not destroyed *just because* it specialized in homosexuality, but because it was a plague center of *every kind of depravity*. The Genesis passage certainly makes it clear that homosexuality was one aspect of moral depravity that was condemned by God.

In 1955, D. S. Bailey, in his book, *Homosexuality and the Western Tradition*, put forth the argument that the crime of the men of Sodom was *not* homosexuality, but *inhospitality*. He argued that the Hebrew word <u>yadha</u>, translated "to know," is rarely used in the sexual sense in the Bible and in only 10 of its 943 uses does it have a sense of carnal knowledge.

But any beginning student in hermeneutics knows that you cannot take frequency of usage over and above context. Certainly, in Genesis 4:1 Adam had more of a relationship that just making Eve's acquaintance, because Cain was the direct result of that "knowing." For centuries, this usage of the word in this passage (Gen 19:5) was understood to mean homosexual relations.[268]

Also, if it was only inhospitality, why did Lot offer his virgin daughters? That would not have satisfied any "hospitality" requests.

Even those who are gay advocates will admit that the passage must be taken in a sexual sense. But they will argue from three different standpoints. In the first, they refer to Jude 6 and 7 and argue that it was not the condemnation of homosexuality among men that was condemned, but the fact that men were going to be intimate with angels, thus they interpret the phrase "strange flesh," in the KJV.

The second way they will rationalize it away is to say that it is only condemning homosexual rape, and not homosexual practice per se. Any kind of rape, homosexual or heterosexual should be condemned, but not acts among consenting couples.

The third way they attempt to rationalize away the text is to say that this was dealing with homosexual perverts, or bisexuals and not true homosexual inverts. They appeal to the fact that Lot offered them his daughters. A true homosexual invert would not be interested at all in such an offer. These were condemned because they went against their "natural order," not like those who are homosexual in orientation. This interpretation is based upon the questionable and unproven theory of constitutional makeup. The Bible makes no such distinctions, and clearly condemns all acts of homosexuality.

The incident at Gibeah has many similarities with the account of Sodom and Gomorrah. A man and his concubine are shown hospitality as they travel through a town and in the evening the men of the city demand to have the man turned over to them. Judges 19:22 reads: ". . . Bring out the man who came to your house so we can have sex with him." NIV The Hebrew word *yadha* is used in this passage just as it was in Genesis 19 and it is the same word that is used in verse 25 which describes the rape of the man's concubine. As with the account of Sodom, the main thrust of this passage has to do with homosexual rape. The one added piece of information here is that these men were very capable of having heterosexual relations because they ravished the man's concubine. This shows that these men were capable of heterosexual sex and were only homosexual by choice. This has to weigh as evidence against the constitutional theory of homosexuality in which the homosexual is only supposed to be able to relate to the same sex and is supposed to be incapable of heterosexual relations.

Leviticus 18:22 and 20:13 - These are two verses which specifically condemn homosexual relations. It is important to note that this condemnation of homosexuality comes in the context of defining what is the sexual norm and what it not.

The homosexual community tries to do away with these verses in several ways. First, they try to say that this is in Leviticus, and that it was meant only for Priests. The purpose was to keep them from becoming idolatrous and participating in other religions, since homosexuality was a large part of cultic Canaanite worship. The fault with that interpretation is that it says specifically in 18:1-2 "The Lord said to Moses, Speak to the Israelites and say to them. . ." Notice that this passage is addressed to the *whole nation.*

Others will admit that it was indeed directed to the whole nation, but its main purpose was still the same, to keep them from participating in other religions. In other words, if they could practice homosexuality in a loving and caring way and not go after other religions, then it would be acceptable. But that logic would mean that you could do any of the other things in the same context. Bestiality, incest, and adultery would be acceptable as long as it didn't cause one to worship other gods.

The final way the homosexual community will try to negate the force of this passage is to say that it is a part of the Law that is done away with--the old covenant. They will point to the fact that we eat shellfish which is forbidden in the same code and do not have any qualms about that activity. The answer is that while it is true we are no longer under the old covenant as a means of salvation, the ethical standards of God never change, especially when the same standards for sexuality are reiterated in the New Testament.

While it is true that Jesus never mentioned homosexuality as a sin, he never spoke in favor of it either and when he did speak on human sexuality, he always presupposed heterosexuality.

The Gospels – The Gospels are basically a reaffirmation of Genesis 1-3. Advocates of homosexuality take great delight in pointing out that Jesus never mentioned homosexuality as a sin. From his silence on the subject, they argue that he was not condemning of the practice. The fault with this argument is that it draws too much from silence. While it is true that Jesus never mentioned homosexuality as a sin, he never spoke in favor of it either and when he did speak on human sexuality, he always presupposed heterosexuality (See: Matt 5:27-28; 19:4-6) as the norm, going back to the creation accounts and stressing God's original intentions for sexuality.

The only alternative which Jesus offers to marriage is celibacy, making oneself a "eunuch" for the kingdom of heaven (Matt 19:12). Furthermore, he probably never spoke on the issue of homosexuality because it was not a major problem for Palestinian Jews who followed the Old Testament commandments and standards and who distanced themselves from Hellenistic culture.

Also, there are many other subjects Jesus did not mention (incest, rape, bestiality, S & M), but that doesn't mean they are permissible! Jesus always upheld the Old Testament law (Matt 5:17-19) which strictly condemned homosexuality and other deviant sexual expression. Jesus spoke of legitimate sexuality only in a heterosexual context, affirming celibacy as the only legitimate alternative to marriage (Matt 19:12).

Romans 1:26-27 - Romans 1:26-27 is the only place in the Bible where both homosexuality and lesbianism are condemned together. Again, the basis of the judgment is that it goes against the created order.

Homosexual advocates will try and say that this is only condemning homosexual promiscuity and that only in heterosexual people who are simply looking for a sexual thrill and not those who are constitutionally homosexual. They claim that if they were "made that way" then it would be a violation of what Paul had written for them to engage in heterosexual relations because it would be for them "unnatural."

> **For Paul, orientation or natural desire would have no bearing on his condemnation of homosexuality.**

For Paul, orientation or natural desire would have no bearing on his condemnation of homosexuality. "Homosexual behavior is a sin, not according to who practices it or by what motivation they seek it, but because that act itself, as a truth-suppressing exchange, is contrary to God's good design."[269]

I Corinthians 6:9-11 - This passage contains two different Greek words which are translated in the NIV as "male prostitutes nor homosexual offenders." The two Greek words are *malakos* and *arsenokoites*. These are very significant words in that they describe both the passive and active partners in homosexual acts. Thayer defines *malakos* as "effeminate, of a catamite, a male who submits his body to unnatural lewdness."[270] *Arsenokoites* is defined by Bauer, Arndt and Gingrich as "a male who practices homosexuality, pederast, sodomite."[271] Don't miss the hope found in this passage; "and such *were* some of you." Paul knew that people could choose to change by the transforming power and forgiveness of Jesus Christ.

I Timothy 1:9-10 - These words were used consistently by Greek authors to apply to the full spectrum of homosexuality, both promiscuous and monogamous. Only by the wildest rationalization can you avoid the conclusion that Paul knew exactly what he meant and how he would be understood when he used and condemned these two words.

> "God does not alter His message to fit the culture. It is the same in every culture. He calls his people to live in contrast to the culture."

From the Old Testament to the New the scriptures are unanimous in condemning acts of homosexuality. Heterosexuality is the created norm and deviation from that is always condemned. When man fell, his entire being, including his sexuality, was affected. Homosexuality is the result of a fallen world. "God does not alter His message to fit the culture. It is the same in every culture. He calls his people to live in contrast to the culture."[272]

When attempts at reinterpreting or twisting the text fail, what do you do? You create a new hermeneutic. The July 1991 issue of *Sojourners* carried an article entitled "A Love That Won't Let Go" written by Melanie Morrison. This article is especially significant because Ms. Morrison at one time was a contributing editor of *Sojourners* but asked to have her name removed two years previous to this article because she was offended by an article written by Richard Foster against homosexuality. This proved to be a turning point in her life as she also decided to come out of the closet at this time and take an open stand in favor of homosexuality. In this article, she details her pilgrimage. Listen for key thoughts and concepts which make up her hermeneutic. She writes:

> It feels particularly appropriate that I should be writing this article during Holy Week, because coming out of the closet has been a resurrection experience. Every time the stone of fear is rolled away, and I can step out of the shadows of invisibility and silence into the light of daring to be seen and known and heard as a lesbian, I know once again in my bones that resurrection is real. . . No amount

of teaching, preaching, or theologizing will convince (me) of the reality of resurrection unless (I) have walked into the valley of the shadow of death and experienced a presence that did not let (me) go.[273]

Did you catch the focus of her hermeneutic? It was "feelings" and "experience." These over and above, preaching, teaching or exegeting scripture. This hermeneutic was developed because she couldn't make scripture say what she wanted it to say. Listen again to her words as she tells of her Seminary experience at Gordon-Conwell.

I studied every Pauline passage in depth, wanting to believe that Paul was being misinterpreted by these students. While I believe there was some misinterpretation, I also concluded that I could not make Paul say everything I wanted him to say. . . Having come to this conclusion, I lost neither my fervor for biblical study nor my love of scripture. I was, however, both forced and freed to adopt a new hermeneutic. With a feminist hermeneutic, I did not stop with the question, What does the Bible say about women? but moved on to ask, What do women have to tell us about the Bible? . . . I came to similar conclusions with regard to homosexuality and the Bible.[274]

Do you hear what she is saying? When the clear message of scripture doesn't agree with what I feel and what I experience, rather than change my feelings and experience to come into line with scripture, I reinterpret scripture through the authority of my feelings and experience. That is the bottom line. What is going to constitute authority? Is scripture going to be allowed to speak for itself authoritatively or will feelings and experience take the position of primacy?

The Homosexual and The Behavioral Sciences

In 1974, the American Psychiatric Association removed homosexuality from its approved list of pathological psychiatric conditions. *The Diagnostical and Statistical Manual III of Mental Disorders*, commonly known as DSM III, was rewritten to state that "Homosexuality that is egosytonic is not classified as a mental disorder." Homosexuality was only seen as a mental disorder when the person was subjectively distressed by his or her homosexual impulses and strongly desired a heterosexual orientation.

This move was probably the single most powerful decision in making homosexuality an "acceptable alternative lifestyle" in the eyes of the world. "The "experts" no longer consider us sick, just different," said the proponents of Gay Rights.

Some little-known facts about the decision may change the way that one regards its validity and its power. First of all, while the deletion of homosexuality from DSM III did take place in response to a majority vote of the APA, later studies showed that *the majority of the APA membership viewed homosexuality as pathological, in spite of the vote!* Four years after the vote, a survey found that 69% of psychiatrists believed that homosexuality "usually represents a pathological adaptation."[275]

Further investigation showed that the vote was taken under political pressure and under explicit threats from the gay rights establishment to continue disruptive demonstrations at APA conventions if the vote didn't pass.

Even at the very convention where the vote was taken, a large voice of protest went up from specialists in the field of homosexuality. These protests resulted in a referendum vote by the entire APA body. Shortly before the ballots were due, a letter was sent out by the officers of the APA urging the members to let the decision stand. Later it was learned that the letter was paid for by the National Gay Task Force.[276]

Even from a purely humanistic standpoint, this decision loses validity when it is learned that the very people who passed the vote, did not really believe in the vote themselves. It appears that the change took place because of political pressure from Gay Rights groups and not because of any discoveries or new theories about homosexuality from within the group of researchers and counselors themselves.[277]

Constitutional Theory--"I was born this way" "I can't help the way I feel." "God made me this way." There are several ways that researchers have suggested that one is "made" homosexual.

Dr. Franz J. Kallman of Columbia University did a study of homosexuality among twins. He studied 63 homosexual men, each with a twin brother. Of these 63 pairs of brothers, 26 pairs were genetically different, while 37 pairs were genetically identical. His studies showed that of the 26 twins who were genetically different, there seemed to be no unusual amount of homosexuality among them. But, in the 37 pairs of identical twins, 100% of them had a homosexual experience, with 28% being exclusively homosexual. He concluded that the cause of homosexuality was genetic.

Kallman's theory seemed sound, but his conclusions were soon discounted by doctors and scientists for the following reasons: 1) Others who worked with homosexuals in clinical research reported *many* cases of identical twins where one was exclusively heterosexual and the other exclusively homosexual; 2) The results of Kallman's study have never been able to be duplicated. (Indication of faulty research or purposeful manipulation of the facts); 3) Kallman could not prove that the fathers and/or other relatives of the identical twins were homosexual, which would have to have been the case if a conclusive genetic cause existed; and 4) All of the twins studied were raised in the same home, and therefore he could not rule out the influence of mother/father relationships or other external factors.[278]

> While demonstrating that homosexuality is familial (occurs more frequently in families) is no proof that genetics alone play a role in such behavior, it does suggest the possibility of genetic influences. In the study with men, homosexuals had a higher incidence of homosexual brothers (22%) than did heterosexual men (4%). In like manner, the study with women reported that homosexual subjects had a significantly higher proportion of homosexual sisters (34%) than did heterosexual subjects (13.8%). Why the figures for both homosexual and heterosexual females are larger than those for their male counterparts is not clear.[279]

Genetics — A DNA transplant in fruit flies was undertaken by biologists Ward Odenwald and Shang-Ding Zhang at the National Institutes of Health in Bethesda, Maryland. They transplanted a single gene into male fruit flies that caused them to display homosexual behavior.

> In some experiments, the female flies are cowering in groups at the top and bottom of the jars. The males, meanwhile, are having a party--no, an orgy--among themselves. With a frenzy usually reserved for chasing females, the males link up end-to-end in big circles or in long, winding rows that look like winged conga lines. As the buzz of the characteristic fruit fly "love song" fills the air, the males repeatedly lurch forward and rub genitals with the next ones in line.[280]

They said the findings were significant because a related gene exists in human beings, although there is no evidence yet that the human gene has an effect on sexual preference.

> Odenwald and Zhang do not pretend to have any easy answers. In fact, the type of gene they've been studying in fruit flies could not begin to account for the complex variations in human homosexual behavior. For one thing, the gene does not cause flies to renounce heterosexuality altogether. If a "gay" fly is surrounded by females instead of males, he'll fertilize the lady flies. So strictly speaking, the genetically altered flies are not homosexual but bisexual. And the gene produces no unusual behavior when transplanted into females: the scientists have produced no lesbian fruit flies.[281]

To complicate the issue, Odenwald and Zhang found that some of their results actually pointed to the environment in addition to genetics as influencing sexual behavior. In one experiment, a small group of "straight" flies was mixed with a larger group of genetically altered "gay" flies. While the gays formed their conga lines, the straights stayed to the side, but only temporarily. After a few hours, the straights joined in and, for the time being, acted gay. They had to conclude that in fruit flies, and certainly in humans, sexual orientation is just not a simple matter.[282]

The research of Odenwald and Zhang finds mixed support in the gay community. On the one hand, gays and lesbians have always believed they were "born that way" and welcome any kind of scientific verification because then they could more easily convince the world that they must be accepted and they deserve legal protection with laws similar to those that prohibit racial discrimination.

> **Many gays are wary of the genetic hypothesis. They fear that the rest of the world will interpret homosexuality as a "defect" in need of "fixing."**

On the other hand, many gays are wary of the genetic hypothesis. They fear that the rest of the world will interpret homosexuality as a "defect" in need of "fixing." They do not want to see these results as justification to come up with some kind of reparative therapy to correct that genetic defect.

Hormone imbalance due to improper endocrine functioning - Another suggestion that was raised early in the research is that homosexuality is the result of a hormone imbalance due to improper endocrine functioning. Male homosexuals were thought to be endowed with too much estrogen (female sex hormone) and too little androgens (male sex hormones). It was thought that this imbalance tended to make the person be sexually drawn toward members of the same sex.

However, the research showed that there were many cases of men with a severe imbalance who had normal, active sex lives and who were totally heterosexual, while homosexuals proved to have a perfectly normal hormonal balance. Also, injections of female sex hormones into normal men did not bring about an attraction to other men, neither did injections of male sex hormones cure anyone of their homosexual desire.[283]

Prenatal hormonal factors - The most recent theory dealing with hormonal factors has to do with prenatal hormonal factors. Studies introducing abnormal hormone levels into animal fetuses have shown that prenatal hormones do affect sexual differentiation and erotic development in animals. An abnormal dose of sex hormones given to an animal fetus at a critical time can result in that animal showing sexually inverted behavior when mature, including homosexual erotic preferences.

Several considerations should be taken into account concerning these prenatal hormonal tests in animals. First of all, what you can do with an animal in a laboratory does not denote conclusive evidence that it causes human homosexual orientation. Secondly, if it did, then it would make homosexual orientation the result of an *abnormal* maternal hormonal environment, which would make homosexuality *abnormal* in itself, a kind of "birth-defect" which should be treated in the same way that you handle all other birth-defects. You try to find a cure. Thirdly, other researchers have concluded that there is no human evidence that prenatal hormonalization *alone*, independently of postnatal history, inexorably preordains one to a homosexual orientation.[284]

Size of hypothalamus - In the September 9, 1991 issue of *Time* an article appeared which focused on a new theory concerning homosexual origins. In this article, the research of Simon LeVay on the brains of homosexual men, suggested that the interstitial nuclei of the anterior hypothalamus was different in homosexual men implying that it was the cause of homosexual desire.

But there are several objections to this research. First of all, the sample was small. He only studied 41 brains in all. Of those, only 19 were known homosexuals. Secondly, all 19 of the homosexual men had died from AIDS and so had six of the 16 presumed heterosexual men and one of the six women. Since the AIDS virus does attack the brain, there is no way of knowing the extent to which the AIDS virus may have contributed to the difference in size.

It is also questionable whether the portion of the hypothalamus LeVay studied (the INAH 3) can be accurately measured. It is smaller than a snowflake, and scientists are not in agreement as to how its size should be determined. According to *Newsweek*, "Measuring brain structures is notoriously difficult and controversial-neuroscientists cannot agree on whether the most meaningful gauge is the volume of the region (LeVay's method) or its number of neurons."[285]

Also, LeVay has admitted to being a homosexual. This causes one to wonder exactly how neutral and unbiased is his research. "It is also possible that the difference actually has nothing to do with sexual orientation or that it is the result rather than the cause of homosexuality."[286]

Even if a neuroanatomical, biochemical, or genetic basis for a behavior is found, it does not make that behavior normal or societally acceptable. Though heterosexual behavior is shaped by biology, not all expressions of the heterosexual urge are acceptable in civilized society. Though aggressive behaviors have known biological foundations, society sets limits on how aggression may be expressed.

> Even if a neuroanatomical, biochemical, genetic basis for a behavior is found, it does not make that behavior normal or societally acceptable.

Dysfunctional parent-child relationships – The development of the personality and sexual orientation is a complex process with many issues interacting to bring about the final result. Dysfunctional parent-child relationships occur in many case studies of gays and lesbians, but it is not absolute. There are those who have healthy, supportive relationships with their parents, but still have a homosexual orientation. But for a good number of gays and lesbians the following issues seem to be significant and may contribute to the development of a homosexual orientation.

1. Imprinting at a young and critical age.
2. Specifically raised to dislike members of the opposite sex and love own sex.
3. Unpleasant experiences with members of own sex within the family structure.
4. Raised exclusively with members of the other sex--acquire their tastes and interests.
5. Raised exclusively with members of the same sex and most comfortable with them and uncomfortable in the presence of the opposite sex.
6. Parents of male homosexuals:
   Mother: Dominates, controls, discourages masculine attitudes and activities; favors this son and demands to be the center of his

attention; overly intimate with this son; frequently allies with the son against the father; unduly concerned about the son's health, tends to be overly protective and interfering

Father: Detached; rejecting; unaffectionate; demeaning this son, unavailable, spending little time with this son; favors other children.

7. Parents of lesbians:

Mother: Hostile and competitive with this daughter; defeminized daughter; interferes with an easy, natural relationship between daughter and father; prefers sons to daughters; unaffectionate with daughter.

Father: Detached, rejecting, unaffectionate and unprotective; overly submissive to wife; generally ineffectual.

This suggestion that homosexuality is caused by dysfunctional parent-child relationships is not without its problems. As stated previously, there are cases where there seemed to be a very healthy relationship in the home and between the parents and the children. Also, it is hard to explain why in a family of three boys who had the same father and mother and grew up in the same environment, that only one is homosexual in orientation. This suggested explanation can cause undue heartache and guilt in the parents of a young man or women struggling with their sexual identity.

External factors – Even if the relationships in the immediate family is healthy, if a person has their first satisfying sexual relations with a member of their own sex they may consequently become fixated in homosexual-type relationships.

Not all young males who are seduced by an older male become homosexual. Most will go on to later try heterosexual experiences and become exclusively heterosexual. But in the case of the boy who has had some difficulty in competing for heterosexual favors, his early pleasant homosexual experiences will be an inducement for him to become totally homosexually oriented.

People, especially adolescents, who have had a traumatic or less than satisfying experience with their first heterosexual experience may later retreat to exclusively homosexual relationships because of the bad initial experience.

> The "interaction model" suggests that genes and hormones do not specify sexual orientation per se, but instead result in the development of certain *temperamental* and *personality* traits.

225

Interaction Theory - One interesting twist on the nature of biological predisposing influences on homosexuality is that presented by Byne and Parsons. These authors propose an "interaction model" in which genes and hormones do not specify sexual orientation per se (much as the previously reviewed evidence might suggest), but instead result in the development of certain *temperamental* and *personality* traits. These personality traits and their interactions with the environment, then, result in the unfolding of homosexuality. This model proposes that biological factors influence sexual orientation *indirectly* rather than in a direct manner by which genes and hormones act on the development of a homosexual brain.[287]

The interaction Theory is very closely tied to developmental theory. Normal development takes place at about ages 1 and 2. Kids begin separating from their mothers and begin to understand that they are their own person and begin a healthy separation attachment. Boys detach from the mother and need to attach to the father and begin to develop a masculine identity. What are boys all about? How am I supposed to act, walk, talk, etc. This all takes place at an unconscious level. The father answers these questions by spending time with his son, verbally affirming his son, showing interest in his son and through physical touch, rough play and wrestling.

At age 5-6 the developing boy now looks to peers to answer the same questions that his father previously answered. He needs to be accepted, included and affirmed by his peers. He needs to spend several years bonding with members of his own sex. We cannot become interested in the opposite sex until we understand our own sex.

At puberty, the boy can now begin to be interested in the opposite sex because he now understands his own sex. This is how normal development is supposed to take place.

For males who develop a homosexual orientation, the normal development is somehow derailed. About the age of 1 1/2 to 2 the young boy is not able to separate from his mother and bond with his father. The father is absent somehow. This

> "The exotic becomes the erotic."

can be a real absence or even a perceived absence. Temperament affects perception. The temperament of a child who goes on to have same sex attraction is sensitive, very intelligent, more artistic than athletic. The boy perceives that the father doesn't want to connect with them. Some fathers truly love their sons, but are loud and this scares the sensitive son and causes him to remain with the mother. Fathers sometimes mean well, but unintentionally cause harm by saying things such as: "Quit acting like a baby or a sissy." This causes the young boy to feel rejected because he doesn't measure up. If the boy senses rejection, he will detach from the father and what he represents and attaches to the mother. He has rejected masculinity. He stays connected to the mother and soaks in femininity instead of masculinity. He learns all about girls, but craves to know about masculinity. When this boy starts school, he ends up rejected by his peers because of his feminine traits. So, his needs for same sex connection go unmet. He wishes his peers would accept him, but he is on the outside. By the time he reaches puberty, he knows all about girls and femininity and has no interest to spend more time with girls but wants to learn about boys. He needs emotionally deep, nonsexual relationships with other boys. But what can happen has been described as "The exotic becomes the erotic." As same-sex peers become familiar to the growing child, peers of the opposite sex are commonly deemed dissimilar and exotic. The exotic leads to a heightened level of arousal, which in turn is transformed into sexual attraction.[288]

The development of lesbianism can be more complicated because there can be a number of different factors which become influential developmentally. The girl may grow up being more of a tom-boy but craves femininity. This is very similar to the gay development. The exotic becomes the erotic.

But there could be other issues that affect development as well. There could be a healthy and normal development with the mother, but at a crucial time there was a break in the bonding early on. The result is a void in the girl's life. One could say that lesbianism, in this case, is a search for motherly love.

Another issue that contributes to the development of lesbianism is if there is physical or sexual abuse by a male. The girl learns that being female is not safe. So, she begins to identify with males because it is seen as a place of strength and safety. Femininity is seen as a place of weakness and shame and something to be avoided.

No "authorities" seem to agree upon one certain factor which is *solely responsible* for a person becoming homosexual in orientation.

A lesbian relationship can develop between two females who were heterosexual in orientation and who had no original intention of heading down this path. This is typically seen in college with dorm mates. They spend much time together, sharing secrets, dreams and disappointments. They are in the same study group and become very close. They develop this intense emotional bond which then evolves into a physical relationship.

Conclusion: No "authorities" seem to agree upon one certain factor which is *solely responsible* for a person becoming homosexual in orientation. The theories about the origins of homosexuality are legion. Rather than landing on one theory which explains it all, same-sex attraction seems to be more of a multi-faceted problem with amazing complexities.

> While agreeing that homosexuality is neither genetic nor hormonal in origin, some people still feel it could be constitutional or somehow inborn. To date, there is no conclusive evidence to support this theory. But this does not mean that hereditary physical and/or emotional makeup are unimportant. Some people may be born with a predisposition toward homosexuality. Put simply this means a person may have a tendency to experience a greater sexual attraction toward one's own sex rather than the opposite sex. But this predisposition does not automatically mean a person will become a homosexual. Predisposition is only important in the development of homosexuality if those urges are cultivated and homosexual behavior patterns are developed. If homosexual behavior patterns are not cultivated, the person will not become homosexual regardless of predisposition.[289]

> We do not know the causes of same-sex attractions or homosexual orientation (nor do we know the causes of attraction to the opposite-sex, as such). Most experts today seem to believe that sexual orientation is the result of many possible contributing factors, both from nature (broadly understood) and from nurture (also broadly understood). These factors are likely weighted differently for different people.[290]

Behavior sciences have shown that homosexuals *can* change if they have the desire to change.

> Medically, homosexuality is changeable. Since the advent of psychology, the medical community has consistently reported successful treatment of this problem. Listed here are six doctors who, as part of their psychological or psychiatric practices, have treated homosexuals and written books about changing homosexuality: Dr. Jeffrey Satinover, *Homosexuality and the Politics of Truth* (1996);

Dr. Joseph Nicolosi, *Reparative Therapy of Male Homosexuality* (1991); Dr. Gerard van den Aardweg, *On the Origins and* treatment of Homosexuality: A Psychoanalytic Reinterpretation (1986); Dr. Irving Bieber et al., *Homosexuality: A Psychoanalytic Study of Male Homosexuals (1988); Dr. Ruth Tiffany Barnhouse,* Homosexuality: A Symbolic Confusion (1977); and Dr. Lawrence Hatterer, *Changing* Homosexuality in the Male: Treatment for Men Troubled by Homosexuality (1970). In 1992, the National Association for Research and Therapy of Homosexuality (NARTH) was formed. This group exists to advance the field of treatment for homosexuality.[291]

Even the American Psychological Association (APA) has now come to a position where it recognizes that sexual orientation is not static but is fluid. The APA (2011) officially recognized sexual fluidity or sexual orientation change. Dr. Lisa Diamond, a self-avowed lesbian, is co-editor-in-chief of the *APA Handbook of Sexuality and Psychology* and has written many chapters in the handbook. She is one of the APA's most respected members.

In her *APA Handbook* chapters, her book, and a YouTube lecture, she says sexual orientation does not come in two types—exclusively homosexual and exclusively heterosexual—that are rigid and unchangeable. The battle to disprove "born that way and can't change" is now over, and she is telling LGBT activists to stop promoting the myth.[292]

Counseling Teens Who Struggle with Same-Sex Attraction

Because of our political and social climate, along with the influence of Hollywood and the media, an increasing number of young people who do not believe it is wrong or sinful to engage in homosexual behavior. This includes those who go to church regularly and identify themselves as "Christian." How do you convince them that this behavior

> When debating the "correctness" or the "error" of any behavior or belief one must first decide on what is going to be the basis of authority for determining the truth of the topic in question.

is not acceptable in God's eyes and is not in their best interests to pursue it?

When debating the "correctness" or the "error" of any behavior or belief one must first decide on what is going to be the basis of authority for determining the truth of the topic in question. When debating the issue of same-sex attraction there are basically four different or competing sources of authority: 1) Scripture; 2) Church tradition (both Catholic and Protestant); 3) Science or Reason; and 4) Personal experience. One's conclusions about the acceptability of homosexual behavior is going to be determined by which basis of authority one chooses.

Scripture forms the basis for Christian tradition. A thorough presentation of all the pertinent scriptural passages has already been presented and the overwhelming conclusion is that scripture affirms the marriage of a man and a woman and condemns all homosexual behavior.

When it comes to church tradition there is a lot of variation within the different denominations. Roman Catholicism has historically held that the purpose of marriage includes the good of the spouses as well as the procreation and education of children. "Historically, more emphasis has been placed on procreation; more recently, however, there has been an emphasis on the relationship of husband and wife as a covenant that symbolizes the love Christ has for the church."[293] The Catholic Church does recognize homosexuality as a real sexual orientation, meaning that it is an enduring pattern of sexual and emotional attraction. But, in spite of this view, the Catholic Church holds that same-sex behavior is against natural law and that homosexuality itself goes against God's original design for sex.

A Roman Catholic view takes seriously the fact that same-sex relationships do not allow for procreation or reflect God's plan for marriage. "Therefore, the person who experiences same-sex attraction is called upon to live a chaste life, accepting their same-sex attractions as a personal trial in their walk with God."[294]

Protestant Christianity has for the most part expressed basically the same views on marriage as the Catholic Church but with a decreased emphasis on procreation within marriage in order to take a more companionship-oriented stance. In Protestant Christianity, the primary purpose of marriage is the love and companionship between husband and wife. Having children has become secondary and an outflow of the marriage relationship. Protestant tradition sees sex within the context of marriage as a normal and positive product of humanity's creation as male and female. In other words, sex is good and proper in the context of heterosexuality marriage, but only in that context.

> **Political correctness has shaped many conclusions concerning this issue and it has purposely suppressed any findings that contradict the pro-gay stance.**

A recent departure from this traditional stance on marriage has been seen to develop in some of the "mainline" denominations, i.e. Episcopal, Methodist, and Presbyterian. Some of these denominations have decided to bless same-sex unions. This decision comes out of questioning the authority of Scripture and an embracing of societal mores.

When people cite "reason" as a source of authority, they are typically thinking of scientific advances that have furthered our understanding of homosexuality. Scientific studies concerning homosexuality have usually centered around four issues: 1) the commonness of homosexuality; 2) the causes of homosexuality; 3) whether it is a mental health issue; and 4) whether sexual orientation can change from homosexual to heterosexual.

The bottom line with the scientific studies is that they are often contradictory, poorly understood, overstated and sometimes misused by those who are trying to challenge the church's traditional stance on homosexuality. Political correctness has shaped many conclusions concerning this issue and it has purposely suppressed any findings that contradict the pro-gay stance.

Personal experience is the last source of authority that many people turn to in trying to decide the correctness of homosexual behavior. In our postmodern worldview, personal experience seems to reign supreme. No one has the right to question another's experience. Many of those who experience same-sex attraction have then made this their primary "identity." Thus, I am gay or lesbian because my sexual orientation is my identity.

While all truths and equally true, not all truths are equally important. One must decide which of the sources of truth or authority is going to have the most "weight" when deciding the appropriateness of homosexual behavior.

> **While all truths and equally true, not all truths are equally important.**

For most evangelicals and Christians, scripture and church tradition trumps science and personal experience. However, there are those individuals who will say that their personal experience is the most important consideration and will, therefore, form their identity and beliefs about homosexuality from it.

Unfortunately, the gay community has convinced many people in society, and especially those who struggle with same-sex attraction, that one's sexual orientation is the equivalent to one's identity. Dr. Mark

Yarhouse makes a good case for arguing that same-sex attraction is *not* identical to one's identity. Yarhouse suggests that there should be a three-tiered distinction made between same-sex attraction, a homosexual orientation, and a gay identity. Same-sex attraction refers to sexual/emotional preferences for the same sex. Orientation describes the enduring pattern of sexual and emotional attraction experienced by a person. Orientation is basically the same as attraction only it has persisted over a longer period of time, and the feelings have not diminished at all, and in fact, may have grown stronger. A gay identity is a contemporary phenomenon, a self-defining attribution ("I am gay."), and it often collapses the three tiers, treating attractions as synonymous with identity.[295]

> **Your job as a counselor is to help the young person who is experiencing same-sex attraction to realize that one's sexual orientation does NOT have to determine their identity.**

Yarhouse presents the view that one's same-sex attraction is only one part of person's total identity. Identity is made up of a number of key issues such as: race, gender, gifts and talents, religious beliefs and commitments, nationality, childhood experiences, body type and sexuality. Since all the pieces of the pie cannot be equal, something must dominate and determine one's overall identity. For some Christians who struggle with same-sex attraction their sexuality is subordinate to their commitment to the authority of scripture and their identity as a Christian. Others will say that their same-sex attraction is the dominating issue and will thus have to find a way to bring scripture and church tradition into this choice. These are the ones who work at creative interpretive schemes that go against the historical-critical method of interpreting scripture and thousands of years of church tradition.

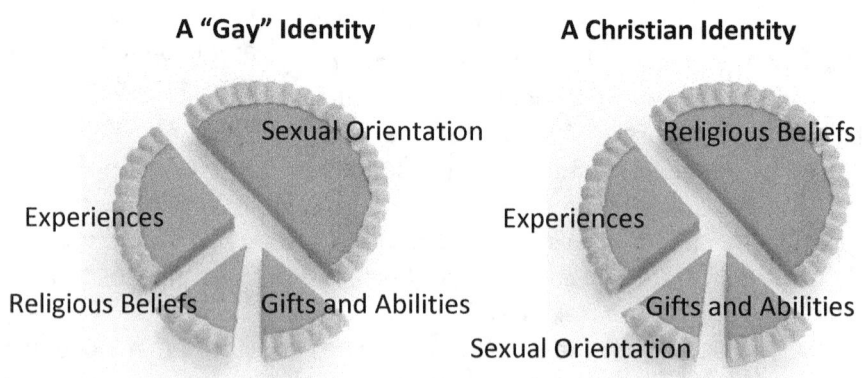

A "Gay" Identity — Sexual Orientation, Experiences, Religious Beliefs, Gifts and Abilities

A Christian Identity — Religious Beliefs, Experiences, Gifts and Abilities, Sexual Orientation

Your job as a counselor is to help the young person who is experiencing same-sex attraction to realize that one's sexual orientation does NOT have to determine their identity. You can be honest and recognize that the same-sex attraction is present, to whatever degree, but it doesn't have to dominate one's life or become their sole identifying factor. There are many other aspects of identity that one can choose to be his or her dominant identifying factor. We do not choose our attractions, but we do choose our behaviors.

Historically the church has failed to minister Christ's love and forgiveness to those who struggle with same-sex attraction. As strongly as we might want to take a stand against homosexual behavior, we must also just as strongly take a stand against our unwillingness to reach out and understand, counsel, disciple, support and love those struggling with same-sex attraction.

> **Historically the church has failed to minister Christ's love and forgiveness to those who struggle with same-sex attraction.**

The church's failure in this area is absolutely embarrassing. During the 16th century the Church of England used men accused of homosexual acts as "faggots" or the kindling wood for witch burnings. The label still remains.

> A young man from Grand Rapids, Michigan, approached his pastor for help--he was told not to return until he had gotten his life straightened out. Two new Christians approached a pastor for help with same-sex attraction issues. They were told, "Commit suicide! God understands suicide better than homosexuality." One jumped off Seattle's George Washington Bridge, the other is drinking himself to death.[296]

People dealing with same-sex attraction issues too often get the message that the church is incapable or unwilling to respond to their need. In despair, they come to believe that they are beyond the saving grace of God. They feel like their only alternative is to embrace the gay community and everything it stands for.

> **I do not think it's possible for the church to pray, "Oh, God, heal that person, but please do not involve me."**

Surely, we can do better. We *must* do better or we may lose a large segment of an entire generation. Heed the words of Doug

Houck, founder and director of Metanoia Ministries, himself someone who once struggled with same-sex attraction:

> I do not think it's possible for the church to pray, "Oh, God, heal that person, but please do not involve me." I want to challenge all heterosexual Christians not to run away, but to become constructively involved--to offer good same-sex friendships to homosexuals. . . Love, both in prayer and in relationships, is the basic therapy. . . Love is the basic problem, the great need, and the only true solution. If we are willing to seek and to mediate the healing and redeeming love of Christ, then healing for the homosexual will become a great and glorious reality.[297]

What should our attitude be? Dr. Mark Yarhouse suggests that most helpful stance that a Christian and the church as a community should take is that of "convicted civility." The phrase "convicted civility" refers to a balance between holding convictions as a Christian and communicating those convictions with civility and compassion.

I Corinthians 6:9-11 is a testimony that those who once practiced homosexuality *can* be delivered of that bondage. There is hope. There is healing. If you want to minister to those struggling with same-sex attraction, consider the following principles and insights.

Avoid shock and express acceptance. Expressing shock or revulsion at the revelation of having same-sex desires will greatly hamper any healthy exploration that might lead to healing. You need to convey an attitude and atmosphere of safety and security.

Address their fears directly. You will not cause a young person to become homosexual by allowing them to explore their anxieties in an open and accepting way. You do not have to "tip-toe" around their true concerns or behaviors. Reassure them that their fears are not uncommon and that many times the same-sex feelings of attraction during the teen years are actually a form of "pseudo-homosexuality."

As you listen to their narrative, in a patient and compassionate way, you need to correct any misinformation that they express. Sometimes this is expressed in erroneous beliefs about what Scripture says about homosexuality or "scientific" inaccuracies such as "homosexuals cannot change their orientation." Perhaps they feel they are beyond redemption and there is no hope. Correcting misunderstandings is appropriate counsel and an enlightened attitude may change the teen's attitude about their struggle and empower them to overcome their difficulties.

Allow for emotional release. Teens who struggle with same-sex attraction will have repressed fears, hostilities and painful memories stored up. They have been hesitant to share them with others because they fear the rejection or ridicule they may receive. They need to release these feelings to resolve internal conflicts and ease the tension in their life.

> You must see them as whole people, not just homosexuals.

Both you as the counselor and the young person must realize that this struggle will not go away overnight. It was a "lifetime" in developing and it is going to take significant time to work through it. You both must make a long-term commitment to see the process through to a healthy conclusion.

You must see them as whole people, not just homosexuals. You don't label and see other people as gossips, liars, adulterers, thieves, or porn addicts. You see them as people, loved by God, who struggle with a particular sin. But they are *not* their sin. It is not their identity. This is extremely important for those who struggle with same-sex attraction because the gay community *wants* them to find their identity in their sexual orientation, but identity is so much more than that.

Be genuine. When necessary confront, share feelings, point out concrete and specific pitfalls, hold the person accountable for their behavior.

You must realize that the healing of those who struggle with same-sex attraction is no different than the restoration of any type of struggle or sin. Although the symptoms of inner brokenness may differ, the source of restoration, Jesus Christ and his church remain the same. The principles that work for straight Christians in conquering this problem will also be effective for believers with same-sex desires.

Convey hope. Share how God has helped you through various trials and struggle in life. In general, the identical spiritual disciplines of accountability, purifying the thought life, prayer, Bible study, all work for the homosexual as well.

The counselor, through using the resources of the church, must make available some new avenues for developing relationships for the one coming out of the gay and lesbian lifestyle. Experiencing same-sex attraction or having a homosexual orientation often leads to a person to experience isolation. Being able to safely tell another person of your struggle can change all that. If someone discloses to you about their struggle with same-sex attraction the first way to respond is by listening, and when appropriate, conveying to the person that they are not alone.

When you come away from homosexuality, there may be a huge vacuum left in your social life. Some other group of people must replace your gay social circles, or you will be drawn back in. Few, if any, people leave homosexuality on their own. Nearly all the ex-gays we know have made this difficult transition with the strong support of Christian friends.[298]

Realize that you will not have, nor do you need to have, all the answers. Be willing to admit your limitations. It is God who will bring about the changes, not you. Be aware that there is no identical plan of action for healing, no quick fix or one-two-three formula that is going to work for everyone. Deal with each case on an individual basis.

> **Realize that you will not have, nor do you need to have, all the answers.**

"Our deliverance from homosexuality comes from a Person, rather than a method," says Frank Worthen, who spent more than twenty years in homosexuality before leaving that lifestyle and starting Love In Action in 1973. As Frank discovered, the interesting thing about the change process is that change itself is not our goal. Change is what *results* as we pursue a far more important and compelling goal: knowing, loving and "beholding' Jesus.[299]

Because the issue of sexual orientation is so complex, the young person is most likely going to need special help in sorting it all out and making sense of the issue. Same-sex attraction is such a strong issue that historically those who have desired change and entered into therapy have still experienced many painful relapses. They need professional Christian counselors who specialize in this area who understand the dynamics of everything that is involved and who can commit to the long-term counseling relationship. The youth pastor should inquire about local Christian counselors or agencies that would best serve the needs of the teen struggling with same-sex attraction and make the proper referral.

Overview of the Counseling Process for Teens Struggling with Same-Sex Attraction

Connect with the Teen
- They may call you and ask for help--if so, set up a meeting giving them instructions on location, time and length of session.
- You may hear concerns from parents about their sexual identity--if so, take pastoral initiative and go to them or call and set up a meeting.
- Prepare your meeting place and yourself by reviewing how to counsel those who struggle with same-sex attraction. Don't forget to pray and ask the Holy Spirit for guidance and insight!

Understand the Teen
- Communicate empathy by your posture, position and active listening skills.
- Communicate nonjudgmental, unconditional love and genuineness.
- Ask yourself the empathy question: "How would I feel if I was this student in this situation?"
- Avoid shock and express acceptance.
- Address their fears directly.
- Allow for emotional release.

Explore with the Teen
- Gently encourage the teen to tell their story. It is important that you listen respectfully and with genuine concern.
- Explore with the teen when their feelings of attraction for their same sex first began. How did these manifest themselves?
- Have they acted on these feelings? Has there been any physical or sexual contact? If so, with whom?
- Help the teen to understand the difference between same-sex attraction, same-sex orientation and a gay identity.

Initiate a Plan with the Teen
- Realize that you will not have, nor do you need to have, all the answers. Be willing to admit your limitations. It is God who will bring about the changes, not you.
- If there is a Christian support group for those struggling with same-sex attraction in the area, provide them with the appropriate information.

- Both you and the teen must realize that this will not go away overnight.
- Provide healthy same-sex relationships within the church.
- Help them practice the spiritual disciplines and to grow in the knowledge of how a follower of Jesus lives.
- Provide any Christian resources that may help them understand their situation.

<u>Finish with the Teen</u>
- Refer to a professional Christian counselor who specializes in same-sex attraction.
- Maintain your relationship with the teen.

Helpful Resources

Homosexuals Anonymous - A national 12-step recovery group for homosexuals.
PO Box 7881,
Reading, PA 19603.
Phone: 610-376-1146.

NARTH - The National Association for the Research and Therapy of Homosexuality
16633 Ventura Blvd. Suite 1340,
Encino, CA 91436-1801.
Phone: 818-789-4440.
Joseph Nicolosi, Ph.D. Fax: 805-373-5084
http://www.narth.com

Kent Paris
Nehemiah Ministries
P.O. Box 773
Urbana, IL 61803
217-344-4636
Nehemiah76@comcast.net

Selected Bibliography

Barr, Adam T. and Citlau, Ron. *Compassion Without Compromise: How the Gospel Frees Us to Love Our Gay Friends Without Losing the Truth.* Minneapolis, MN: Bethany House Publishers, 2014.

Dallas, Joe and Heche, Nancy, Gen Eds. *The Complete Christian Guide to Understanding Homosexuality: A Biblical and Compassionate Response to Same-Sex Attraction.* Eugene, OR: Harvest House Publishers, 2010.

DeYoung, Kevin. *What Does the Bible Really Teach About Homosexuality?* Wheaton, IL: Crossway, 2015.

Yarhouse, Mark A. *Homosexuality and the Christian. A Guide for Parents, Pastors, and Friends.* Minneapolis, MN: Bethany House Publishers, 2010.

Yarhouse, Mark A. *Understanding Sexual Identity: A Resource For Youth Ministry.* Grand Rapids, MI: Zondervan, 2013.

Exercise 13.1 - Understanding Same-Sex Attraction

Rate yourself on your knowledge and understanding same sex attraction. Use the scale provided: 1 = poor; 2 = below average; 3 = Average; 4 = Above average; 5 = Excellent. Simply check the box that best describes you. Be honest with yourself. Work on the areas that need improvement—it's not an assignment, it's a life that you might save!

Understanding Same-Sex Attraction	1	2	3	4	5
I am knowledgeable with the percent of men and women who struggle with same-sex attraction					
I am familiar with the passages of Scripture that deal specifically with homosexuality.					
I am able to refute or correct any errors in interpretation of scripture regarding homosexual behavior.					
I understand the different theories/explanations that are given by the scientific community to explain the development of same-sex attraction.					
I understand that the development of same-sex attraction cannot be explained by just one theory but that it is a complicated issue with many factors contributing to it.					
I am familiar with the four competing positions of authority that people take in trying to determine truth.					
I understand the importance of differentiating between one's sexual orientation and one's identity.					
I understand and can confidently put into practice					

the general principles and guidelines for working with teens who struggle with same-sex attraction.					

CHAPTER FOURTEEN

THE PORNOGRAPHY PLAGUE

Men seem to be wired in such a way that pornography hijacks the proper functioning of their brains and has a long-lasting effect on their thoughts and lives. . . But calls to pray harder, move the computer to the living room and get plugged into an accountability group only go so far. They come across as hollow to many men whose brains have been altered and rewired by their experiences with pornography.[300] –William M. Struthers.

If you are losing the battle, please read closely: following Jesus consists of so much more than trying harder and white-knuckling your way through it. You can be free. God has charted a path to freedom that men before you have walked.   You can discover this path leading to authentic transformation in your soul, a path that consists of so much more than sin management. You also need to know that your masculine soul is deeper and truer than your desire for porn. Part of you longs to walk intimately with God.[301] -- Michael John Cusick

A Case Study

Derek wasn't looking for porn the first time he encountered it. He was simply doing some research for a school assignment and one of the websites that came up as a possible site of information contained a provocative looking ad embedded in it. He clicked on it out of curiosity and that was the start of his porn addiction. Derek was all of eleven years old when it started. At first it was just looking at pictures of semi-naked and fully naked women. Later, when he was older, he discovered there were free videos on the internet that showed people in actual intercourse. His excitement knew no bounds. Pretty soon he was spending hours on the internet and he began to masturbate compulsively.

After a while he found that the "soft porn" just didn't excite him as much as it used to. He began searching for sites that offered more "hard core sex." He was now filling his mind with scenes of rape, group sex, anal sex, sado-masochistic sex, and homosexual sex.

He felt guilty about his involvement with porn and tried to quit from time to time, and though he might go for days or weeks without looking at porn, he would eventually succumb to it promise of cheap thrills. Eventually his mother caught him looking at porn and made him go talk with the youth pastor at a local church. Derek was hoping he could help, but he wasn't sure that anything would be able to free him from his addition to porn.

Statistics

The U.S. Department of Justice made the following statement: "Never before in the history of telecommunications media in the United States has so much indecent (and obscene) material been so easily accessible by so many minors in so many American homes with so few restrictions."[302]

According to a survey conducted by the Barna Group in the U.S. in 2014:

- The following percentages of men say they view pornography at least once a month: 18-30-year-olds, 79%; 31-49-year-olds, 67%; 50-68-year-olds, 49%.
- The following percentages of men say they view pornography at least several times a week: 18-30-year-olds, 63%; 31-49-year-olds, 38%; 50-68-year-olds, 25%.
- The following percentages of women say they view pornography at least once a month: 18-30-year-olds, 76%; 31-49-year-olds, 16%; 50-68-year-olds, 4%.
- The following percentages of women say they view pornography at least several times a week: 18-30-year-olds, 21%; 31-49-year-olds, 5%; 50-68-year-olds, 0%.
- 55% of married men say they watch porn at least once a month, compared to 70% of not married men.
- 25% of married women say they watch porn at least once a month, compared to 16% of not married women.
- 32% of teens admit to intentionally accessing nude or pornographic content online. Of these, 43% do so on a weekly basis.[303]
- Every second 28,258 users are watching pornography on the internet.
- 35% of all internet downloads are related to pornography.
- 25% of all search engine queries are related to pornography, or about 68 million search queries a day.
- One third of porn viewers are women.
- Search engines get 116,000 queries every day related to child pornography.

- 34% of internet users have experienced unwanted exposure to pornographic content through ads, pop up ads, misdirected links or emails.[304]
- Almost half (46%) of teenagers say "sending sexual or naked photos or videos is part of everyday life for teenagers nowadays."
- Seven out of 10 (72%) 18 year olds say "pornography leads to unrealistic attitudes to sex" and that "pornography can have a damaging impact on young people's views of sex or relationships."
- Two thirds of young women (66%) and almost half of young men (49%) agree, "it would be easier growing up if pornography was less easy to access..."[305]
- Internet Safety is now the 4th top ranked issue in the list of health concerns for U.S. children.[306]
- 42% of sextortion victims met their abuser online.[307]
- The largest consumers of internet pornography are kids ages 12-17.
- 9% of girls and 15% of boys have seen child pornography.
- 18% of girls and 32% of boys have viewed bestiality on the internet.[308]

According to Craig Gross, founder and spokesperson for xxxchurch.com, pornography is a "57-billion-dollar, worldwide industry, making more than the combined revenues of all the professional football, baseball, and basketball teams in America. Porn revenue in the United States (12 billion dollars) exceeds the combined revenues of ABC, CBS, and NBC (6.2 billion dollars), and disgustingly enough, child pornography alone generates 3 billion dollars annually."[309]

Porn's Effect on the Adolescent Brain

Watching porn actually short-circuits the neural pathway that associates pleasure with one's spouse and now centers it on screen stimulation and masturbation.

The viewing of pornography is especially problematic for the developing adolescent brain. Every event, every sensation that a person experiences creates a neural pathway in the brain. The more times a person experiences a particular event or feeling, the stronger that neural pathway becomes. God has designed us so that our sexuality, and pleasure associated with it, is supposed to be connected to our spouse. This association of sexual pleasure with our spouse creates a strong bond and helps to deepen the love, affection and commitment of a husband and wife for each other.

Because the developing brain exhibits a remarkable amount of plasticity or the ability to change, watching porn actually short-circuits the neural pathway that associates pleasure with one's spouse and now centers it on screen stimulation and masturbation. "Instead of bonding to a real mate, the porn viewer's brain bonds to the image, video, or situation, especially when the activity is reinforced through repetition."[310]

Both having sex and watching porn causes dopamine, the neurotransmitter responsible for reward and pleasure, to be released. But repeatedly causing this surge in dopamine, by regularly watching pornography, means the brain become desensitized to its effects.

William M. Struthers, in his book, *Wired For Intimacy: How Pornography Hijacks the Male Brain*, makes the case that "men seem to be wired in such a way that pornography hijacks the proper functioning of their brains and has a long-lasting effect on their thoughts and lives."[311] Many others agree with his findings.

> Pornography triggers certain hormones in our bodies, such as adrenaline, and stimulates the production of testosterone, oxytocin, dopamine, and serotonin. Indulging in pornography is like indulging in a chemical cocktail. It gets you going. Like any drug, though, once the "rush" is over, there is invariably a letdown or a bombardment of negative emotions. To get the rush again, you have to take another hit later. Therefore, the addiction potential for pornography is enormous. Like drugs or alcohol, some get addicted after one time.[312]

There is a correlation between the amount of time spent viewing porn and reduced grey matter in the brains' reward circuitry, which governs motivation and appetites. The reward circuitry, which lights up in response to sexual stimuli, shows less activation the more porn the adolescent watches. The connection between the

The brains of compulsive porn users react to cues much like alcoholics and drug addicts.

prefrontal cortex, the "executive control" part of the brain, and the reward circuitry becomes weaker the more porn the adolescent watches, which becomes a risk for impaired decision making. The brains of compulsive porn users react to cues much like alcoholics and drug addicts.

Reduced grey matter is associated with needing greater stimulation to achieve the same effect.

> Between the ages of 12 and 20, the human brain undergoes a period of great neuroplasticity. The brain is in a malleable phase during which billions of new synaptic connections are made. This leaves us vulnerable to the influence of our surroundings and leads our brains to be "wired" around the experiences and information that we receive during that time period.
>
> When an adolescent boy compulsively views pornography, his brain chemistry can become shaped around the attitudes and situations that he is watching. Sadly, pornography paints an unrealistic picture of sexuality and relationships that can create an expectation for real-life experiences that will never be fulfilled.[313]

Not only does viewing porn affect adolescent brain development with respect to normal sexual response, it has contributed to the growing problem of porn induced erectile dysfunction. PIED is the inability to maintain an erection when attempting to engage in sex. The problem is related to The Coolidge Effect. The Coolidge Effect was first used to describe a phenomenon seen in animal species whereby males, and to a lesser extent females, exhibit renewed sexual interest if introduced to new receptive sexual partners. The concept central to the Coolidge Effect is that of novelty. The introduction of a new and different partner brings about a renewed interest.

> **The good news is that the neural plasticity of the brain allows the brain to "re-wire" and correct the neural pathways that had been short-circuited by viewing porn.**

The way this is applied to porn watching is that in order to maintain the same level of sexual arousal, the porn user has to constantly switch from one site to the next, seeking out something that is different from what he has been watching. The problem develops when the porn user is with a real person, but only one person, that one person cannot hold his interest because his brain has become accustomed to frequent and novel sexual stimulation. The result is porn induced erectile dysfunction.

This phenomenon of porn induced erectile dysfunction is becoming so common that there are actual web sites and programs for men who have experienced this to make a commitment to give up watching porn completely. What they have found is that after 90 days of abstinence from watching porn they "get their mojo back." "One online community claims 50,000 members, and their goal is to encourage each other to avoid pornography and masturbation for 90 days in the hope of never going back."[314] The good news is that the neural plasticity of the brain allows the brain to "re-wire" and correct the neural pathways that had been short-circuited by viewing porn. "Rewiring your brain allows it to unlearn the addictive patterns and relearn impulse control."[315]

Not only does the viewing of porn affect the mind of the viewer by short-circuiting the neuro pathways and negatively affecting the reward response, but it hurts intimacy and causes the user to view women as objects of their lust rather than as a person whom God has created in His image.

> Pornographers want people to believe that viewing porn is harmless entertainment and that it can even spice up one's love life, but the opposite is true. Rather than encouraging intimacy, research shows that porn steals it away. Porn encourages selfishness rather than an exchange of intimacy. Especially among men, who are more visually stimulated than women, porn teaches that women are objects for their lust. Women are just body parts, used for personal gratification.[316]

The Church and the Porn Addict

Pornography is destructive to the developing adolescent brain for a number of reasons, as we have seen. So how do you help or convince a young person that viewing porn in not in their best interests; that it is, in fact, destructive? What is the best way to help?

> **Churches need to do a better job of becoming communities of grace. Otherwise sin just stays hidden and grows and propagates and destroys Christ's beautiful bride.**

My observation is that we have a cultural problem in many of our churches. While it is "okay" to ask for help with a drinking problem, drug addiction or financial problems, the church is not a place where it is safe to talk about struggles of a sexual nature. If the church is going to be a place where people who struggle with pornography can get help, it must communicate a culture of grace.

There's rarely a place where men feel they can confess and be treated appropriately. I knew other men in seminary were struggling, but none of us would talk about it because we'd be pushed to the side rather than walked with in a relationship through the struggle to victory. Churches need to do a better job of becoming communities of grace. Otherwise sin just stays hidden and grows and propagates and destroys Christ's beautiful bride.[317]

John Piper wrote a very helpful article for *Christianity Today* entitled "Gutsy Guilt" which did an excellent job of addressing the importance of understanding God's grace and forgiveness when dealing with the problem of pornography. The entire article is worth reading, but here are a few key excerpts from it.

Many young people are being lost to the cause of Christ's mission because they are not taught how to deal with the guilt of sexual failure. The problem is not just how *not* to fail. The problem is how to deal with failure so that it doesn't sweep away your whole life into wasted mediocrity with no impact for Christ.

The great tragedy is not masturbation or fornication or pornography. The tragedy is that Satan uses guilt from these failures to strip you of every radical dream you ever had or might have. In their place, he gives you a happy, safe, secure, American life of superficial pleasures, until you die in your lakeside rocking chair.

I have a passion that you do not waste your life. My aim is not mainly to cure you of sexual misconduct. I would like that to happen. But mostly I want to take out of the Devil's hand the weapon that exploits your sin and makes your life a wasted, worldly success. Satan wants that for you. But you don't!

What breaks my heart today, is not that you have sinned sexually. It's that this morning Satan took your 2 A.M. encounter—whether on TV or in bed—and told you: "See, you're a loser. You may as well not even worship. No way are you going to make any serious commitment of your life to Jesus Christ! You may as well get a good job so you can buy yourself a big widescreen and watch sex till you drop."

I want to take that weapon out of his hand.[318]

Piper goes on to do an exegesis of Colossians 2:13-14 and Micah 7:8-9 which shows in a very powerful and practical way how Christ's substitutiary sacrifice has defeated Satan and given us the victory through the death of Christ on the cross.

> When you learn to deal with the guilt of sexual failure by this kind brokenhearted boldness, this kind of theology, this kind of justification by faith, this kind of substitutionary atonement, this kind of gutsy guilt, you will fall less often. Why is this so? Because Christ will become increasingly precious to you.[319]

Symptoms of a Sex Addict

Not every person you encounter in a counseling situation will be convinced that porn is bad or that they have a problem with it. Denial is one of the major characteristics of addiction, whether it is alcohol, drugs, gambling or porn. Ask the young person you are counseling to look at the following symptoms and be as honest as possible. The more symptoms that are present, the greater the indication that the person has an addiction problem that needs to be addressed.

> Denial is one of the major characteristics of addiction, whether it is alcohol, drugs, gambling or porn.

- Sexual acting out despite serious consequences and repeated attempts at control.
- Inability to stop (or powerlessness) despite adverse consequences, with frequent use of denial, rationalization, and minimization to hide both the problem and the underlying shame.
- Neglect or sacrifice of important social, family, occupational, or recreational activities because of sexual behavior.
- An ongoing desire or effort to limit sexual behavior.
- An inordinate amount of time spent in obtaining sex, being sexual, or recovering from sexual experience.

- Risk taking.
- Living a double life.
- Decrease in one's spiritual or religious life. A constant violation of one's value system.
- Endangering one's professional and family life.

"Sexual addiction has been described as 'the athlete's foot of the mind.' It never goes away. It is always asking to be scratched, promising relief. To scratch, however, is to cause pain and to intensify the itch."[320] "Problems for cybersex addicts often develop rapidly. Many of these addicts quickly find themselves doing the unthinkable."[321]

The following criteria for a porn addiction are given by Dr. Kevin B. Skinner, in his book, *Treating Pornography Addiction: The Essential Tools for Recovery*. He states that a minimum of three of the ten symptoms must be present in the person's life in order to diagnose them as having a pornography addiction. "Most sex addicts will have five signs, while over 50 percent have seven."[322]

1. Recurrent failure to resist impulses to view pornography
2. More extensive/longer viewing of pornography than intended
3. Ongoing, but unsuccessful, efforts to stop, reduce, or control behavior
4. Inordinate amount of time spent obtaining pornography, viewing pornography, and/or being sexual—either through masturbation, or with another person or object, or recovering from sexual experiences
5. Feeling preoccupied with fantasy, sexualized thoughts, and/or preparatory activities
6. Viewing pornography takes significant time away from obligations: occupational, academic, domestic, or social
7. Continuation of behavior despite consequences
8. Tolerance—more frequent or intense pornography is needed over time to obtain the desired result
9. Deliberately limiting social, occupational, or recreational activities in order to keep time open for finding and viewing pornography
10. Distress, restlessness, or irritability if unable to view pornography (withdrawal)
11. dizziness
12. body aches
13. headaches
14. sleeplessness
15. restlessness

16. anxiety
17. mood swings
18. depression[323]

If you have a client who is in denial about his addiction to pornography, there are several excellent tests that can be given that will help you access the situation. Of course, you must keep in mind that they all depend upon the honesty of the person taking the test.[324]

The Seven Levels of Pornography Addiction

> **A curious observation about a porn addiction is that rarely is a person's involvement static—in other words it rarely stays at the same level.**

Dr. Skinner prefers to understand pornography addiction as a place on a continuum, rather than arbitrarily labeling one person "addicted" and another as not—even though they both are viewing pornography. With an addiction, it becomes compulsive behavior and includes a loss of control. Secondly, negative consequences are associated with having an addiction. But a curious observation about a porn addiction is that rarely is a person's involvement static—in other words it rarely stays at the same level. It is more common for the person's commitment and desire to stop viewing pornography increase and decrease with time and circumstances.

For example, some individuals will binge for days or weeks at a time and then remain abstinent for months and even years at a time. This begs the question of why this happens. A clear answer comes from understanding what is happening in each individual's life. His involvement generally fluctuates based on stress, family circumstances, emotional well-being, relationship status, and a host of other reasons. With this understanding, it is helpful to view a person's pornography involvement on levels of a continuum.[325]

Skinner suggests seven levels of pornography addiction. In each of these levels there are common behaviors that distinguish each level from the others. The most significant differences can be found in the consequences of the behaviors: the compulsivity, the frequency and

250

intensity of the behavior, and the beliefs an individual forms about himself.

Level 1 – Generally those at level one have just recently been exposed to pornography or they only look at pornography once or twice a year. These people have a very limited exposure to pornography. Their thoughts and everyday actions are not focused on pornography.

Level 2 – This level does not indicate an addiction as the viewing of pornography is not a compulsive act nor has it created problems for the individual. The desire to view pornography does not dominate day-in and day-out thinking. Generally, those at this level have recently had an increase in exposure to pornography and are questioning the growing curiosity they feel inside. The challenge at this level is growing curiosity.

Level 3 – "Level three pornography involvement is on the borderline between a growing problem and a compulsive behavior—a sign of addiction."[326] Individuals at this level are looking at pornography about once a month and it has been going on a while. Those at this level try to restrain themselves from more exposure, but about once a month it becomes unbearable and they give in. Once they do give it, it is likely they will binge for a day or two before attempting to stop again.

> Some individuals at this level don't consider their involvement to be a problem. They feel like they can manage their behaviors on their own, and in most instances, they try to monitor their behavior and limit their exposure. These individuals are at a crossroads, as further involvement is more likely to become compulsive in nature. Generally speaking, individuals at level three have to put extra effort into quitting entirely because they have been exposed to stronger forms of pornography (R-rated videos, nude pictures, sexual movies, etc.).[327]

Fantasizing is also a part of the battle at level three. As their mind tries to avoid thinking about pornography, they still find themselves fantasizing about viewing it. The challenge is that fantasizing at this level makes it more and more difficult to *not* give in to viewing pornography. It is common for individuals at level three to start spending extra time and energy fighting off thoughts of pornography and the desire to view it.

Level 4 – At this level it is impacting more and more aspects of a person's life. They are viewing pornography a few times each month and are looking at more hard-core types of pornography. They are likely viewing movies or downloading clips from the Internet. Individuals at this level will spend time fantasizing about sexual things even if they do not act out their fantasies. It is common for individuals at level four to fight off strong urges and desires to view pornography. Individuals at this level may be viewing pornography even other week or so, but their desire to give in between episodes is often strong and challenging. Generally speaking, individuals at level four have been fighting pornography for many years. They may have tried to cut back or tried to stop, but find they can only go a couple of weeks without giving in to the desire.

Level 5 – At this level pornography is impacting regular day-to-day living. There isn't a day that goes by when they don't think about looking at pornography or give in and looking at it. They are viewing pornography three to five times a week. Pornography and sexual behaviors are probably among the top seven things they think about each day. Pornography has probably affected some aspect of their lives negatively at this point (e.g., work, education, relationships, religious involvement). Individuals at this level begin to experience more intense withdrawal symptoms the longer they go without pornography. They are on the brink of giving up the fight. When a person begins to feel helpless and throws caution to the wind that he transitions to level six. At level six there are no barriers. Level six is when pornography consumes all of a person's daily activities.

Level 6 – "At level six, pornography beings to dominate a person's life. There are very few days he doesn't view pornography. Initially, pornography was for excitement and entertainment, but over time pornography has become more than just entertainment—it has become a compulsive addiction."[328] It is common for individuals at this level to have been caught and they are starting to feel the negative consequences that are often associated with this level of addiction. But even with the potential negative consequences, they are still willing to take risks and give in to compulsive desires. Often at level six the person is likely to have lost something in their life due to their involvement with pornography. Some people lose a job, others their spouses, God and others lose their desire for other passions.

> Level 7 – At level seven, viewing pornography and sexually acting out are almost daily occurrences. There is a deep seeded compulsive feeling to act out. These feelings impact a person's ability to focus, except on pornography and sex. There is a feeling of powerlessness and hopelessness at this level. There are very few days when pornography is not viewed at this level.[329]

Each day is generally filled with finding and viewing pornography. The images seen are often hardcore and may be filled with violence, rape, incest, bestiality, and other extremely hardcore material. The reason for this escalation is that previous images are no longer stimulating. Most individuals at level seven are engaged in acting out their sexual fantasies. Those who try to limit or curtail how much they view pornography at this level have found that it is virtually impossible to do so on their own.

Individuals at this level feel out of control. They spend hours each day looking for and finding pornography or sex. Pornography has definitely hindered the following areas of this person's life: relationships, work, school, fun and enjoyment, spirituality, and finances.

Lying is a frequent behavior of individuals at level seven. There are many situations each day in which lying must take place in order to cover up the time spent on pornography and acting out. If caught at this level, there is a good chance this person will minimize his level of involvement because of the potential consequences.

"Once a person starts acting out his fantasies and what he is seeing in pornographic films, he is in a dangerous place because of the risky behaviors in which he is engaged."[330]

How Is a Pornography Addiction Maintained?

> **Dishonesty is a major aspect of a porn addiction.**

Many factors contribute to the fall of a person into pornography addiction. The following factors can be true of all pornography addicts, but may be seen more prominently in men.

Pride is the first issue. This is manifested by an unwillingness to admit that he is out of control and that pornography is a significant problem in his life.

Selfishness is the next issue. The painful reality about his situation is that everything the person does is geared toward satisfying his own desires, regardless of how lurid or deviant they may be.

Dishonesty is a major aspect of a porn addiction. This is part of the defense mechanism that is built into most pornography addicts. They usually do not know how to be honest with themselves about their own conditions, and find it all but impossible to be honest with anyone else when confronted with the issue.

Fear is another issue. The closer a person is emotionally to the addict, the more difficulty the addict will have in being totally candid with that person about his condition. The addict commonly fears rejection, being ostracized, or even the threat of legal action if his addiction has taken him to the point that he is acting out possible criminal activity that he has seen portrayed in pornography.

Masturbation is probably the single most prevalent activity in the perpetuation of pornography addiction. Masturbation can play a very significant role in maintaining the natural neurochemical activity that accompanies pornography addiction.

All of these issues, when combined, make a pornography addiction very difficult to overcome. But, the good news is that it can be done and there are many who were once slaves to their addiction who have found freedom.

Defeating A Pornography Addiction

Flee from sexual immorality. All other sins a man commits are outside his body, but he who sins sexually sins against his own body. . . You are not your own; you were bought at a price. Therefore, honor God with your body. - 1 Corinthians 6: 18-19 NIV

There is hope. A porn addiction can be defeated—but it is going to be a difficult struggle. Many men have made a genuine decision to quit, found release for several days or weeks, only to fall back into the habit feeling more defeated and discouraged than before. Michael Cusick refers to this as the "lather, rinse, repeat" cycle.

> First, it begins with getting clean—genuine remorse and sincere repentance. Promising God that we won't go there again. Then, for reasons we don't really understand, we go there again. Eventually, when our shame overwhelms us, or perhaps we've been discovered, we come clean again. But this time we tell somebody and find an accountability partner. Finally, we commit to a new strategy by redoubling our efforts, trying even harder, checking in more often with our accountability partner, and maybe reading our Bibles more. It's lather, rinse, repeat—with the emphasis on repeat. And the saddest part of this cycle is that most men see no alternative. We're seemingly stuck with two choices: either suppress our passions or give in and indulge them. We know in our hearts that porn is not God's best for our lives. But in the heat of the moment, it seems as if there's nothing better than porn. *We desperately need another way to live.*[331]

The good news is that there *is* a better way. But it doesn't come from trying harder, or getting more accountability partners or managing your time better. (Although there is nothing wrong with those things, they are not the ultimate answer) The ultimate answer is in recognizing and appropriating Jesus' promise of freedom and the power of his grace to help find victory.

The good news is that there *is* a better way. But it doesn't come from trying harder, or getting more accountability partners or managing your time better.

If you are losing the battle, please read closely: *following Jesus consists of so much more than trying harder and white-knuckling your way through it*. You can be free. God has charted a path to freedom that men before you have walked. You can discover this path leading to authentic transformation in your soul, a path that consists of so much more than sin management.[332]

Victory over pornography is realizing that you were created for something bigger than yourself.

Victory over pornography is realizing that you were created for something bigger than yourself. You were called to live an abundant life—a life that flows from the center of God's will for your life. But it comes down to desire. Thomas Merton has said: "Life is shaped by the end you live for. You are made in the image of what you desire."[333] Your deepest desire must be for God. Jesus said that the greatest commandment was to "Love the Lord your God with all your heart and with all your soul and with all your mind."[334] Victory over a porn addiction is not just breaking free from the compulsions to visit XXX sites on the internet, it is also the freedom to run towards God and to become the person that you truly want to be. "God is concerned with so much more than giving you the energy to keep you from looking at porn. Obviously, He wants you free from any bondage—including porn and lust—that stands in the way of your relationship with Him."[335]

In order to defeat a pornography addiction, it is helpful to be able to identify one's "triggers" which seem to lead a person into viewing porn. Most people who struggle with a pornography addiction will mention the following as common triggers:[336]

- Boredom

- Exposure
- Loneliness
- Opportunity
- Stress
- Tiredness
- Rejection

It is very common to hear someone who struggles with porn say something like, "When I'm bored and alone—that's the number one trigger." "When I am tired, depressed and lonely I just don't seem to be able to stand up to the temptation."

While it is true that circumstances can trigger our sin and shape the form it takes, they don't really cause it. The root cause is always our hearts and their sinful desires. If the problem were simply with our eyes, then the solution would be to avert our eyes. But if the problem begins in the heart, then the solution must be something different entirely. A person must be willing to take responsibility for his sin and desire to be free from it.

> God wants more than just weepy prayers. Yes, He will forgive but if you are honest, you are looking for more than just forgiveness. If you have a righteous heart then you are longing for personal integrity, longing to build a legacy of uncompromising purity. You desire to be a man of God. The alternative is persistent shame and feeling like a fraud. Thank God for shame, it is a sign of a soft heart.[337]

There are two types of temptation, the kind we have no control over and the kind we can do something about. God gives us strength over temptation but grace is not given to overcome the temptation we seek out or allow in by laziness. We are to flee, not walk or loiter but run from temptation.

> **A person must be willing to take responsibility for his sin and desire to be free from it. God wants more than just weepy prayers.**

Loitering around a temptation then desperately praying for more strength is ridiculous. God will not be mocked; He is not a crutch for inaction.[338]

Paul admonished Timothy to "Flee the evil desires of youth, and pursue righteousness, faith, love and peace. . ."[339] This is the time to take personal responsibility and to take action—running away from temptation and towards the things that are helpful and will lead you to a closer walk with God. "You must stop complaining about the things you have no control over such as the way women dress, the content of movies and commercials that use sex to sell a product. You need to start focusing on the things you can do something about."[340]

Tim Chester, in his book, *Closing the Window: Steps to Living Porn Free*, suggests there are five key ingredients that need to be in place if a person is going to win the battle against a pornography addiction.[341]

1	Abhorrence of porn	A hatred of porn itself (not just the shame it brings) and a genuine longing for change
2	Adoration of God	A desire for God, arising from a confidence that He offers more than porn
3	Assurance of grace	An assurance that you are loved by God and right with God through faith in the work of Jesus
4	Avoidance of temptation	A commitment to do all in your power to avoid temptation, starting with controls on your computer
5	Accountability to others	A community of Christians who are holding you accountable and supporting you in your struggle

Porn is a sin of the imagination. We need to counter it by enlarging our imaginations. The answer to porn is to believe the truth. But that's so much more than an intellectual process. We need to let the truth capture our imaginations: to meditate, ponder, wonder at and sing the truth. We need to feel the truth, glory in the truth delight in the truth. Discipline yourself to start each day by cultivating your affections for God. Remind yourself of Christ's goodness, glory, grace and greatness until your heart is warmed again by those truths and Christ is supreme in your heart.[342]

Breaking this pervasive addiction will demand a cost.

Change takes place when you, after counting the cost of remaining in sin and the cost of walking away forever, decide one way or another. You cannot sit on the fence refusing to make a choice because sooner or later that choice will be made for you.

Jesus tells us to count the cost. Breaking this pervasive addiction will demand a cost. Are you willing to pay the price? Is your reputation, you family name and most of all, your relationship with God worth it?

Here are some costs and rewards of remaining addicted to pornography or choosing to give it up. Consider them carefully.[343]

Cost of Staying in Pornography

- alienation from those closest to you including God
- guilt, shame and remorse
- hurt the people you love
- desensitized conscience and detachment
- never discovering your full spiritual potential
- jaded view of women
- loneliness
- controlled
- intimacy issues
- low self esteem
- insecurity
- a constant feeling of hypocrisy

Rewards of Staying in Pornography

- a temporary high
- something to fall back on when feeling bored
- sexual fulfillment on demand

Cost of Walking Away from Pornography

- temporarily grieving the loss of an old friend
- temporary feeling of depression and emptiness
- feeling restricted in following a strong impulse
- no longer having an escape when feeling out of control
- not having sexual fulfillment on demand
- enduring withdrawals to a powerful addiction
- the arduous job of working through unresolved issues
- putting restrictive measures in place

Rewards of Walking Away from Pornography

- a growing contentment
- freedom from shame, guilt and remorse
- nothing to hide
- building a legacy of holiness
- blessing your family
- marital healing
- even emotions
- able to grow into emotional and spiritual maturity
- single-minded ministering with a clear conscience
- enjoying God's favor
- rediscovering your spouse
- intimacy with God
- life of integrity

> "If you want to stay stuck in your sin, confess it only to God. If you want to overcome it, confess it to someone else."

Once the decision has been made to give up pornography then you must clean house. This means getting rid of all forms of temptation that are accessible to you—magazines, books, DVDs, and cable channels that have sexual content. Accountability must be built into your computer, tablet, phone use and Netflix account. I would highly suggest adding accountability software to your computer that can be obtained through XXXchurch.[344]

Part of cleaning house is asking several men whom you trust to be your accountability partners. You will probably not have much success at overcoming this sin if you keep it hidden, known only to yourself. "Most relationships with porn thrive on isolation, secrecy, and denial. By talking openly and honestly with another person about your problem you automatically weaken your connection to porn."[345] Steve Gallagher has said: "If you want to stay stuck in your sin, confess it only to God. If you want to overcome it, confess it to someone else."[346] However, you must realize these men will only be as valuable to you as you are honest with them.

Having honest friendships with spiritually mature men where accountability is as natural as conversation, guards from dangerous subjective justification. Good friendship will encourage and challenge, uplift and rebuke. "Like an earring of gold or an ornament of fine gold is a wise man's rebuke to a listening ear" (Proverbs 25:12). A well-placed rebuke can save a man's life. These kinds of friendships are vital and worth seeking out. They demand honesty and courage, resulting in the fruit of mutual spiritual protection.[347]

While accountability has its place, it is not the be all and end all of overcoming a pornography addiction. The ultimate focus must be on Christ. Accountability groups too easily revert to legalism in which a person is pressured into religious conformity. A man can end up fighting sin (or denying his sin) because he fears the group's disapproval and not because he treasures Christ. The message again and again must not be simply, "You should not use porn," but "You need not use porn because God offers more."

One of the greatest fears of someone who wants to overcome a pornography addiction is the fear of failure or relapse. Some obsess about this and will even stop trying to overcome their addiction because they believe in trying they are only setting themselves up for more disappointment and failure. This fear of failure is putting the focus upon you instead of on God! God is a loving father who delights in forgiveness and in offering grace. Plus, victory is not found in your efforts, but in what the Holy Spirit will do through you. Your choice to defeat this addiction opens the door so that God can inhabit your lifestyle and enable you to focus on God and not your problems or your addiction.

If you don't know how to appropriate God's grace and power in your life for defeating sin and temptation, I would refer you back to an excellent article mentioned earlier in this chapter by John Piper entitled, "Gutsy Guilt," which appeared in *Christianity Today*.[348] In this article Piper gives a step-by-step process of defeating shame and guilt through an understanding and application of Colossians 2:13-15 and Micah 7:8-9.

> The more you say no to porn, the weaker the temptation will be. Not filling your mind with enticing images means you're less likely to recall them in moments of pressure. Sin is habit-forming, but so too is purity. . . Temptations come less frequently, and when they come they are weaker—less appealing and less powerful.[349]

The message again and again must not be simply, "You should not use porn," but "You need not use porn because God offers more."

I would encourage you to challenge anyone who is addicted to porn but who wants to be free from it, to take the forty-day challenge.

This means that the person will not look at porn or masturbate for at least forty days. Some people say this can be accomplished in 30-90 days, depending on the person and the strength of the addiction. What this accomplishes is a re-setting of the neuropathways in the brain.

> Neuro-chemical tolerance that is a factor in Internet addiction can be reversed if the addict is willing and able to establish a period of total sexual abstinence. This can usually be achieved in 30-90 days, the first 14 of which will be the most difficult. . . The abstinence period achieves a noticeable detoxification effect. It also begins to reverse a core belief of addicts that sex is their most important need.[350]

> **This re-setting of the brain is important because it allows you to focus on what is of supreme importance in your life.**

This re-setting of the brain is important because it allows you to focus on what is of supreme importance in your life. It is not enough to break the porn addiction, important as that is. "You must get a vision for something much bigger: a vision of reflecting Christ's glory in the world. Only this will be big enough to eclipse the appeals of porn."[351]

"But thanks be to God! He gives us the victory through our Lord Jesus Christ." --1 Corinthians 15:57.

Overview of the Counseling Process for A Pornography Addiction

Connect with the Teen
- They may call you and ask for help--if so, set up a meeting giving them instructions on location, time and length of session.
- You may hear from others about their pornography problem--if so, take pastoral initiative and go to them or call and set up a meeting.
- Prepare your meeting place and yourself by reviewing how to help someone with a pornography addiction. Don't forget to pray and ask the Holy Spirit for guidance and insight!
- Familiarize yourself with the symptoms of a porn addict.

Understand the Teen
- Communicate empathy by your posture, position and active listening skills.

- Communicate nonjudgmental, unconditional love and genuineness.
- Ask yourself the empathy question: "How would I feel if I was this student in this situation?"
- Prepare for denial because of the shame associated with a pornography addiction.

Explore with the Teen
- Find out when they first started using porn.
- Explore what kind of porn they are using, magazine, movies, internet sites, chat rooms, etc.
- Explore how much time they spend looking at porn.
- Discover if they have started "acting out" porn scenarios.
- Look for "exceptions"—times when they are not looking at porn. Try to schedule more times that will encourage exceptions.
- Help the teen identify "triggers" and help the teen avoid them.
- Help the teen understand that only God can fill the void in their life that they have been using porn to fill.
- Explore with the teen the costs of staying addicted to pornography and the rewards of giving it up.

Initiate a Plan with the Teen
- Lead them in confession of sin and assurance of forgiveness.
- Clean house—get rid of all movies, magazines, books and internet accounts that promote pornography.
- Teach them how to resist temptation.
- Involve the teen in an accountability group.
- Encourage the use of accountability software.
- Encourage them to take the 40-day challenge.

Finish with the Teen.
- Prepare for a relapse and take appropriate measures if one occurs.
- Maintain a continued relationship with the teen.

Helpful Resources

Ron Lagerquist, "Pornography Addiction." Freedom You: Health Is a Choice.
     http://www.freedomyou.com/pornography_addiction_intro_free domyou.aspx

Covenant Eyes—Internet Accountability and Filtering.
http://www.covenanteyes.com/
X3Watch. Accountability software. https://x3watch.com/

Selected Bibliography

Carnes, Patrick; Delmonico, David L.; and Griffin, Elizabeth. *In the Shadows of the Net: Breaking Free of Compulsive Online Sexual Behavior.* Center City, MN: Hazelden, 2001.

Chester, Tim. *Closing the Window: Steps to Living Porn Free.* Downers Grove, IL: InterVarsity Press, 2010.

Maltz, Wendy, and Maltz, Larry. *The Porn Trap: The Essential Guide to Overcoming Problems Caused by Pornography.* New York, NY: Harper, 2010.

Skinner, Kevin B. *Treating Pornography Addiction: The Essential Tools For Recovery.* Provo, UT: GrowthClimate, 2005.

Struthers, William M. *Wired For Intimacy: How Pornography Hijacks the Mail Brain.* Downers Grove, IL: IVP Books, 2009.

Exercise 14.1 - Understanding Pornography Addiction

Rate yourself on your knowledge and understanding pornography addiction. Use the scale provided: 1 = poor; 2 = below average; 3 = Average; 4 = Above average; 5 = Excellent. Simply check the box that best describes you. Be honest with yourself. Work on the areas that need improvement—it's not an assignment, it's a life that you might save!

Understanding Pornography Addiction	1	2	3	4	5
I am knowledgeable with the percentages of men and women who struggle with a pornography addiction.					
I understand how pornography short-circuits the brain and creates new neural pathways.					
I understand how early pornography viewing in adolescents contributes to PIED and is related to the Coolidge Effect.					
I am familiar with the symptoms of a sexual addiction.					
I am knowledgeable of the seven levels of a pornography addiction.					
I understand why and how a pornography addiction is maintained.					

I can identify the most common triggers that lead to pornography viewing.				
I am familiar with the five key ingredients that need to be in place if a person is going to win the battle against a pornography addiction.				
I am knowledgeable of the costs and rewards of giving up a pornography addiction.				
I understand the importance of cleaning house and accountability in defeating a pornography addiction.				

CHAPTER FIFTEEN

SELF-ESTEEM AND IDENTITY ISSUES

Self-esteem is an individual's overall and specific positive and negative self-evaluation. Whereas self-concept reflects beliefs and cognitions about the self (*I am good at trumpet; I am not so good at social studies*), self-esteem is more emotionally oriented (*Everybody thinks I'm a nerd*). – Robert S. Feldman[352]

From my view in family counseling, self-esteem can have significant impact on relationships. It generally seems that family members are more prone to act badly toward each other when they are feeling bad about themselves. The worse they feel about themselves, the worse they often treat others, the worse they get treated in return, the worse they end up feeling about themselves, the worse they treat others, and round and round the cycle of unhappiness goes. In low-esteem families, relationships can become mutually destructive. –Carl E. Pickhardt[353]

A Case Study

Kay is sixteen years old and has struggled with weight all her life. As far back as she can remember she has been teased about her weight. On the playground in grade school the other students would call her names like "fatty" and "tubby" and very few of the other students would want to play with her or sit by her in the lunch room. She was always picked last in gym class. The taunting and rejection continued throughout junior high school and into high school although it was more subtle. Kay found it difficult to make friends and found herself excluded from most social events. She didn't feel like attending the school ball games or concerts because she didn't have anyone to sit with.

Although Kay's mother is very loving and supportive towards her, there are still negative comments made at home. Kay's father would say things like, "Why don't you go on a diet?" or "What, are you snacking again? You know that is only going to make you fatter!" Her older brother, Jim, was embarrassed to be seen with her at school. Jim was very good looking, athletic and popular.

Kay is filled with negative thoughts about herself and is filled with self-doubt concerning her abilities to do anything. Anytime she looks in the mirror she only thinks about how ugly and fat she is. She wonders if any boy would ever like her and if marriage is even in her future.

Kay is very typical of many adolescents who struggle with self-esteem. Body issues are especially critical for adolescent girls as they constantly feel the need to compare themselves to the pictures of models on the glossy covers of the fashion magazines. She needs to learn that her self-esteem in not found in comparing herself to others, or some unrealistic standard, but in her relationship to God.

Statistics Relating to Adolescent Self-Esteem

- Among high school students, 44% of girls and 15% of guys are attempting to lose weight.
- Over 70% of girls age 15 to 17 avoid normal daily activities, such as attending school, when they feel bad about their looks.
- 75% of girls with low self-esteem reported engaging in negative activities like cutting, bullying, smoking, drinking, or disordered eating. This compares to 25% of girls with high self-esteem.
- About 20% of teens will experience depression before they reach adulthood.
- Teen girls that have a negative view of themselves are 4 times more likely to take part in activities with boys that they've ended up regretting later.
- 38% of boys in middle school and high school reported using protein supplements and nearly 6% admitted to experimenting with steroids.
- 7 in 10 girls believe that they are not good enough or don't measure up in some way, including their looks, performance in school and relationships with friends and family members.

> 7 in 10 girls believe that they are not good enough or don't measure up in some way, including their looks, performance in school and relationships with friends and family members.

- A girl's self-esteem is more strongly related to how she views her own body shape and body weight, than how much she actually weighs.[354]
- 74% of girls say they are under pressure to please everyone.
- 98% of girls feel there is an immense pressure from external sources to look a certain way.
- 92% of teen girls would like to change something about the way they look, with body weight ranking the highest.
- 90% of eating disorders are found in girls.

- 1 in 4 girls today fall into a clinical diagnosis – depression, eating disorders, cutting, and other mental/emotional disorders. On top of these, many more report being constantly anxious, sleep deprived, and under significant pressure.
- By age thirteen, 53% of American girls are "unhappy with their bodies." This grows to 78% by the time girls reach seventeen.[355]
- Teenage girls with negative views of themselves are four times more likely to engage in activities with boys that they later regret.
- 95% of teenagers have at some point in their lives felt inferior. The reasons for these feelings were most commonly connected to appearance, ability in a certain area, intelligence and size.
- A study conducted in 2013 found that 47% of girls age 11 to 14 refuse to take part in activities, such as swimming or performing in a play, that show their bodies to others. The study also showed that 23% of these girls are afraid to put their hands up in class.[356]

Characteristics of Students with Low Self-Esteem

Research has shown key differences between individuals with high and low self-esteem. For example, people with high self-esteem focus on growth and improvement, whereas people with low self-esteem focus on not making mistakes in life. Low self-esteem has been shown to be correlated with a number of negative outcomes, such as depression.[357]

> 95% of teenagers have at some point in their lives felt inferior. The reasons for these feelings were most commonly connected to appearance, ability in a certain area, intelligence and size.

People with low self-esteem have been found to model the following characteristics:

- They are more troubled by failure and tend to exaggerate events as being negative.
- They often interpret non-critical comments as critical.
- They are more likely to experience social anxiety and low levels of interpersonal confidence.
- They feel awkward, shy, conspicuous, and unable to adequately express themselves when interacting with others.
- They tend to be pessimistic towards people and groups within society.
- Research has also shown that low self-esteem has been linked to an increased risk of teenage pregnancy.

- They are at a higher risk for depression and suicide.

While boys and girls report similar levels of self-esteem during childhood, a gender gap emerges by adolescence, in that adolescent boys have higher self-esteem than adolescent girls. This drop in self-esteem seems to be related to body issues which seems to affect girls much more seriously than boys in adolescence.

> A study carried out by Dr Zimet (professor of pediatrics and clinical psychology) revealed that Adolescent boys with high self-esteem are almost 2 and a half times more likely to initiate sexual intercourse than boys with low self-esteem, while Girls with a high self-esteem are three times more likely to delay sexual intercourse than girls with low self-esteem.[358]

As you can see from the statistics and characteristics, a teenager who struggles with low self-esteem is at risk in a number of critical areas. Body image issues seem to be particularly problematic, especially for teenage girls. The best way to help a student who is struggling with self-esteem issues, is to help change their worldview. Instead of trying to develop self-esteem through worldly standards, the pastoral counselor must help the student develop a biblical sense of self-esteem. They must see themselves as God sees them.

Adolescents who attended church or other religious institutions are more likely to have a higher self-esteem than their peers who have no religious affiliation.

> Adolescents who attended church or other religious institutions are more likely to have a higher self-esteem than their peers who have no religious affiliation. It suggests that religious institutions play a part in teaching people how to have a positive self-esteem and have a healthy view of themselves.[359]

You Are What You Commit Yourself To

At the start of my senior year in high school, I had saved up enough money from working at the local Safeway that I was able to purchase my first car. I do have to say that it was sweet! It was a 1962 Chevy Impala Super Sport. It had a 327-cubic inch engine in it, a three-speed stick on the floor, a Holley four-barrel carburetor, and a Corvette clutch. It was custom painted metal-flake blue with chrome wheels all the way around, and a Muncie 8-track tape player under the dash. (Most of you reading this won't even know what an 8-track tape player is. Yes, I know. I'm old! Deal with it.) But the piece-de-resistance was the dual glass-pack Hollywood mufflers that I had installed. For those of who are automobile challenged, glass pack mufflers are barely legal and they make a lot of noise! I wanted people to hear me coming and to take notice of my cool car.

In the first week that I had purchased the car, I made plans for my glorious entrance to our youth group meeting. It was summertime and we were meeting outdoors at one of the elder's houses in town. I waited until I could be "fashionably late," and showed up revving the engine for all it was worth. They could hear me coming three blocks away.

Sure enough, as soon as I pulled into the driveway the whole group gathered around to admire my car. All the while I was secretly thinking, "Yeah, I'm cool! Just look at my car!" I craved the attention that I was getting.

Well, one of the other teens, Boyd, didn't like the attention I was getting. He was jealous so he started talking to the group about his newly purchased stereo. He was jabbering on about woofers and tweeters and a diamond stylus on his turn-table. I couldn't believe it—they were actually losing interest in my car and were fascinated by his stupid stereo!

Jeff, another teen from the youth group, felt left out and unimportant, so he started talking about his athletic scholarship to the U of O. He was describing in detail about how cool the athletic dormitory was, how well equipped the weight and training room was and the amount of tuition money that he was going to receive just to play football. It wasn't long before the group wasn't paying any attention to me or Boyd, but were focused on what Jeff was saying.

I was totally frustrated. This was supposed to be my moment of glory and these other guys were messing it up for me. All the while the preacher was just watching the interaction that was taking place. He knew what we were all trying to do and how we were trying to do it. When we all sat down to start the meeting and everyone was quiet, he just looked at us, smiled, and said: "Well, I'm a child of the King. Top that!"

In that moment, I knew he was right. He brought rebuke and conviction to my soul. I learned that night that genuine self-esteem didn't come from possessions or accomplishment or comparison to others. My self-esteem needed to come from my relationship to God. I was made in His image, loved, redeemed and adopted into His forever family and I could cry out, "Abba Father."[360]

I first heard Tony Campolo talk about the issue of identity and self-esteem at a National Youth Leader's Convention. He said that many teens and twenty-somethings who are confused about their identity or self-esteem make decisions based on the belief that the "self" is some separate entity, out somewhere in the world waiting to be discovered. Year after year, frustrated and confused college students drop out of school and take off on some trek to "go and find themselves."

> The self is not some separate entity "out there" waiting to be discovered. The self is found within, waiting to be created.

Why is it when someone feels the need to go and find themselves, they usually end up in Boulder, Colorado or Big Sur, California sitting on rock and contemplating their navel? Why don't they go to Fargo, North Dakota or downtown Detroit? In all my years of teaching college, when a student has dropped out to go and find themselves, I have never had one come back to me and say: "Dr. Zus, you wouldn't believe it. I was on my way to Boulder, Colorado to find myself and I stopped in Kansas City at a 7-11 to get a Slurpee, and guess who I found in there playing video games? It was my self! We had a happy reunion and now I feel whole!"

That will never happen because the self is not some separate entity "out there" waiting to be discovered. The self is found within, waiting to be created. Because you are what you commit yourself to. Think about all of the different demographic groups that you find in a typical high school. There are jocks, preps, stoners, goths, band nerds, computer geeks, skaters, artsy-fartsy types, and the list goes on. I will just take one of these groups for illustration purposes. I will take jocks.

What makes a jock a jock? His entire life revolves around sports. He wakes up in the morning thinking about the big game that night. He has a bowl of Wheaties for breakfast, looking at the champion on the box, dreaming about the day that his picture will be there for everyone to see. He goes to school and his locker is with the other jocks. He sits with like-minded jocks in all of his classes. At lunch the jocks all sit together at the same lunch table, and no other group dare invade their space or suffer the consequences. When classes are done, he heads to gym and puts on his uniform and gets psyched for the game. After the game is over he heads home and thinks about every aspect of the game. He watches a little ESPN before going to sleep and dreaming about the day when he will become a professional athlete. In other words, he eats, breaths, sleeps and lives for sports. You are what you commit yourself to.

In Jeremiah 2:5 the prophet says this about the people of Israel: "They followed worthless idols and became worthless themselves." (NIV)

You see, they became what they committed themselves to. They committed themselves to worthless idols and they became worthless themselves.

The path to developing a healthy self-esteem and self-image is found in making a wise choice in what you commit yourself to. If you commit yourself to Jesus Christ, you will reflect his love and grace. The fruit of the spirit will be manifest in your life.[361] How can you not have a healthy self-image when you are reflecting Christ?

> **You are what you commit yourself to.**

Dangers or Problems Related to the Issue of Self-Esteem

As we have shown previously, low self-esteem has been implicated in problems with being overweight and obesity, anxiety, depression, suicide and delinquency in middle and late childhood and adolescence. Youth with low self-esteem who were followed through life were discovered to have a lower life satisfaction at 30 years of age. The negative aspects of having a low self-esteem can follow you through your life!

Low and decreasing self-esteem in adolescence was linked to adult depression, poor physical health, worse economic prospects and higher levels of criminal behavior.

On the other side of the coin, having a healthy sense of self-esteem is no guarantee of success in life because self-esteem perceptions do not always match reality! Have you ever watched the tryouts for American Idol? Case closed! The results of international math tests from eight different counties were examined. Results? The investigators found that mathematical self-esteem had an inverse relation to actual mathematical accomplishment.

Sociological studies found that sometimes students with high self-esteem exhibit arrogance and a grandiose sense of superiority over others. Some with high self-esteem end up exhibiting antisocial behavior in that they become bullies.

No matter how much the public school system is concerned about trying to develop a positive self-esteem in their students, it was found that there are only moderate correlations between school performance and self-esteem and these correlations do not suggest that high self-esteem produces better school performance. Efforts to increase students' self-esteem have not always led to improved school performance. In fact, it was found that when students advanced to college and received genuine critique of their work, the students had a melt down because they had never received any negative feedback before. They were emotionally soft and unprepared for the real world.

Too many of today's young people are growing up receiving praise for mediocre or even poor performance, and as a consequence have an inflated sense of self-esteem. This in turn causes them to have problems handling competition and criticism.

Researchers have also found that inflated praise, although well-intended may cause children with low self-esteem to avoid important learning experiences and life challenges.

> Sociological studies found that sometimes students with high self-esteem exhibit arrogance and a grandiose sense of superiority over others.

Another serious problem with the self-esteem movement is that society has begun to excuse evil or destructive behavior on the grounds of low self-esteem. But self-esteem, whether high or low, does not determine one's actions. We are accountable for them and we are responsible for trying to do good and to avoid evil.

Exposing False Ideas of Self-Worth

One of contributing factors to students struggling with their self-esteem is that they compare themselves with others and end up feeling inferior by comparison. The problem with using this as a standard is that you can always find someone who is worse than you at something, and you can always find someone who is better than you at something. 2 Corinthians 10:12 states, "We do not dare to classify or compare ourselves with some who commend themselves. When they measure themselves by themselves and compare themselves with themselves, they are not wise." (NIV) Trying to gain a healthy sense of self-esteem by making comparisons of yourself with others is a losing proposition. The standard is ever changing. You must look for an unchanging standard instead. More about that is to come.

Physical attractiveness is probably the greatest source of self-esteem problems. Between 70-80 percent of teenage girls are not satisfied with their appearance. Society has such an unrealistic standard that no one could possibly live up to it and maintain it. Students don't realize that all of the photos of the gorgeous models on the covers of the fashion magazine have all been photo-shopped. There are a number of videos on the internet which show how much the models have been enhanced and how unrealistic it would be to try and match it.[362]

Dove Real Beauty sketches took random volunteers and had them describe themselves to a professional sketch artist who then drew a picture of them only from their own description. Then a total stranger described them to the sketch artist who drew them from that description. Then they compared pictures and showed them to the volunteers. It was an eye-opening experience. The volunteers realized they had a tendency to over-emphasize their perceived flaws and understate their natural beauty.[363]

From a biblical standpoint, beauty and outward features are not to be desired over inward transformation or character. For example, Saul was chosen as the first king over Israel. What stood out that impressed the people? Saul was "an impressive young man without equal among the Israelites—a head taller than any of the others."[364] Even though he had this impressive beginning God quickly rejected him. "I am grieved that I have made Saul king, because he has turned away from me and has not carried out my instructions."[365]

Who did God choose to take Saul's place? David. While he was also handsome in appearance (1 Samuel 16:12), that is not what motivated God to choose him over all others. "But the Lord said to Samuel, 'Do not consider his appearance or his height, for I have rejected him. The Lord does not look at the things man looks at. Man looks at the outward appearance, but the Lord looks at the heart.'"[366]

The Bible reiterates the importance of character over outward beauty for women, also. "Charm is deceptive, and beauty is fleeting, but a woman who fears the Lord is to be praised."[367] "Your beauty should not come from outward adornment, such as braided hair and the wearing of gold jewelry and fine clothes. Instead, it should be that of your inner self, the unfading beauty of a gentle and quiet spirit, which is a great worth in God's sight."[368]

Another source of self-esteem that teens turn to is intelligence or getting good grades. Of course, this backfires if you are a girl because most boys won't ask an intelligent girl out on a date because they lack self-confidence themselves and smart girls intimidate them. So, if a girl wants to be asked out, she has to play "dumb" in order to placate the boy's fragile ego.[369]

My wife has always been an intelligent woman, but she will verify that it isn't always to a person's advantage to be smart. When she was in college studying for her RN degree, she had a number of challenging courses such as Anatomy and Physiology and Microbiology. She studied hard for the tests in order to do well. When the grades came back, she was ridiculed and teased as a "curve-wrecker" because of her high score. She felt like she wasn't allowed to feel good about her ability because it made others jealous or mad.

God's view of the world's wisdom teaches us that there are other things which we should hold in higher esteem, such as the salvation of our souls through the sacrifice of Christ.

> [18] For the message of the cross is foolishness to those who are perishing, but to us who are being saved it is the power of God. [19] For it is written:
>
> "I will destroy the wisdom of the wise; the intelligence of the intelligent I will frustrate."
>
> [20] Where is the wise person? Where is the teacher of the law? Where is the philosopher of this age? Has not God made foolish the wisdom of the world? [21] For since in the wisdom of God the world through its wisdom did not know him, God was pleased through the foolishness of what was preached to save those who believe. [22] Jews demand signs and Greeks look for wisdom, [23] but we preach Christ crucified: a stumbling block to Jews and foolishness to Gentiles, [24] but to those whom God has called, both Jews and Greeks, Christ the power of God and the wisdom of God. [25] For the foolishness of God is wiser than human wisdom, and the weakness of God is stronger than human strength. (I Corinthians 1:19-25 NIV)

Another area where students try to gain a positive sense of self-esteem is through success. This can be in any arena; academic, athletic, arts, music or math. The problem with trying to gain a healthy sense of self-esteem through the avenue of success is that it is competitively achieved. This means it is not enough for you to succeed, others must fail! What teen feels good about himself, when he is secretly praying for the failure of his peers in order that he might succeed?

I have seen the proof of this issue in my own classrooms. I have set up a hypothetical situation where I told a student that he received a B-on his final exam. I ask him how he feels about it. The student will always say that he is very disappointed. When I tell him that it is the highest grade in the class, he quickly changes his mind and is happy with his score. What made the difference? When competitively compared to the other students in the class, he came out on top—the best. So, he feels good about himself.

The last area I will cover concerning self-esteem among teenagers is that of popularity. If a teen sees herself as popular with her peers and the boys, then she will generally have high self-esteem. If she feels that she is on the outside looking in at the social scene, then she will have low self-esteem. Because teens want to be popular, they will generally do whatever it takes to fit in and be popular with the "in" crowd. Unfortunately, that usually means breaking their own moral code, even though the Bible admonishes us: "Do not follow the crowd in doing wrong."[370]

The Correct Basis for Self-Esteem

> The truest facts about you are what God says about you, *not* what your emotions say about you.

The Bible teaches that men and women have a special worth because we were the only creatures in all of God's creation who were made in His image and likeness.[371] Some would argue that when Adam and Eve sinned in the Garden, we lost that image and that after the fall there was nothing that God saw as worthwhile in all of humankind. But that thought is in error because in Psalm 8:4-5 the Bible declares: "What is man that you are mindful of him, the son of man that you care for him? You have made him a little lower than the heavenly beings and crowned him with glory and honor." (NIV) Note that this statement was written after the fall in the Garden. God still sees people as having great value and a purpose in God's kingdom.

In Romans 5:6-8 Paul writes: "You see, at just the right time, when we were still powerless, Christ died for the ungodly. Very rarely will anyone die for a righteous man, though for a good man someone might possibly dare to die. But God demonstrates his own love for us in this: While we were still sinners, Christ died for us." (NIV) Notice that Paul does not say that we are "worthless," but that we are "powerless." The Greek word that is translated "powerless" can also be translated as "helpless," "sick," or "weak."[372] This is why we need Jesus, because we are powerless or helpless to save ourselves from our sin. But what we could not do, God did through the sacrificial death of His son. We were sick with sin—a sickness that leads to death if untreated. As serious as that is, it still doesn't make us worthless!

When my wife and I were new parents, our oldest son was only about three days old and I remember how horrified I was to see my firstborn perform projectile vomiting! I mean it came out of his nose and out of his mouth and shot all the way across the room. It was like something out of the Exorcist! Horrified and scared as I was, I didn't say to my wife, "This baby is worthless, send him back." No, he wasn't worthless, but he was sick and in need of some loving attention. It is the same with us. Though we are diseased with sin, God doesn't see us as worthless, but as sick, weak, and helpless. In his great love, he sent Jesus to redeem and heal us.

The truest facts about you are what God says about you, *not* what your emotions say about you. Don't misunderstand me. I am not saying that emotions are not important—I am saying that emotions are easily manipulated by circumstances, hormones, health and a host of other things. Because they are so easily manipulated, you cannot rely on them 100% of the time as a valid judge of your self-worth.

When I was first married, for my Christmas present that year my father-in-law, who was a certified flight instructor, told me that he would give me enough free flying lessons until I received my private pilot's license. My brother-in-law owned his own plane and his gift to me was that I could use his plane for free. All I had to do was pay for the gas and oil until I had logged enough hours until I received my private pilot's license. It was a really sweet deal.

One of the first lessons that my flight instructor drilled into my head was always "Trust your instruments." What he was especially referring to was the horizon on the instrument panel. The horizon told you if the plane was flying level or not. This is important because the weather could change unexpectedly and you would find yourself totally surrounded by white clouds. When that happens, you may experience a phenomenon known as vertigo. Vertigo is a disorienting sensation that tricks your senses into thinking that you are actually flying upside down! Everything in your guts and your bodily experience screams out to you that you are flying upside down. At this point, you must make a decision. You have to decide if you are going to trust your sensations or your emotions or trust your instruments. If you decide to trust your emotions, you will make a decision that will cost you your life because you will actually turn the plan upside down and crash into the ground and die a fiery death. But trusting your instruments will save your life! They will guide you down through the clouds, level and safe so that you may live to fly again.

As it is with flying, so it is with your self-esteem. You must learn to trust your instruments and *not* your feelings. What is your primary instrument that can be trusted in every situation? It is the Bible. The Bible declares that you have worth. 1 Peter 1:18-19 declares: "For you know that it was not with perishable things such as silver or gold that you were redeemed from the empty way of life handed down to you from your ancestors, but with the precious blood of Christ, a lamb without blemish or defect." (NIV) God loves you enough that he sent his son to die for you. That indicates great worth. Trust your instruments!

Another choice you can make that will improve your self-esteem is to compensate for your weaknesses by concentrating on your strengths. Instead of comparing yourself to other people and focusing in on the abilities or characteristics that you don't have, learn to identify the gifts that God has given you and then use them to the best of your ability for His glory. The great missionary to China and Olympic gold medalist, Eric Liddell is quoted as saying: "I believe God made me for a purpose, but he also made me fast! And when I run I feel his pleasure."[373]

When I was a teenager growing up, I was always one of the smallest boys in my class. I tried out for basketball with the rest of the boys in the seventh grade, but I knew very quickly there was no way that I was going to get any playing time or be any good at the game simply because I was too small. The other players towered over me and I couldn't get a shot off to save my soul. If I would have fixated on my failure as a basketball player, my self-esteem would have taken a nosedive. Luckily for me, our school also

> **You must learn to trust your instruments and *not* your feelings.**

had a gymnastics team. I was very strong for my age, flexible and agile and quickly adapted to all the events and routines. Floor exercise and the pommel horse were my strongest events, even though I entered the all-around competition. I was good enough that I received a Varsity letter my Freshman year in high school. That was quite an achievement "back in the old days." It definitely helped bolster my self-esteem.

Not only do we receive natural gifts and abilities inherited from our parents, but God also bestows on us special spiritual gifts. We are to use these gifts for the building up of the body of Christ. No one is to look down on someone else's gift, or despise their own. Each person should use their gift for the benefit of others and find fulfillment in doing so, knowing that you are carrying out part of God's purpose for your life.[374]

> **The value of an object is often determined by what someone is willing to pay for it.**

The value of an object is often determined by what someone is willing to pay for it. I have seen works of modern art sell for millions of dollars. I certainly didn't see that much value in the abstract forms on the canvas—but somebody did and they were willing to pay an exorbitant price to own it! Please understand that you have been purchased at a great cost also--the ultimate sacrifice. God sent his son to die an excruciating death that you might be saved. God values you enough that he would personally experience the death that was meant for you and me in order that we might have eternal life.[375]

Your worth is not based upon comparison with others, but upon your response to God and *his* judgment.[376] In the parable of the talents, God doesn't compare the men with each other, but with the opportunity and ability that each was given. He gives the same praise to the one who gained ten talents and the one who gained five. His condemnation of the man who only was given one talent, was not because he didn't do as well compared to the other men, but because he didn't do anything with what he was given. Success in life is not measured by what we are or what we have done, but rather by what we are and have done compared to what we *could* have been and *could* have done according to God's gifts to us and opportunities to serve.[377]

I will share some concluding insights on self-acceptance that every teen who struggles with self-esteem issues needs to understand. First of all, each and every person has been personally designed by God. You are the perfect you! No one else can be as good of a "you," as you can. God doesn't want you to be your best imitation of some model or Hollywood star. He wants you to be the you that he prescribed before your birth.[378] You must also realize that you are a work in progress. God isn't finished with you yet, but he has promised that he will not stop until you are complete.[379] God wants to do more with your life than you could ever think of in your wildest imagination.[380] Last of all, keep in mind that outward beauty is not related to inward happiness or satisfaction. Jesus Christ was the most complete, loving, patient, compassionate, joyful man who ever walked the face of the earth. Yet scripture says, "He had no beauty or majesty to attract us to him, nothing in his appearance that we should desire him."[381] Your personal fulfillment and self-esteem should not depend on your physical attributes, but on your inward character and relationship to Jesus Christ.

My good friend, Steve Thomas, wrote a short story that does the very best job of explaining how much God loves you and his plans for your life. It is called, "The Gift."

> If I could give you a gift, I'd give you what you already have. . . Jesus. More of Him, more believably in your life. Which is a difficult thing to do. The way I would try it would be to give you a few words I think Jesus would say to you.

> **Your worth is not based upon comparison with others, but upon your response to God and *his* judgment.**

He would call you by your name and wouldn't start talking until you looked Him straight in the eyes. Then once your eyes were on Him, He'd say:

I *like* you. I'm not stuck with you. I *chose* you. Before I ever made this planet and spun it into orbit, I had you in mind. I picked you. I think you count. I have plans for you that you might not be able to imagine or believe.

You are my workmanship, my work of art, my poem, my sculpture. But I'm not finished with you. I don't make "instant masterpieces." I go a little at a time. Sometimes I know you wish I would hurry up and finish. But don't forget, I get my pleasure from the process as well as the finished product.

And please don't misunderstand this! When I re-shape and re-fashion you--when I bend and shape you to make changes I want--don't forget I am doing this because I love you! I want your life to show the beauty of my craftsmanship. Sometimes when I fashion you, it will hurt. Especially when you resist my hand. But sometimes, even when you cooperate, it will hurt. Some changes are just painful.

When I am working one of those painful changes--especially then--don't forget that it is I, not "chance," at work. You can't trust "chance" when it hurts, but you can trust me. I know how far to go--just how much pressure and stress you can take. Please trust me to never go past that point. Sometimes you will think I have. But trust me. I won't.

And don't be discouraged by the fact that this stress point is different for you than for someone else. I know you. I made you. And because of that, I know where I can do my most profound work in you. I don't love you less or someone else more because I'm not doing the same things in both of your lives.

Believe this: the masterpiece I am shaping in you is *already* wonderful beyond your belief. The finished work will go beyond that.

For when I am finished, *YOU'LL LOOK LIKE ME!*[382]

Doesn't that thought bring joy to your heart? "Dear friends, now we are children of God, and what we will be has not yet been made known. But we know that when he appears, we shall be like him, for we shall see him as he is."[383] How can you *not* but feel good about yourself, when you look in the mirror and see Jesus staring back at you?

Overview of the Counseling Process for Self-Esteem and Identity Issues

Connect with the Teen
- They may call you and ask for help--if so, set up a meeting giving them instructions on location, time and length of session.
- You may receive a referral from concerned parents about their teen's self-esteem --if so, take pastoral initiative and go to them or call and set up a meeting.
- Prepare your meeting place and yourself by reviewing how to deal with self-esteem and identity issues. Don't forget to pray and ask the Holy Spirit for guidance and insight!

Understand the Teen
- Communicate empathy by your posture, position and active listening skills.
- Communicate nonjudgmental, unconditional love and genuineness.
- Ask yourself the empathy question: "How would I feel if I was this student in this situation?"
- Be familiar with the characteristics of a teen who struggles with a low self-esteem.

Explore with the Teen
- Listen for false ideas of self-worth and help the teen identify and correct them.
- Explore inaccurate perceptions of body image—especially with teenage girls.
- Teach the correct basis for self-esteem from a Christian perspective.

Initiate a Plan with the Teen

- Replace false ideas of self-worth with correct ones.
- Eliminate any false perceptions concerning physical beauty and comparisons to magazine models.
- Teach them to trust what God says about them, not necessarily their feelings.
- Help them to trust in God's continuing work to transform them into the image of Christ.
- Compensate for any weaknesses by emphasizing their strengths.

Finish with the Teen

- If needed, refer to a professional Christian counselor.
- Maintain a continuing relationship with the teen.

Helpful Resources

Amy LaTour. "8 Common Causes of Low Self-Esteem." *Good Choices Good Life.* http://www.goodchoicesgoodlife.org/choices-for-young-people/boosting-self-esteem/

Carl E. Pickhardt. "Adolescence and Self-Esteem." *Psychology Today.* (September 6, 2010) https://www.psychologytoday.com/blog/surviving-your-childs-adolescence/201009/adolescence-and-self-esteem.

"Self-Esteem and Teenagers." *Reach Out.com.* https://parents.au.reachout.com/common-concerns/everyday-issues/self-esteem-and-teenagers

Selected Bibliography

Dobson, James. *Preparing for Adolescence: How to Survive the Coming Years of Change.* Ada, MI: Revell, 2005.

Goff, Sissy. *Growing Up Without Getting Lost: Discovering Your Identity in Christ.* Grand Rapids, MI: Zondervan, 2008.

McDowell, Josh. *Building Your Self-Image.* Wheaton, IL: Tyndale House Publishers, 1986.

Exercise 15.1 Understanding Self-Esteem and Identity Issues

Rate yourself on your knowledge and understanding of self-esteem and identity issues. Use the scale provided: 1 = poor; 2 = below average; 3 = Average; 4 = Above average; 5 = Excellent. Simply check the box that best describes you. Be honest with yourself. Work on the areas that need improvement—it's not an assignment, it's a life that you might save!

Understanding Self-Esteem and Identity Issues	1	2	3	4	5
I am knowledgeable with the percentages of adolescents, both male and female, who struggle with self-esteem issues.					
I understand how having a low self-esteem can negatively affect a developing adolescent.					
I understand the impact that body image has on an adolescent's self-esteem--especially females.					
I am familiar with the characteristics of adolescents who struggle with a low self-esteem.					
I understand that one's identity is not some separate entity waiting to be discovered, but that identity comes from what one is committed to.					
I understand that negative consequences concerning one's self-esteem is not limited to those who have a poor self-esteem. Those with a high self-esteem may struggle with problematic issues, also.					
I am familiar with all of the false or unhealthy ways that students try to build up their self-esteem.					
I am familiar with the correct basis for building a healthy self-esteem.					
I have confidence that I can show students how God sees them from a biblical standpoint.					

CHAPTER SIXTEEN

CONCLUSION

When a student opens up to you about spiritual, emotional, or relational problems, it can often feel like "holy ground" as you become the loving presence of Christ in the teenager's life. –Les Parrot III[384]

Listening to the stories of pain and heartache from a young person can be overwhelming at times. You may wonder if you are up to the task. You may even feel completely lost and wonder how you can help at all. If you resonate with this, I hope you will allow me to encourage you. The very fact that a young person has confided in you regarding their problems and concerns communicates a special trust and respect that will positively aid in the counseling process. While you may not feel fully equipped to deal with the complicated mental health issues that you are presented with, remember that the very presence of a caring individual who practices basic listening skills and who has a good relationship with the teenager can still make a huge difference in that person's life by simply helping them clarify their feelings and looking for available solutions.

"Addressing the barriers that interfere with a student's spiritual development is a crucial part of ministry. Counseling teenagers on personal or emotional difficulties can go hand in hand with attending to their spiritual needs."[385]

I would offer five hindrances that the youth counselor must be aware of in order to maintain a healthy and helpful counseling relationship with the young people that you are called to serve and help.

First, resist the lure to rescue. Because of your age and experience, you may truly know the choices that would be in the best interests of the young person, but you must not make those choices for them. You must listen and guide them so that they make the choice for themselves. When you rescue a young person by making choices for them you subtly communicate to the young person that they are incapable of dealing with the problem themselves. This damages their self-esteem, self-confidence and keeps them from maturing and learning through taking responsibility for their own actions. If you continually rescue them, then the next time a problem comes along the young person is no better prepared to solve the problem than the first time.

Secondly, avoid overdoing advice giving. There is a time and place to provide information and insight that the young person is not capable of obtaining for themselves. But a good counselor needs to be careful not to overuse advice giving and concentrate primarily on listening, understanding and providing emotional support.

Third, be careful of excessive emotional involvement. Being a successful counselor requires a certain amount of empathy, genuineness, and unconditional love. But becoming too involved emotionally will hinder your ability to stay circumspect concerning the teen's problems and may hinder your ability to confront sin or destructive behavioral choices.

Fourth, guard your purity and integrity and do not let the closeness of the counseling relationship become sexual. Because transference will often take place in a counseling relationship, this can be misunderstood for sexual attraction and illicit sexual involvement is the result. "Sexually intimate behavior between therapists and their clients has emerged as an increasingly serious problem within the profession, as revealed by an examination of the records in three arenas—ethics cases, malpractice suits, and licensing board hearings."[386] This is especially heinous when it occurs within the church. The psychological and emotional devastation that results from this violation of trust is deep and the scars remain for years.

Last of all, guard yourself against feelings of inadequacy when a problem isn't solved. Emotional, psychological and relational issues are complicated and there are no quick and easy solutions. Even when a significant amount of time is spent on a particular problem, it still may not be resolved for a number of reasons outside of your control. Even professional counselors do not have a 100% success rate!

Allow yourself to be used by God and guided by the Holy Spirit to bring comfort and healing to the teenagers entrusted to your care. Keep in mind the following principles when engaging with a young person to help them with a counseling issue, whether it is emotional, spiritual, behavioral or relational.

- Depend upon the Holy Spirit's ministry as Counselor and Comforter. Go to Him in prayer for guidance, wisdom and healing power. (John 14:16-17)
- The Bible should be your basic reference tool for helping students with problems. You should use it wisely and appropriately. (2 Tim 3:16-17)
- Remember that prayer is a crucial part of effective biblical counseling. Pray with and for the student you are counseling when possible. (James 5:16)
- The ultimate goal of counseling is to help students become more like Jesus—not necessarily to make them happy. Our counseling

efforts and involvement should enable the Christian students to grow into spiritual maturity and holiness and to introduce non-Christian students to the invitation and call of Christ. (Rom 8:29; 2 Cor 3:18; Matt 28:18-20)

- The style or approach in counseling that you use should be flexible depending upon the counselee and the specific problem that needs addressed.
- Whatever techniques or methods of counseling that you employ should be consistent with the Bible's teaching and values. (1 Thess 5:21)
- Be aware of your own limitations and know how and when to make a referral to a professional.[387]

Index of Topics

Endnotes for the Introduction

[1] Josh McDowell and Bob Hostetler, *Handbook on Counseling Youth* (Nashville, TN: W Publishing Group, 1996), p. 12.

[2] Les Parrott III, *The Comprehensive Guide to Youth Ministry Counseling* (Loveland, CO: Group Publishing, 2002), p. 6.

[3] All of the names have been changed to protect the privacy of these individuals. Some represent a combination of young people I have encountered, but all represent very real people and situations that the average youth worker will encounter.

[4] G. Wade Rowatt Jr. *Adolescents In Crisis: A Guide For Parents, Teachers, Ministers, and Counselors*. (Louisville, KY: Westminster John Knox Press, 2001), p. 3.

[5] Joan Sturkie and Siang-Yang Tan. *Advanced Peer Counseling In Youth Groups* (Grand Rapids, MI: Zondervan, 1993), p. 11.

[6] "Mental Health Facts: Children and Teens." National Alliance on Mental Illness. www.nami.org. accessed October 30, 2016. https://www.nami.org/getattachment/Learn-More/Mental-Health-by-the-Numbers/childrenmhfacts.pdf

[7] Clyde M. Narramore, *Counseling Youth* (Grand Rapids, MI: Zondervan, 1966) p. 7.

[8] Josh McDowell and Bob Hostetler, *Handbook on Counseling Youth* (Nashville, TN: W Publishing Group, 1996), pp. v-vii.

[9] Clyde M. Narramore, *Counseling Youth* (Grand Rapids, MI: Zondervan, 1966) p. 12.

[10] Proverbs 15:23 and 25:11. All scripture is from the New International Version.

Endnotes for Chapter One

[11] Rich Van Pelt. *Intensive Care: Helping Teenagers in Crisis* (Grand Rapids, MI: Zondervan, 1988), p. 32.

[12] Les Parrott III, "How Can We Help Hurting Adolescents?" in Richard R. Dunn and Mark H. Senter III *Reaching a Generation For Christ* (Chicago, IL: Moody Press, 1997), p. 515.

[13] Not his real name.

[14] Les Parrott III. *Helping the Struggling Adolescent* (Grand Rapids, MI: Zondervan, 2000), p. 25.

[15] Keith Olson, *Counseling Teenagers* (Loveland, CO: Group Books, 1984), p. 1.

[16] Siang-Yang Tan, *Counseling and Psychotherapy: A Christian Perspective* (Grand Rapids, MI: Baker Academic, 2011), p. 14.

[17] This exercise is suggested by Keith Olson in *Counseling Teenagers* (Loveland, CO: Group Books, 1984), p. 2.

[18] Keith Olson, *Counseling Teenagers* (Loveland, CO: Group Books, 1984), pp. 1-2.

[19] Carl R. Rogers et al., *The Therapeutic Relationship and Its Impact* (Madison: University of Wisconsin Press, 1967); Douglas A. Bernstein and Peggy W. Nash, *Essentials of Psychology*, 3rd ed. (Boston, MA: Houghton Mifflin Company, 2008), pp. 506-507; Josh McDowell and Bob Hostetler, *Handbook On Counseling Youth* (Nashville, TN: W Publishing Group, 1996), pp. 10-11; Keith Olson, *Counseling Teenagers* (Loveland, CO: Group Books, 1984), p. 3.

[20] Graham A. Barker, and Clifford J. Powell. *From Woe to Go: A Training Text For Christian Counselors.* (Bloomington, IN: Balboa Press, 2014), p. 43.

[21] Les Parrott III. *Helping the Struggling Adolescent* (Grand Rapids, MI: Zondervan, 2000), p. 32.

[22] Les Parrott III. *Helping the Struggling Adolescent* (Grand Rapids, MI: Zondervan, 2000), p. 30.

[23] Gary Collins, *How to Be a People Helper* (Ventura, CA: Regal Books, 1976) p. 34.

[24] Keith Olson, *Counseling Teenagers.* (Loveland, CO: Group Books, 1984), p. 5.

[25] Graham A. Barker, and Clifford J. Powell. *From Woe to Go: A Training Text For Christian Counselors.* (Bloomington, IN: Balboa Press, 2014), p. 45.

[26] Gary Collins, *How to Be a People Helper.* (Ventura, CA: Regal Books, 1976) p. 34.

[27] Les Parrott III. *Helping the Struggling Adolescent.* (Grand Rapids, MI: Zondervan, 2000), p. 31.

[28] Les Parrott III. *Helping the Struggling Adolescent.* (Grand Rapids, MI: Zondervan, 2000), p. 35.

[29] Les Parrott III. *Helping the Struggling Adolescent.* (Grand Rapids, MI: Zondervan, 2000), pp. 46-47.

[30] Rich Van Pelt. *Intensive Care: Helping Teenagers in Crisis.* (Grand Rapids, MI: Zondervan, 1988), p. 33.

[31] "The Benefits of Laughter" http://www.cnn.com/2007/HEALTH/06/04/pl.laughter/index.html

[32] Keith Olson, *Counseling Teenagers.* (Loveland, CO: Group Books, 1984), p. 8.

[33] Graham A. Barker, and Clifford J. Powell. *From Woe to Go: A Training Text For Christian Counselors.* (Bloomington, IN: Balboa Press, 2014), p. 49.

[34] Graham A. Barker, and Clifford J. Powell. *From Woe to Go: A Training Text For Christian Counselors.* (Bloomington, IN: Balboa Press, 2014), p. 41.

[35] David G. Benner, *Strategic Pastoral Counseling: A Short-Term Structured Model.* (Grand Rapids, MI: Baker Publishing, 1992, 2003), p. 15.

[36] David G. Benner, *Strategic Pastoral Counseling: A Short-Term Structured Model.* (Grand Rapids, MI: Baker Publishing, 1992, 2003), p. 15.

[37] David G. Benner, *Strategic Pastoral Counseling: A Short-Term Structured Model.* (Grand Rapids, MI: Baker Publishing, 1992, 2003), p. 37.

[38] David G. Benner, *Strategic Pastoral Counseling: A Short-Term Structured Model.* (Grand Rapids, MI: Baker Publishing, 1992, 2003), p. 37.

[39] Les Parrott III. *Helping the Struggling Adolescent.* (Grand Rapids, MI:

Zondervan, 2000), pp. 50.

Endnotes for Chapter Two

[40] Josh McDowell and Bob Hostetler. *Handbook on Counseling Youth* (Nashville, TN: W Publishing Group, 1996), p.7.

[41] Rich Van Pelt. *Intensive Care: Helping Teenagers in Crisis* (Grand Rapids, MI: Zondervan, 1988), p. 21.

[42] Gary Collins, *How to Be a People Helper* (Ventura, CA: Regal Books, 1976), p. 71.

[43] Keith Olson, *Counseling Teenagers* (Loveland, CO: Group Books, 1984), p. 485.

[44] "Catharsis" comes from the Greek, meaning purification. Aristotle used it to refer to the emotional purgation which spectators experience while viewing a tragic play. Freud understood catharsis as a discharge of painful memories from early childhood. In other therapies such as Gestalt, the focus is frequently on the ventilation of anger. T.L. Brink, "Catharsis" in *Baker Encyclopedia of Psychology*, David G. Benner, Ed. (Grand Rapids, MI: Baker Book House, 1985), pp. 150-151.

[45] Rich Van Pelt. *Intensive Care: Helping Teenagers in Crisis* (Grand Rapids, MI: Zondervan, 1988), p. 46.

[46] Rich Van Pelt. *Intensive Care: Helping Teenagers in Crisis* (Grand Rapids, MI: Zondervan, 1988), p. 56.

[47] H. Norman Wright. *Crisis Counseling* (Ventura, CA: Regal Books, 1993), p. 55.

[48] Rich Van Pelt. *Intensive Care: Helping Teenagers in Crisis* (Grand Rapids, MI: Zondervan, 1988), p. 46.

[49] See: Genesis 39:2, 21, 23. Later Joseph told his brothers that all of his misfortunes had occurred as a part of God's plan to preserve the family (Genesis 45:5-8).

Endnotes for Chapter Three

[50] Dave Carlson, "Principles of Informal Counseling," in *The Youth Leader's Sourcebook*, ed. Gary Dausey. (Grand Rapids, MI: Zondervan, 1983), p. 303.

[51] G. Keith Olson, *Counseling Teenagers*. (Loveland, CO: Group Books, 1984), p. 165.

[52] In 1961, the Joint commission on Mental Illness found that 42% of people who sought help with an emotional problem, first went to a member of the clergy, while 29% sought out a local physician, 18% sought psychologists and psychiatrists, and 10% sought social services. In 1981, a University of Michigan research team replicated the previous study, surveying 2,267 Americans. The study found that despite the increase in the use of mental health specialists in the 1960s and 1970s, about four out of ten Americans continued to choose a

minister for help with counseling issues. The actual number of people seeking help from a member of the clergy increased by approximately 50% between 1957 and 1967. The researchers summarized the results of their study by stating, "One cannot fail to be impressed by the continuing role that clergy play in assisting many Americans in dealing with personal problems." Andrew J. Weaver, "Has There Been A Failure to Prepare and Support Parish-Based Clergy in Their Role as Frontline Community Mental Health Workers: A Review." *The Journal of Pastoral Care*. Summer 1995, Vol 49, No 2. pp. 129-147.

[53] Richard Dayringer. *The Heart of Pastoral Counseling*. (New York, NY: The Haworth Pastoral Press, 1998), pp. 57-58.

[54] Helen Harris Perlman, *Relationships: The Heart of Helping People*. (Chicago, IL: University of Chicago Press, 1979), p. 12.

[55] Richard Dayringer. *The Heart of Pastoral Counseling*. (New York, NY: The Haworth Pastoral Press, 1998), p. 5.

[56] Petruska Clarkson, "Integrative Psychotherapy, Integrating Psychotherapies, or Psychotherapy after 'Schoolism;?" In Colin Feltham, *Which Psychotherapy?* (Thousand Oaks, CA: Sage, 1997), p. 35.

[57] I. D. Yalom. *Existential Psychotherapy*. (New York: Basic Books, 1980), p. 401.

[58] I.V. Coleman. "Patient-Physician Relationships in Psychotherapy." *American Journal of Psychiatry* 104. April 1948, p. 641.

[59] Dave Carlson, "Principles of Informal Counseling," in *The Youth Leader's Sourcebook*, ed. Gary Dausey. (Grand Rapids, MI: Zondervan, 1983), p. 298.

[60] Dave Carlson, "Principles of Informal Counseling," in *The Youth Leader's Sourcebook*, ed. Gary Dausey. (Grand Rapids, MI: Zondervan, 1983), p. 299.

[61] Rich Van Pelt, *Intensive Care*. (Grand Rapids, MI: Zondervan, 1988), pp. 41-59; David E. Carlson, "Principles of Student Counseling" in Warren S. Benson and Mark H. Senter III, *The Complete Book of Youth Ministry*. (Chicago, IL: Moody Press, 1987), pp. 409-420; G. Keith Olson, *Counseling Teenagers*. (Loveland, CO: Group Books, 1984), pp. 147-163; Robert E. Doyle, *Essential Skills Strategies in the Helping Process*. (Pacific Grove, CA: Brooks/Cole Publishing Company, 1992), pp. 46-61; Robert R. Carkhuff, *The Art of Helping VII*. (Amherst, MA: Human Resource Development Press, 1993), pp. 31-192; Josh McDowell and Bob Hostetler, *Josh McDowell's Handbook on Counseling Youth*. (Nashville, TN: W Publishing Group, 1996), pp. 12-14.

[62] Van Pelt, *Intensive Care*. (Grand Rapids, MI: Zondervan, 1988), pp. 45.

[63] Leona E. Tyler, *The Work of the Counselor*. (New York, NY: Appleton-Centure-Crofts, 1969) quoted in G. Keith Olson, *Counseling Teenagers*. (Loveland, CO: Group Books, 1984), p. 202.

[64] Barbara B. Varenhorst, *Training Teenagers For Peer Ministry: A Step-by Step Program Teaching Kids How to Care for Each Other*. (Loveland, CO: Group Books, 1988), p. 42.

[65] "Active Listening." Skills You Need. skillsyouneed.com. accessed

October 5, 2016, http://www.skillsyouneed.com/ips/active-listening.html.

[66] David G. Martin, *Counseling and Therapy Skills*. (Prospect Heights, IL: Waveland Press, Inc., 1983, 1989), p. 22.

[67] Josh McDowell and Bob Hostetler, *Josh McDowell's Handbook on Counseling Youth*. (Nashville, TN: W Publishing Group, 1996), p. 13.

[68] Gerard Egan, *The Skilled Helper: A Problem-Management Approach to Helping*. 5th ed. (Pacific Grove, CA: Books/Cole Publishing Company, 1994), pp. 91-92.

[69] David Dillon, *Short-Term Counseling: Utilizing Short-Term Therapy In Your Counseling Ministry*. (Waco, TX: Word, Inc., 1992), pp. 70-71.

[70] Carol Lesser Baldwin, *Friendship Counseling: Biblical Foundations for Helping Others*. (Grand Rapids, MI: Zondervan, 1988), pp. 128-129.

[71] Robert R. Carkhuff, *The Art of Helping VII*. (Amherst, MA: Human Resource Development Press, 1993), p. 92.

[72] Robert R. Carkhuff, *The Art of Helping VII*. (Amherst, MA: Human Resource Development Press, 1993), p. 97.

[73] Robert R. Carkhuff, *The Art of Helping VII*. (Amherst, MA: Human Resource Development Press, 1993), p. 107.

[74] Charles Allen Kollar, *Solution-Focused Pastoral Counseling: An Effective Short-Term Approach for Getting People Back on Track*. (Grand Rapids, MI: Zondervan, 1997, 2011), p. 38.

[75] Charles Allen Kollar, *Solution-Focused Pastoral Counseling: An Effective Short-Term Approach for Getting People Back on Track*. (Grand Rapids, MI: Zondervan, 1997, 2011), pp. 80-81, 151.

[76] Charles Allen Kollar, *Solution-Focused Pastoral Counseling: An Effective Short-Term Approach for Getting People Back on Track*. (Grand Rapids, MI: Zondervan, 1997, 2011), pp. 81, 151.

[77] Charles Allen Kollar, *Solution-Focused Pastoral Counseling: An Effective Short-Term Approach for Getting People Back on Track*. (Grand Rapids, MI: Zondervan, 1997, 2011), pp. 81, 151.

[78] Joel Latner, *The Gestalt Therapy Book*. (New York, NY: The Julian Press, 1973), p. 70.

[79] Robert R. Carkhuff, *The Art of Helping VI*. (Amherst, MA: Human Resource Development Press, 1987), p. 141.

[80] Robert R. Carkhuff, *The Art of Helping VI*. (Amherst, MA: Human Resource Development Press, 1987), p. 144,146.

[81] Charles Allen Kollar, *Solution-Focused Pastoral Counseling: An Effective Short-Term Approach for Getting People Back on Track*. (Grand Rapids, MI: Zondervan, 1997, 2011), p. 67.

[82] Charles Allen Kollar, *Solution-Focused Pastoral Counseling: An Effective Short-Term Approach for Getting People Back on Track*. (Grand Rapids, MI: Zondervan, 1997, 2011), p. 105.

[83] Robert R. Carkhuff, *The Art of Helping VI*. (Amherst, MA: Human Resource Development Press, 1987), p. 162.

[84] Adapted from: Robert R. Carkhuff, *The Art of Helping VI*. (Amherst,

MA: Human Resource Development Press, 1987).

Endnotes for Chapter Four

[85] Rich Van Pelt, *Intensive Care* (Grand Rapids, MI: Zondervan, 1988), p. 91.

[86] G. Keith Olson, *Counseling Teenagers* (Loveland, CO: Group Books, 1984), p. 235.

[87] Gary Collins, *How to Be A People Helper: You Can Help The Others In Your Life*. (Ventura, CA: Regal Books, 1976), pp. 66-67.

[88] Wayne Oates, *Protestant Pastoral Counseling* (Philadelphia, PA: The Westminster Press, 1962), p. 112.

[89] Rich Van Pelt, *Intensive Care* (Grand Rapids, MI: Zondervan, 1988), p. 91.

[90] Rich Van Pelt, *Intensive Care* (Grand Rapids, MI: Zondervan, 1988), p. 92.

[91] Gary Collins, *How to Be A People Helper: You Can Help The Others In Your Life*. (Ventura, CA: Regal Books, 1976), p. 112.

[92] Howard J. Clinebell, *Community Mental Health: The Role of Church and Temple*. (Nashville, TN: Abingdon Press, 1970), p. 247.

[93] Howard J. Clinebell, *Basic Types of Pastoral Counseling* (Nashville, TN: Abingdon Press, 1966), p. 178; Gary R. Collins, *Christian Counseling* (Dallas, TX: Word Publishing, 1988), p. 70.

Endnotes for Chapter Five

[94] Paul G. Quinnett, *Suicide: The Forever Decision*. (New York, NY: The Crossroad Publishing Company, 2011), p. 5.

[95] As quoted in: Josh McDowell & Bob Hostetler, *Josh McDowell's Handbook on Counseling Youth*. (Nashville, TN: Thomas Nelson, 1996), p. 103.

[96] This case study is a composite of several teenage suicides but is a fair representation of what a teenage suicide looks like.

[97] American Association of Suicidology. "U.S.A. Suicide: 2014 Official Final Data." Accessed: October 28, 2016. http://www.suicidology.org/Portals/14/docs/Resources/FactSheets/2014/2014datapgsv1b.pdf

[98] Catharine Paddock. "Suicide Rates Rising in US, CDC Report." Accessed October 28, 2016. http://www.medicalnewstoday.com/articles/309507.php

[99] Catharine Paddock. "Suicide Rates Rising in US, CDC Report." Accessed October 28, 2016. http://www.medicalnewstoday.com/articles/309507.php

[100] Sally C. Curtain, Margaret Warner, and Holly Hedegaard. "Increase in Suicide in the United States, 1999-2014. NCHS Data Brief No. 241. April 2016. Accessed October 28, 2016. http://www.cdc.gov/nchs/products/databriefs/db241.htm

[101] American Association of Suicidology. "Understanding and Helping the

Suicidal Individual." Accessed: October 28, 2016. http://www.suicidology.org/Portals/14/docs/Resources/FactSheets/Understandi ngHelpingSuicidalIndividual.pdf

[102] The Jason Foundation. "Youth Suicide Statistics." Accessed October 28, 2016. http://jasonfoundation.com/youth-suicide/facts-stats/

[103] American Association of Suicidology. "Depression and Suicide Risk (2014). Accessed October 28, 2016. http://www.suicidology.org/Portals/14/docs/Resources/FactSheets/2011/Depres sionSuicide2014.pdf

[104] American Association of Suicidology. "AAS Childhood Sexual Abuse and Suicide 2014." Accessed October 28, 2016. http://www.suicidology.org/Portals/14/docs/Resources/FactSheets/2011/ChildS exualAbuseSuicide2014.pdf

[105] The Jason Foundation. "Youth Suicide Statistics." Accessed October 28, 2016. http://jasonfoundation.com/youth-suicide/facts-stats/

[106] The Jason Foundation. "Youth Suicide Statistics." Accessed October 28, 2016. http://jasonfoundation.com/youth-suicide/facts-stats/

[107] The Jason Foundation. "Youth Suicide Statistics." Accessed October 28, 2016. http://jasonfoundation.com/youth-suicide/facts-stats/

[108] CDC. "Suicide: Facts at a Glance. 2015." Accessed October 28, 2016. https://www.cdc.gov/violenceprevention/pdf/suicide-datasheet-a.pdf

[109] David Elkind, "The Facts About Teen Suicide," *Parents* magazine, January 1990, p. 111.

[110] Karen Mason, *Preventing Suicide: A Handbook for Pastors, Chaplains and Pastoral Counselors*. (Downers Grove, IL: IVP Books, 2014), p. 52.

[111] Albert Y. Hsu, *Grieving a Suicide: A Loved One's Search for Comfort, Answers and Hope*. (Downers Grove, IL: InterVarsity Press, 2002), p. 29.

[112] Bill Blackburn, *What You Should Know About Suicide*. (Waco, TX: Word Books, 1982), pp. 20-30.

[113] Paul Quinnett, QPR Institute. "What Is QPR?" Accessed October 28, 2016. https://www.qprinstitute.com/about-qpr

[114] Paul Quinnett, *Question, Persuade, Refer: Ask a Question, Save a Life*. (Missouri Department of Mental Health, 1991), p. 16.

[115] Albert Y. Hsu, *Grieving a Suicide: A Loved One's Search for Comfort, Answers and Hope*. (Downers Grove, IL: InterVarsity Press, 2002), p. 100.

[116] Albert Y. Hsu, *Grieving a Suicide: A Loved One's Search for Comfort, Answers and Hope*. (Downers Grove, IL: InterVarsity Press, 2002), p. 100.

[117] Gilbert Meilaender, *Bioethics*. (Grand Rapids, MI: Eerdmans, 1996), p. 59.

[118] Albert Y. Hsu, *Grieving a Suicide: A Loved One's Search for Comfort, Answers and Hope*. (Downers Grove, IL: InterVarsity Press, 2002), p. 99.

[119] Karen Mason, *Preventing Suicide: A Handbook for Pastors, Chaplains and Pastoral Counselors*. (Downers Grove, IL: IVP Books, 2014), p. 18.

[120] Albert Y. Hsu, *Grieving a Suicide: A Loved One's Search for Comfort, Answers and Hope*. (Downers Grove, IL: InterVarsity Press, 2002), p. 9.

[121] Anne-Grace Scheinin as quoted in: Albert Y. Hsu, *Grieving a Suicide: A Loved One's Search for Comfort, Answers and Hope.* (Downers Grove, IL: InterVarsity Press, 2002), p. 13.

[122] Albert Y. Hsu, *Grieving a Suicide: A Loved One's Search for Comfort, Answers and Hope.* (Downers Grove, IL: InterVarsity Press, 2002), p. 18.

[123] Albert Y. Hsu, *Grieving a Suicide: A Loved One's Search for Comfort, Answers and Hope.* (Downers Grove, IL: InterVarsity Press, 2002), p. 27.

[124] Albert Y. Hsu, *Grieving a Suicide: A Loved One's Search for Comfort, Answers and Hope.* (Downers Grove, IL: InterVarsity Press, 2002), p. 27.

[125] American Association of Suicidology. "Surviving After Suicide Fact Sheet - 2010." Accessed October 31, 2016. http://www.suicidology.org/Portals/14/docs/Survivors/Loss%20Survivors/Survivors-of-Suicide-Fact-Sheet_2010.pdf

[126] Albert Y. Hsu, *Grieving a Suicide: A Loved One's Search for Comfort, Answers and Hope.* (Downers Grove, IL: InterVarsity Press, 2002), p. 30.

Endnotes for Chapter Six

[127] Steven Arterburn and Jim Burns. *Drug Proof Your Kids.* (Ventura, CA: Regal Books, 1995) p. 1.

[128] Stephen Van Cleave, Walter Byrd and Kathy Revell. *Counseling for Substance Abuse and Addiction.* (Waco, TX: Word, 1987), pp. 11-12.

[129] Not his real name. All of the names are fictional to protect the identity of the person. While the names are fictional, the case studies are all real.

[130] Research Update. Butler Center For Research. May 2016. "Prevalence of Adolescent Substance Misuse." Hazelden Betty Ford Foundation. Accessed November 2, 2016. https://www.hazelden.org/web/public/document/bcrup_0100.pdf

[131] National Institute on Drug Abuse. "Principles of Adolescent Substance Use Disorder Treatment: A Research Based Guide. Accessed November 1, 2016. https://www.drugabuse.gove/publications/principles-adolescent-substance-use-disorder-treatment-reaserch-based-guide/introduction.

[132] Research Update. Butler Center For Research. May 2016. "Prevalence of Adolescent Substance Misuse." Hazelden Betty Ford Foundation. Accessed November 2, 2016. https://www.hazelden.org/web/public/document/bcrup_0100.pdf

[133] National Institute on Drug Abuse. "DrugFacts—High School and Youth Trends. Revised June 2016. Accessed November 1, 2016. https://www.drugabuse.gov/publications/drugfacts/high-school-youth-trends

[134] Les Parrott III. *Helping the Struggling Adolescent.* (Grand Rapids, MI: Zondervan, 2000), p. 125.

[135] Romans 7:7

[136] National Institute on Drug Abuse for Teens. "Prescription Drugs." Accessed November 2, 2016. https://teens.drugabuse.gov/drug-facts/prescription-drugs

[137] Foundation For a Drug-Free World. "The Truth About Prescription Drug Abuse." Accessed November 2, 2016. http://www.drugfreeworld.org/drugfacts/prescription/abuse-international-statistics.html

[138] National Institute on Drug Abuse. "Preventing Drug Use Among Children and Adolescents (In Brief). Accessed November 2, 2016. https://www.drugabuse.gov/publications/preventing-drug-abuse-among-children-adolescents/chapter-1-risk-factors-protective-factors/what-are-highest-risk

[139] G. Wade Rowatt, Jr. *Adolescents In Crisis: A Guide for Parents, Teachers, Ministers, and Counselors.* (Louisville, KY: Westminster John Knox Press, 2002), p. 170.

[140] For more detailed descriptions of the various drug categories and their effects see: G. Keith Olson, *Counseling Teenagers.* (Loveland, CO: Group Books, 1984) pp. 470-475; Mental Health First Aid, *Mental Health First Aid USA.* (Lutherville, MD: Mental Health Association of Maryland, 2013), pp. 72-85; Casa Palmera. "Top 8 Drug Categories." Accessed November 4, 2016. https://casapalmera.com/top-8-drug-categories.

[141] Beth Polson and Miller Newton, *Not My Kid: A Parent's Guide to Kids and Drugs.* (New York, NY: Avon Books, 1984), p. 54.

[142] Beth Polson and Miller Newton, *Not My Kid: A Parent's Guide to Kids and Drugs.* (New York, NY: Avon Books, 1984), p. 60.

[143] American Psychiatric Association. *Diagnostic and Statistical Manual of Mental Disorders, Fifth Ed. DSM-5.* (Washington, DC: American Psychiatric Publishing, 2013), p. 490.

[144] American Psychiatric Association. *Diagnostic and Statistical Manual of Mental Disorders, Fifth Ed. DSM-5.* (Washington, DC: American Psychiatric Publishing, 2013), pp. 490-491.

[145] Michael B. First, ed. *DSM-IV-TR Mental Disorders: Diagnosis, Etiology, and Treatment.* (Hoboken, NJ: Wiley, 2005), pp. 352-353.

[146] Les Parrott III. *The Comprehensive Guide to Youth Ministry Counseling.* (Loveland, CO: Group Books, 2002), p. 93.

[147] Intervention. - http://www.intervention.com/faqfintv.html#necessary. Accessed 9/25/08.

[148] I would highly recommend the program "Intervention" which can be seen on A & E as an example of how a professional intervention takes place. You can also go to the web site: http://www.aetv.com/intervention/ to learn more about an intervention.

[149] Les Parrott III, *Helping the Struggling Adolescent.* (Grand Rapids, MI: Zondervan, 2000), p. 100.

[150] Stephen Van Cleave, Walter Byrd and Kathy Revell. *Counseling for Substance abuse and Addiction.* (Waco, TX: Word, 1987), p. 143.

[151] Les Parrott III. *The Comprehensive Guide to Youth Ministry Counseling.* (Loveland, CO: Group Books, 2002), p. 91.

[152] Patrick Welsh. "Students' Scars Point to Emotional Pain." Accessed 9/30/08 http://www.usatoday.com/news/opinion/editorials/2004-06-27-oplede_x.htm.

[153] Patrick Welsh. "Students' Scars Point to Emotional Pain." http://www.usatoday.com/news/opinion/editorials/2004-06-27-oplede_x.htm. Accessed 9/30/08

[154] TeenHelp.com. "Cutting Statistics and Self-Injury Treatment." Accessed: November 11, 2016. https://www.teenhelp.com/physical-health/cutting-statistics-and-self-injury-treatment/

[155] Dennis Romboy. "Cutting Away the Pain." Accessed 9/30/08. http://www.toddlertime.com/dx/borderline/cutting-away-pain.htm.

[156] The Refuge: A Healing Place. "Self-Injury: Statistics, Causes, Signs & Symptoms." Accessed: November 11, 2016. http://www.therefuge-ahealingplace.com/co-occurring/self-injury/effects-symptoms-signs/

[157] TeenHelp.com. "Cutting Statistics and Self-Injury Treatment." Accessed: November 11, 2016. https://www.teenhelp.com/physical-health/cutting-statistics-and-self-injury-treatment/

[158] Kristin Magaldi. *Medical Daily*. "Self-Harm Is On the Rise With Teens, And Needing Attention Has Nothing to Do With It." (June 25, 2015). Accessed: November 9, 2016. http://www.medicaldaily.com/self-harm-rise-teens-and-need-attention-has-nothing-to-it-339974.

[159] Walt Mueller. *The Center for Parent/Youth Understanding*. "Crying Through Their Cuts." Accessed November 9, 2016. https://cpyu.org/resource/crying-through-their-cuts/

[160] Samantha Gluck. HealthyPlace. "Self Injury, Self Harm Statistics and Facts." Accessed: November 10, 2016. http://www.healthyplace.com/abuse/self-injury/self-injury-self-harm-statistics-and-facts/

[161] Bill Gaultiere. *Soul Shepherding*. "Caring for People Who Cut Themselves (Help for Self-Injury) Accessed: November 9, 2016. http://www.soulshepherding.org/2012/08/caring-for-people-who-cut-themselves-help-for-self-injury/ and *Mental Health America*. "Self-Injury (Cutting, Self-Harm or Self-Mutilation) Accessed: November 11, 2016. http://www.mentalhealthamerica.net/self-injury

[162] Although 60 percent of self-injurers have never had suicidal thoughts, self-injury can be a harbinger of suicidal behavior. It can also accidentally result in suicide. Jane E. Brody. *The New York Times. (*May 6, 2008) "The Growing Wave of Teenage Self-Injury. Accessed: November 11, 2016. http://www.nytimes.com/2008/05/06/health/06brod.html

[163] "The Problem of Cutting or Self-Harm." http://kidshealth.org/teen/your_mind/mental_health/cutting.html

[164] Opposing viewpoints in Context. "Self-Cutting Is a Serious Problem." Accessed: November 9, 2016.http://ic.galegroup.com/ic/ovic/ViewpointsDetailsPage/ViewpointsDetails

Window?displayGroupName=Viewpoints&prodId=OVIC&action=2&catId=&docu mentId=GALE%7CEJ3010510206&userGroupName=san30851&jsid=3b16b3f6d8b 11a4e60768a8d2e767e62

[165] *The Refuge: A Healing Place.* "Self-Injury: Statistics, Causes, Signs & Symptoms." Accessed: November 11, 2016. http://www.therefuge-ahealingplace.com/co-occurring/self-injury/effects-symptoms-signs/

[166] Crimson Ashes. Accessed 9/30/08 http://members.aol.com/crimsonashes7/page22.html. The Refuge: A Healing Place. "Self-Injury: Statistics, Causes, Signs & Symptoms." Accessed: November 11, 2016. http://www.therefuge-ahealingplace.com/co-occurring/self-injury/effects-symptoms-signs/

[167] Secret Shame. Accessed 9/30/08. http://www.palace.net/~llama/psych/injury.html

[168] *Life In Student Ministry*, posted December 3, 2007." Tips for helping a cutter find relief."
Accessed: November 10, 2016. *http://www.studentministry.org/tips-for-helping-a-cutter-find-relief/*

[169] Ken Mueller. "Cutting to Cope." Accessed 9/30/08 www.cpyu.org/Page.aspx?id=77237

[170] Marilee Strong. *A Bright Red Scream: Self-Mutilation and the Language of Pain.* (New York, NY: Viking, 1998), pp. 161-162.

Endnotes for Chapter Eight

[171] Raymond E. Vath. *Counseling Those With Eating Disorders.* (Waco, TX: Word Books, 1986), pp. 10.

[172] Michele Siegel, Judith Brisman and Margot Weinshel. *Surviving an Eating Disorder: Strategies for Family and Friends.* (New York, NY: HarperCollins, 1997), p. 5.

[173] David Sue, Derald Wing Sue and Stanley Sue. *Understanding Abnormal Behavior.* (Boston, MA: Houghton Mifflin Company, 2006), pp. 527-539.

[174] Eating Disorder Hope. "Teen, Adolescent and Children's Eating Disorders." Accessed: November 18, 2016. https://www.eatingdisorderhope.com/treatment-for-eating-disorders/special-issues/teen-adolescent-children

[175] National Eating Disorders Association. "Parent Toolkit." P. 10. Accessed: November 18, 2016. https://www.nationaleatingdisorders.org/sites/default/files/Toolkits/ParentToolk it.pdf

[176] The Healthy Teen Project. "Adolescent Eating Disorders Such as Anorexia, Bulimia and Binge Eating Disorders Are Treatable." Accessed: November 18, 2016. http://www.healthyteenproject.com/adolescent-eating-disorders-ca

[177] National Eating Disorders Association. "Parent Toolkit." P. 10.

Accessed: November 18, 2016.
https://www.nationaleatingdisorders.org/sites/default/files/Toolkits/ParentToolk
it.pdf

[178] National Eating Disorders Association. "Parent Toolkit." P. 11.
Accessed: November 18, 2016.
https://www.nationaleatingdisorders.org/sites/default/files/Toolkits/ParentToolk
it.pdf

[179] National Eating Disorders Association. "Parent Toolkit." P. 11.
Accessed: November 18, 2016.
https://www.nationaleatingdisorders.org/sites/default/files/Toolkits/ParentToolk
it.pdf

[180] National Eating Disorders Association. "Parent Toolkit." P. 12.
Accessed: November 18, 2016.
https://www.nationaleatingdisorders.org/sites/default/files/Toolkits/ParentToolk
it.pdf

[181] Les Parrott III. *Helping the Struggling Adolescent.* (Grand Rapids, MI:
Zondervan, 2000), p. 138.

[182] P.A. Neuman and P.A. Halvorson. *Anorexia Nervosa and Bulimia: A
Handbook for Counselors and Therapists.* (New York, NY: Guilford Press, 1985), p.
2.

[183] Adapted from *The Diagnostic and Statistical Manual IV TR.*

[184] David Sue, Derald Wing Sue and Stanley Sue. *Understanding
Abnormal Behavior.* (Boston, MA: Houghton Mifflin Company, 2006), p. 534.

[185] American Psychiatric Association. *Diagnostic and Statistical Manual of Mental
Disorders. 5th Ed.* (Washington, DC: American Psychiatric Association, 2013), p.
345.

[186] David Sue, Derald Wing Sue and Stanley Sue. *Understanding
Abnormal Behavior.* (Boston, MA: Houghton Mifflin Company, 2006), p. 536.

[187] "Helping Someone With an Eating Disorder."
http://helpguide.org/mental/eating_disorder_treatment.htm Accessed 10/01/08

[188] There are three tests available in the appendix of Les Parrott's book,
Helping the Struggling Adolescent, which would be very helpful and a good place
to start. There are also a number of free, self-scoring tests available on line, i. e.
http://psychologytoday.psychtests.com/tests/eating_disorders_access.html,
http://anred.com/slf_tst.html.

Endnotes for Chapter Nine

[189] Lynn Heitritter & Jeanette Vought, *Helping Victims of Sexual Abuse.*
(Minneapolis, MN: Bethany House Publishers, 1989), p. 13.

[190] Kay Scott, *Sexual Assault: Will I Ever Feel Okay Again?* (Minneapolis,
MN: Bethany House Publishers, 1993), p. 130.

[191] TeenHelp.com. "Sexual Abuse Statistics" accessed: November 21,
2016 https://www.teenhelp.com/sexual-abuse-trauma/sexual-abuse-statistics/

[192] Dan B. Allender. *The Wounded Heart: Hope For Adult Victims of*

Childhood Sexual Abuse. (Colorado Springs, CO: NavPress, 1990), p. 74.

[193]TeenHelp.com. "Sexual Abuse Statistics" accessed: November 21, 2016 https://www.teenhelp.com/sexual-abuse-trauma/sexual-abuse-statistics/

[194]TeenHelp.com. "Sexual Abuse Statistics" accessed: November 21, 2016 https://www.teenhelp.com/sexual-abuse-trauma/sexual-abuse-statistics/

[195] Josh McDowell & Bob Hostetler, *"Josh McDowell's Handbook on Counseling Youth: A Comprehensive Guide for Equipping Youth Workers, Pastors, Teachers, Parents.* (Nashville, TN: W Publishing Group, 1996), p. 349.

[196] Lynn Heitritter & Jeanette Vought, *Helping Victims of Sexual Abuse.* (Minneapolis, MN: Bethany House Publishers, 1989), pp. 23-27.

[197] Kay Scott, *Sexual Assault: Will I Ever Feel Okay Again?* (Minneapolis, MN: Bethany House Publishers, 1993), p. 128.

[198] Josh McDowell & Bob Hostetler, *Handbook on Counseling Youth.* (Nashville, TN: W Publishing Group, 1996), p. 372.

[199] Lynn Heitritter & Jeanette Vought, *Helping Victims of Sexual Abuse.* (Minneapolis, MN: Bethany House Publishers, 1989), p. 28-32.

[200] Lynn Heitritter & Jeanette Vought, *Helping Victims of Sexual Abuse.* (Minneapolis, MN: Bethany House Publishers, 1989), p. 39.

[201] Scott Gibson, *The Comprehensive Guide to Youth Ministry Counseling.* (Loveland, CO: Group Publishing, 2002), p. 19.

[202] Rape Abuse and Incest National Network. http://www.rainn.org/get-information/statistics/sexual-assault-victims. Accessed: 10/4/08.

[203] Scott Gibson, *The Comprehensive Guide to Youth Ministry Counseling.* (Loveland, CO: Group Publishing, 2002), p. 21.

Endnotes for Chapter Ten

[204] G. Wade Rowatt, Jr. *Adolescents in Crisis: A Guide for Parents, Teachers, Ministers, and Counselors.* (Louisville, KY: Westminster John Knox Press, 2001), p. 147.

[205] Les Parrott III. *Helping the Struggling Adolescent: A Guide to Thirty Common Problems for Parents, Counselors, & Youth Workers.* (Grand Rapids, MI: Zondervan Publishing House, 1993), p. 87.

[206] Josh McDowell & Bob Hostetler, *Josh McDowell's Handbook on Counseling Youth: A Comprehensive Guide for Equipping Youth Workers, Pastors, Teachers, Parents.* (Nashville, TN: W Publishing Group, 1996), p. 60.

[207] TeenHelp.com. "Teen Depression, Statistics & Facts." Accessed: December 5, 2016. https://www.teenhelp.com/teen-depression/teen-depression-statistics/

[208] TeenHelp.com. "Teen Depression, Statistics & Facts." Accessed: December 5, 2016. https://www.teenhelp.com/teen-depression/teen-depression-statistics/

[209] TeenHelp.com. "Teen Depression, Statistics & Facts." Accessed: December 5, 2016. https://www.teenhelp.com/teen-depression/teen-depression-statistics/

[210] American Psychiatric Association. *Diagnostic and Statistical Manual of Mental Disorders, Fifth Edition.* (Arlington, VA: American Psychiatric Association, 2013), pp. 160-161.

[211] Sally Schwer Canning. *The Comprehensive Guide to Youth Ministry Counseling.* (Loveland, CO: Group Publishing, 2002), p. 76; Tim LaHaye. *How to Win Over Depression.* (Grand Rapids, MI: Zondervan Publishing House, 1974) pp. 29-31; Florence Littauer. *Blow Away the Black Clouds: A woman's Answer to Depression.* (Eugene, OR: Harvest House, 1979), pp. 13-21; Siang-Yang Tan and John Ortberg. *Coping With Depression. Revised and Expanded.* (Grand Rapids, MI: Baker Books, 2004), pp. 15-16.

[212] Les Parrott III. *Helping the Struggling Adolescent: A Guide to Thirty Common Problems for Parents, Counselors, & Youth Workers.* (Grand Rapids, MI: Zondervan Publishing House, 1993), p. 89.

[213] H. Norman Wright. *Training Christian to Counsel: A Resource and Training Manual.* (Denver, CO: Christian Marriage Enrichment, 1977), p. 70.

[214] *Mental Health First Aid USA.* (Lutherville, MD: Mental Health Association of Maryland, 2013), p. 24.

Endnotes for Chapter Eleven

[215] G. Wade Rowatt Jr. *Adolescents in Crisis: A Guide for Parents, Teachers, Ministers, and Counselors.* (Louisville, KY: Westminster John Knox Press, 2001), p. 98.

[216] Linda I. Shands, *What Now? Help for Pregnant Teens.* (Downers Grove, IL: InterVarsity Press, 1997), p. 15.

[217] Josh McDowell & Bob Hostetler, *Josh McDowell's Handbook On Counseling Youth: A Comprehensive Guide for Equipping Youth Workers, Pastors, Teachers, Parents.* (Nashville, TN: Word Publishing Group, 1996), p. 292.

[218] CDC Center for Disease Control and Prevention. "Reproductive Health: Teen Pregnancy." Accessed: December 16, 2016. https://www.cdc.gov/TeenPregnancy/index.htm

[219] Teen Pregnancy Statistics. "Teen Pregnancy Facts. Accessed: December 16, 2016. http://www.teenpregnancystatistics.org/content/teen-pregnancy-facts.html

[220] "About Teen Pregnancy" http://www.cdc.gov/TeenPregnancy/AboutTeenPreg.htm

[221] "Teen Pregnancy Statistics" http://unplannedpregnancy.adoptionblogs.com/weblogs/title-212

[222] Kristin Moore, "Teenage Motherhood: Social and Economic Consequences," The Urban Institute, Washington, D.C., 1979, 32.

[223] The most common date rape drugs, also called "club drugs", are flunitrazepam (Rohypnol), also called roofies; gamma hydroxybutyric acid (GHB), also called liquid ecstasy; and ketamine, also called Special K. These drugs may come as pills, liquids, or powders. Medicinenet.com. "Date Rape Drugs. Accessed: December 17, 2016.

[224] Teen Pregnancy Statistics. "Reasons for Teen Pregnancies." Accessed: December 16, 2016. http://www.teenpregnancystatistics.org/content/reasons-for-teen-pregnancies.html

[225] Carolyn Owens and Linda Roggow. *Pregnant and Single: Help for Touch Choices.* (Grand Rapids, MI: Zondervan, 1984), pp. 14-15.

[226] Howard J. Clinebell, Jr., *Basic Types of Pastoral Counseling.* (Nashville, TN: Abingdon Press, 1966), p. 164.

[227] Carolyn Owens and Linda Roggow, *Pregnant and Single: Help for the Tough Choices.* (Grand Rapids, MI: Zondervan, 1984), p. 21.

[228] Linda I. Shands, *What Now? Help for Pregnant Teens.* (Downers Grove, IL: InterVarsity Press, 1997), p. 44.

[229] Carolyn Owens and Linda Roggow, *Pregnant and Single: Help for the Tough Choices.* (Grand Rapids, MI: Zondervan, 1984), p. 81.

[230] Linda I. Shands, *What Now? Help for Pregnant Teens.* (Downers Grove, IL: InterVarsity Press, 1997), p. 28.

[231] Linda Lowen. (Updated June 22, 2015). About.com. "Ten Teen Pregnancy Facts." Accessed: December 16, 2016. http://womensissues.about.com/od/datingandsex/tp/Teenpregancy.htm

[232] Keith Olson, *Counseling Teenagers.* Loveland, CO: Group, 1984, p. 411.

[233] Jayne E. Schooler. *"Mom, Dad. . . I'm Pregnant." When Your Daughter or Son Face an Unplanned Pregnancy.* (Colorado Springs, CO: NavPress, 2004), p. 73.

[234] John 8:44 NIV

[235] Jayne E. Schooler. *"Mom, Dad. . . I'm Pregnant." When Your Daughter or Son Face an Unplanned Pregnancy.* (Colorado Springs, CO: NavPress, 2004), p. 80.

[236] Jayne E. Schooler. *"Mom, Dad. . . I'm Pregnant." When Your Daughter or Son Face an Unplanned Pregnancy.* (Colorado Springs, CO: NavPress, 2004), p. 80.

[237] Jayne E. Schooler. *"Mom, Dad. . . I'm Pregnant." When Your Daughter or Son Face an Unplanned Pregnancy.* (Colorado Springs, CO: NavPress, 2004), p. 83.

End Notes for Chapter Twelve

[238] Les Parrott III. *The Comprehensive Guide to Youth Ministry Counseling.* (Loveland, CO: Group Publishing, 2002), p. 82.

[239] Jen Abbas. *Generation EX: Adult Children of Divorce and the Healing of Our Pain.* (Colorado Springs, CO: WaterBrook Press, 2004), p. xi-xii.

[240] McKinley Irvin Family Law. "32 Shocking Divorce Statistics." October 30, 2012. Accessed: January 4, 2017. https://www.mckinleyirvin.com/Family-Law-Blog/2012/October/32-Shocking-Divorce-Statistics.aspx

[241] McKinley Irvin Family Law. "32 Shocking Divorce Statistics." October 30, 2012. Accessed: January 4, 2017. https://www.mckinleyirvin.com/Family-

Law-Blog/2012/October/32-Shocking-Divorce-Statistics.aspx

[242] McKinley Irvin Family Law. "32 Shocking Divorce Statistics." October 30, 2012. Accessed: January 4, 2017. https://www.mckinleyirvin.com/Family-Law-Blog/2012/October/32-Shocking-Divorce-Statistics.aspx

[243] These questions came from: Carolyn Nystrom. *Mike's Lonely Summer: A Child's Guide Through Divorce*. (Belleville, MI: Lion Publishing, 1986), p. 11 and Edward Teyber. *Helping Your Children With Divorce*. (New York, NY: Pocket Books, 1985), pp. 37-81.

[244] Rich Van Pelt, *Intensive Care*. (Grand Rapids, MI: Zondervan, 1988), p. 135.

[245] Archibald D. Hart. *Children & Divorce: What to Expect. How to Help*. (Waco, TX: Word Books, 1982), p, 27.

[246] (Maria Sullivan. *The Parent/Child Manual On Divorce*. (New York: NY: RGA Publishing Group, 1988), p. 7.

[247] Josh McDowell & Bob Hostetler. *Josh McDowell's Handbook on Counseling Youth*. (Nashville, TN: W Publishing Group, 1996), p. 204.

[248] Rich Van Pelt, *Intensive Care*. (Grand Rapids, MI: Zondervan, 1988), p. 137

[249] Archibald D. Hart. *Children & Divorce: What to Expect. How to Help*. (Waco, TX: Word Books, 1982), p, 28.

[250] *Newsweek*, "The Children of Divorce." February 11, 1980, p. 63.

[251] Archibald D. Hart. *Children & Divorce: What to Expect. How to Help*. (Waco, TX: Word Books, 1982), p, 28.

[252] Barbara Dafoe Whitehead, "Dan Quayle Was Right." *The Atlantic Monthly*, April 1993, p. 47.

[253] Barbara Dafoe Whitehead, "Dan Quayle Was Right." *The Atlantic Monthly*, April 1993, p. 65.

[254] Kyle D. Pruett. "Helping Children Cope With Divorce." *Psychology Today*, May 12, 2016. Accessed: January 6, 2017. https://www.psychologytoday.com/blog/once-upon-child/201605/helping-children-cope-divorce.

[255] *Christianity Today*, May 25, 1979

[256] Les Parrott III. *The Comprehensive Guide to Youth Ministry Counseling*. (Loveland, CO: Group Publishing, 2002), p. 87.

[257] Les Parrott III. *The Comprehensive Guide to Youth Ministry Counseling*. (Loveland, CO: Group Publishing, 2002), p. 84.

[258] Les Parrott III. *The Comprehensive Guide to Youth Ministry Counseling*. (Loveland, CO: Group Publishing, 2002), p. 84.

Endnotes for Chapter Thirteen

[259] Les Parrott III. *Helping the Struggling Adolescent*. (Grand Rapids, MI: Zondervan, 1993), p. 152.

[260] Adam T. Barr and Ron Citlau. *Compassion Without Compromise: How the Gospel Frees Us to Love Our Gay Friends Without Losing the Truth*.

(Minneapolis, MN: Bethany House Publishers, 2014), p. 109.

[261] Robert R. Reilly, *Making Gay Okay: How Rationalizing Homosexual Behavior Is Changing Everything.* (San Francisco, CA: Ignatius Press, 2014), p. 135.

[262] Peter Aldhous, "French Venture Where U.S. Fears to Tread," *Science,* Vol 257 (July 3, 1992), p. 25.

[263] Kim Painter, "Only 1% of Men Say They Are Gay." *USA Today,* April 15, 1993, pp. 1D, 8D.

[264] Sandhya Somashekhar. "Health survey gives government its first large-scale data on gay, bisexual population." *The Washington Post.* (July 15, 2014). Accessed: January 24, 2017. https://www.washingtonpost.com/national/health-science/health-survey-gives-government-its-first-large-scale-data-on-gay-bisexual-population/2014/07/14/2db9f4b0-092f-11e4-bbf1-cc51275e7f8f_story.html?utm_term=.fbcd92d1aeb9

[265] Frank Newport. "Americans Greatly Overestimate Percent Gay, Lesbian in U.S. Gallup. (May 21, 2015) Accessed: January 24, 2017. http://www.gallup.com/poll/183383/americans-greatly-overestimate-percent-gay-lesbian.aspx

[266] Frank Newport. "Americans Greatly Overestimate Percent Gay, Lesbian in U.S. Gallup. (May 21, 2015) Accessed: January 24, 2017. http://www.gallup.com/poll/183383/americans-greatly-overestimate-percent-gay-lesbian.aspx

[267] Tim Stafford, "Issue of the Year," *Christianity Today*, (May 5, 1978), p. 38.

[268] See: Francis Brown, S.R. Driver and Charles A. Briggs, *A Hebrew and English Lexicon of the Old Testament.* (Oxford: Clarendon Press, 1978), p. 394.

[269] Kevin DeYoung. *What Does the Bible Really Teach About Homosexuality?* (Wheaton, IL: Crossway, 2015), p. 53.

[270] Joseph Henry Thayer. *A Greek-English Lexicon of the New Testament.* (Grand Rapids, MI: Baker, 1977), p. 387.

[271] Walter Bauer, William F. Arndt and F. Wilbur Gingrich. *A Greek-English Lexicon of the New Testament and Other Early Christian Literature.* (Chicago, IL: The University of Chicago Press, 1957), p.109.

[272] Jerry Kirk. *The Homosexual Crisis in the Mainline Church.* (Nashville, TN: Thomas Nelson Inc.,1978) p. 61)

[273] Melanie Morrison. "A Love That Won't Let Go." *Sojourners.* (July 1991) p. 12.

[274] Melanie Morrison. "A Love That Won't Let Go." *Sojourners.* (July 1991) pp. 12-13.

[275] R. Bayer. *Homosexuality and American Psychiatry: The Politics of Diagnosis.* (New York, NY: Basic, 1981), p. 167.

[276] See: Ruth Tiffany Barnhouse. *Homosexuality: A Symbolic Confusion.* (New York, NY: Seabury Press, 1977) pp. 42-45.

[277] Stanton L. Jones and Don E Workman. "Homosexuality: the Behavioral Sciences and the Church." *Journal of Psychology and Theology.* Vol

17, No. 3, 1989, pp. 213-225; Douglas A. Houck. "Neglected by Mission: The Homosexual Person." *Urban Mission*. (May 1987), pp. 13-20

[278] Sharon Harrington. *Homosexuality: A Christian Response*. (Seattle, WA: Life Messenger, 1978), pp. 6-7.

[279] Sherwood O. Cole, "The Biological Basis of Homosexuality: A Christian Assessment." *The Journal of Psychology and Theology* (1995) Vol 23, No 2, pp. 89-100.

[280] Larry Thompson. "Search For the Gay Gene." *Time* (June 12, 1995).

[281] Larry Thompson. "Search For the Gay Gene." *Time* (June 12, 1995).

[282] Larry Thompson. "Search For the Gay Gene." *Time* (June 12, 1995).

[283] Rich Deem. "Genetics and Homosexuality: Are People Born Gay? The Biological Basis for Sexual Orientation. Godandscience.org. Accessed: January 24, 2017. http://www.godandscience.org/evolution/genetics_of_homosexuality.html; William H. Perloff. "Hormones and Homosexuality," in *Sexual Inversion: The Multiple Roots of Homosexuality*, ed. Judd Marmor. (New York, NY: Basic, 1965), p. 57.

[284] Stanton L. Jones and Don E. Workman. "Homosexuality: The Behavioral Sciences and The Church. *Journal of Psychology and Theology*. Vol 17 (Fall 1989), pp. 213-225.

[285] Christine Gorman. "Are Gay Men Born That Way?" *Time*. (Sept 9, 1991), p. 60.

[286] Christine Gorman. "Are Gay Men Born That Way?" *Time*. (Sept 9, 1991), p. 61.

[287] William Byne and Bruce Parsons. "Human Sexual Orientation: The Biologic Theories Reappraised." *Arc Gen Psychiatry.* Vol 50. No 3. (June 1993), pp. 228-239.

[288] Daryl J. Bem. "Exotic Becomes Erotic: A Developmental Theory of Sexual Orientation." *Psychological Review*. Vol 103, No. 2. (1996), pp. 320-335.

[289] Sharon Harrington. *Homosexuality: A Christian Response*. (Seattle, WA: Life Messenger, 1978), pp. 8-9.

[290] Mark A. Yarhouse and Erica S. N. Tan, *Sexuality & Sex Therapy: A Comprehensive Christian Appraisal*. (Downers Grove, IL: IVP, 2014), pp. 298-299.

[291] Mario Bergner, "Telling the Truth About Homosexuality." *The Resurrection Light*, Winter 1998, p. 18.

[292] Laura Haynes. "APA on Sexual Orientation." *California Psychologist*. (September 2016), p. 1.

[293] Mark A. Yarhouse. *Homosexuality and the Christian. A Guide for Parents, Pastors, and Friends*. (Minneapolis, MN: Bethany House Publishers, 2010), p. 26.

[294] Mark A. Yarhouse. *Homosexuality and the Christian. A Guide for Parents, Pastors, and Friends*. (Minneapolis, MN: Bethany House Publishers, 2010), p. 27.

[295] Mark A. Yarhouse, "Sexual Identity Therapy: An Innovative Paradigm for Facilitating Congruence." *American Association of Christian Counselors*

Convention. (October 17-18, 2008); Mark A. Yarhouse. *Homosexuality and the Christian. A Guide for Parents, Pastors, and Friends.* (Minneapolis, MN: Bethany House Publishers, 2010), pp. 41-42.

[296] Douglas A. Houck, "Neglected by Mission: The Homosexual Person" *Urban Mission.* (May 1987) p. 15.

[297] Douglas A. Houck, "Neglected by Mission: The Homosexual Person" *Urban Mission.* (May 1987) p. 19.

[298] Bob Davies and Lori Rentzel. *Coming Out of Homosexuality: New Freedom for Men & Women.* (Downers Grove, IL: InterVarsity Press, 1993), p. 38.

[299] Bob Davies and Lori Rentzel. *Coming Out of Homosexuality: New Freedom for Men & Women.* (Downers Grove, IL: InterVarsity Press, 1993), p. 29.

Endnotes for Chapter Fourteen

[300] William M. Struthers. *Wired for Intimacy: How Pornography Hijacks the Male Brain.* (Downers Grove, IL: IVP Books, 2009), pp. 11, 15.

[301] Michael John Cusick. *Surfing For God: Discovering the divine Desire Beneath Sexual Struggle.* (Nashville, TN: Thomas Nelson, 2012), p. xvi.

[302] U.S. Department of Justice. Post Hearing Memorandum of Points and Authorities, at l, ACLU v. Reno, 929 F. Supp. 824, 1996.

[303] 2014 Pornography Survey and Statistics. Proven Men Ministries. Accessed Dec. 29, 2014. http://www.provenmen.org/2014pornsurvey/.

[304] Webroot. "Internet pornography by the numbers; a significant threat to society." Accessed: February 1, 2017. https://www.webroot.com/us/en/home/resources/tips/digital-family-life/internet-pornography-by-the-numbers

[305] Enough-Is-Enough: Making the Internet Safe for Children and Families. "Statistics: Youth & Porn." Accessed: February 1, 2017. http://enough.org/stats-youth-and-porn

[306] C.S. Mott Children's Hospital (2015). "Sexting and internet safety climb top 10 list of health concerns for children across the U.S. National Poll on Children's Health." Accessed: February 1, 2017. http://www.mottchildren.org/news/archive/201508/sexting.

[307] Thorn. "Child Pornography Statistics." Accessed: February 1, 2017. https://www.wearethorn.org/child-pornography-and-abuse-statistics/

[308] Chiara Sabina, Janis Wolak, and David Finkelhor, "The nature and dynamics of Internet pornography exposure for youth," CyberPsychology and Behavior 11 (2008): 691-693.

[309] Craig Gross and Jason Harper. *Eyes of Integrity: The Porn Pandemic and How it Affects You.* (Grand Rapids, MI: Baker Books, 2010), p. 21.

[310] Sam Black, *The Porn Circuit: Understand Your Brain and Break Porn Habits in 90 Days.* (Owosso, MI: Covenant Eyes, 2013), p. 12.

[311] William M. Struthers, *Wired For Intimacy: How Pornography Hijacks the Male Brain.* (Downers, Grove, IL: IVP Books, 2009), p. 11.

[312] Association For Natural Psychology. "Pornography and Mental

Health." (January 7, 2016). Accessed: February 1, 2017. http://aycnp.org/effects.of.pornography.php

313 Alexandra Katehakis. "Effects of Porn on Adolescent Boys." *Psychology Today.* (July 28, 2011). Accessed: February 1, 2017. https://www.psychologytoday.com/blog/sex-lies-trauma/201107/effects-porn-adolescent-boys.

314 Reddit, NoFap - http://www.reddit.com/r/NoFap/ (accessed Feb. 26, 2013).

315 Michael John Cusick. *Surfing For God: Discovering the Divine Desire Beneath Sexual Struggle.* (Nashville, TN: Thomas Nelson, 2012), p. 134.

316 Sam Black, *The Porn Circuit: Understand Your Brain and Break Porn Habits in 90 Days.* (Owosso, MI: Covenant Eyes, 2013), p. 12.

317 Tim Chester, *Closing the Window: Steps to Living Porn Free.* (Downers Grove, IL: IVP Books, 2010), pp. 106-107.

318 John Piper, "Gutsy Guilt: Don't Let Shame Over Sexual Sin Destroy You." *Christianity Today.* (October 2007), pp. 73-74.

319 John Piper, "Gutsy Guilt: Don't Let Shame Over Sexual Sin Destroy You." *Christianity Today.* (October 2007), p. 76.

320 Patrick Carnes, *Out of the Shadows: Understanding Sexual Addiction.* *3rd ed.* (Center City, MN: Hazelden, 2001), p. 3.

321 Patrick Carnes, *Out of the Shadows: Understanding Sexual Addiction.* *3rd ed.* (Center City, MN: Hazelden, 2001), p. 84.

322 Kevin B. Skinner, *Treating Pornography Addiction: The Essential Tools For Recovery.* (Provo, UT: GrowthClimate, Inc., 2005), p. 24.

323 Kevin B. Skinner, *Treating Pornography Addiction: The Essential Tools For Recovery.* (Provo, UT: GrowthClimate, Inc., 2005), pp. 23-24.

324 Kevin B. Skinner, *Treating Pornography Addiction: The Essential Tools For Recovery.* (Provo, UT: GrowthClimate, 2005), pp. 162-171; Tim Clinton and Mark Laaser, *The Fight of Your Life: Manning Up to the Challenge of Sexual Integrity.* (Shippensburg, PA: Destiny Image Publishers, 2015), pp. 227-232; Michael Leahy, *Porn University.* (Chicago, IL: Northfield Publishing, 2009), pp. 39-43.

325 Kevin B. Skinner, *Treating Pornography Addiction: The Essential Tools For Recovery.* (Provo, UT: GrowthClimate, Inc., 2005), p. 25.

326Kevin B. Skinner, *Treating Pornography Addiction: The Essential Tools For Recovery.* (Provo, UT: GrowthClimate, Inc., 2005), p. 26.

327 Kevin B. Skinner, *Treating Pornography Addiction: The Essential Tools For Recovery.* (Provo, UT: GrowthClimate, Inc., 2005), p. 26.

328 Kevin B. Skinner, *Treating Pornography Addiction: The Essential Tools For Recovery.* (Provo, UT: GrowthClimate, Inc., 2005), p. 29.

329Kevin B. Skinner, *Treating Pornography Addiction: The Essential Tools For Recovery.* (Provo, UT: GrowthClimate, Inc., 2005), p. 31.

330 Kevin B. Skinner, *Treating Pornography Addiction: The Essential Tools For Recovery.* (Provo, UT: GrowthClimate, Inc., 2005), p. 34.

331 Michael John Cusick. *Surfing For God: Discovering the Divine Desire*

Beneath Sexual Struggle. (Nashville, TN: Thomas Nelson, 2012), p. xv.

[332] Michael John Cusick. *Surfing For God: Discovering the Divine Desire Beneath Sexual Struggle.* (Nashville, TN: Thomas Nelson, 2012), p. xvi.

[333] Michael John Cusick. *Surfing For God: Discovering the Divine Desire Beneath Sexual Struggle.* (Nashville, TN: Thomas Nelson, 2012), p. 151.

[334] Matthew 22:37 NIV

[335] Michael John Cusick. *Surfing For God: Discovering the Divine Desire Beneath Sexual Struggle.* (Nashville, TN: Thomas Nelson, 2012), p. 151.

[336] Tim Chester, *Closing the Window: Steps to Living Porn Free.* (Downers Grove, IL: IVP Books, 2010), p. 37.

[337] Ron Lagerquist, "Pornography Addiction." Freedom You: Health Is a Choice. Accessed: March 10, 2017.
http://www.freedomyou.com/pornography_addiction_intro_freedomyou.aspx

[338] Ron Lagerquist, "Pornography Addiction." Freedom You: Health Is a Choice. Accessed: March 10, 2017.
http://www.freedomyou.com/pornography_addiction_intro_freedomyou.aspx

[339] 2 Timothy 2:22 NIV

[340]Ron Lagerquist, "Pornography Addiction." Freedom You: Health Is a Choice. Accessed: March 10, 2017.
http://www.freedomyou.com/pornography_addiction_intro_freedomyou.aspx

[341] Tim Chester, *Closing the Window: Steps to Living Porn Free.* (Downers Grove, IL: IVP Books, 2010), p. 17.

[342] Tim Chester, *Closing the Window: Steps to Living Porn Free.* (Downers Grove, IL: IVP Books, 2010), p. 64.

[343] Ron Lagerquist, "Breaking Porn Addiction – Action 1 – Make a Decision." Freedom You: Health Is a Choice. Accessed: March 10, 2017.
http://www.freedomyou.com/breaking_porn_addiction__action_1__make_a_de cision_freedomyou.aspx

[344] See: https://x3watch.com/blog/xxxchurch-software/#.WMgJsRIrKRs

[345]Wendy Maltz and Larry Maltz. *The Porn Trap: The Essential Guide to Overcoming Problems Caused by Pornography.* (New York, NY: Harper, 2008), p. 159.

[346] Tim Chester, *Closing the Window: Steps to Living Porn Free.* (Downers Grove, IL: IVP Books, 2010), p. 101.

[347] Ron Lagerquist, "Pornography Addiction." Freedom You: Health Is a Choice. Accessed: March 10, 2017.
http://www.freedomyou.com/pornography_addiction_intro_freedomyou.aspx

[348] John Piper, "Gutsy Guilt" *Christianity Today* (October 2007), pp. 73-76.

[349]Tim Chester, *Closing the Window: Steps to Living Porn Free.* (Downers Grove, IL: IVP Books, 2010), p. 91.

[350] Mark R. Laaser and Louis J. Gregoire, "Pastors and Cybersex Addiction," *Sexual and Relationship Therapy* 18, no. 3 (2003): p. 401.

[351]Tim Chester, *Closing the Window: Steps to Living Porn Free.* (Downers Grove, IL: IVP Books, 2010), p. 137.

Endnotes for Chapter Fifteen

[352] Robert S. Feldman, *Development Across the Life Span.* (Upper Saddle River, NJ: Pearson Prentice Hall, 2008), p. 335.

[353] Carl E. Pickhardt. "Adolescence and Self-Esteem." *Psychology Today.* (September 6, 2010) Accessed: March 16, 2017. https://www.psychologytoday.com/blog/surviving-your-childs-adolescence/201009/adolescence-and-self-esteem.

[354] "11 Facts About Teens and Self-Esteem." DoSomething.org. Accessed: March 16, 2017. https://www.dosomething.org/us/facts/11-facts-about-teens-and-self-esteem.

[355] "Statistics on Girls & Women's Self Esteem, Pressures & Leadership." Heart of Leadership. Accessed: March 16, 2017. http://www.heartofleadership.org/statistics/

[356] "What Are the Statistics Regarding Low Self-Esteem In Teenagers?" Reference.com. Accessed: March 16, 2071. https://www.reference.com/family/statistics-regarding-low-self-esteem-teenagers-ff6eeec305c3e21b.

[357] Saul McLeod. "Low Self-Esteem." *Simply Psychology.* (2012) Accessed: March 16, 2017. http://www.simplypsychology.org/self-esteem.html.

[358] Some Interesting Self-Esteem Statistics and Facts You Might Not Be Aware Of." Self-Esteem-School.com. Accessed: March 16, 2017. http://www.self-esteem-school.com/self-esteem-statistics.html.

[359] "Some Interesting Self-Esteem Statistics and Facts You Might Not Be Aware Of." Self-Esteem-School.com. Accessed: March 16, 2017. http://www.self-esteem-school.com/self-esteem-statistics.html.

[360] Romans 8:15.

[361] Galatians 5:22-23.

[362] See: http://abcnews.go.com/GMA/video/time-lapse-video-shows-models-photoshop-transformation-20738180; https://www.youtube.com/watch?v=hibyAJOSW8U; https://www.youtube.com/watch?v=XRbcE-VTsQM;

[363] https://www.youtube.com/watch?v=litXW91UauE

[364] 1 Samuel 9:2 NIV

[365] 1 Samuel 15:11 NIV

[366] 1 Samuel 16:7 NIV

[367] Proverbs 31:30 NIV

[368] 1 Peter 3:3-4 NIV

[369] Yes, I know this isn't always the case and I am using exaggeration to make a point. Chill!

[370] Exodus 23:2 NIV

[371] See: Genesis 1:26-27

[372] ἀσθενῶν, "without strength, feeble" – David H. Wheaton. *New Bible Commentary.* Accordance Bible software.

[373] Eric Liddell. "Eric Liddell Quotes." *Good Reads.* Accessed: March 20, 2017. https://www.goodreads.com/author/quotes/802465.Eric_Liddell

[374] See: Romans 12:3-8 and 1 Corinthians 12:7-31.

[375] See: John 3:16; 1 Peter 1:18-19; Isaiah 53:5-7.

[376] See: 2 Corinthians 10:17-18; Jeremiah 9:23-24.

[377] See: Matthew 25:14-46 and Luke 19:12-27.

[378] See: Psalm 139:1-5, 13-16; Isaiah 45:9-12.

[379] See: Philippians 1:6.

[380] See: Ephesians 3:20.

[381] Isaiah 53:2 NIV.

[382] Steve Thomas. "The Gift." Used by permission.

[383] I John 3:2.

End Notes For Chapter Sixteen

[384] Les Parrott III. *The Comprehensive Guide to Youth Ministry Counseling.* (Loveland, CO: Group, 2002), p. 10.

[385] Les Parrott III. *The Comprehensive Guide to Youth Ministry Counseling.* (Loveland, CO: Group, 2002), p. 10-11.

[386] Kenneth S. Pope, Barbara G. Tabachnick, and Patricia Keith-Spiege. "Sexual Attraction to Clients: The Human Therapist and the (Sometimes) Inhuman Training System." Kspope.com. Accessed: April 7, 2017. http://kspope.com/sexiss/research5.php

[387] Adapted from: Joan Sturkie and Siang-Yang Tan. *Peer Counseling in Youth Groups: Equipping Your Kids to Help Each Other.* (Grand Rapids, MI: Zondervan, 1992), p. 92.

www.ingramcontent.com/pod-product-compliance
Lightning Source LLC
Chambersburg PA
CBHW061957280526
45787CB00005B/1900